Antique and Twentieth Century Jewellery

Antique and Twentieth Century Jewellery

A Guide for Collectors

Vivienne Becker

VNR VAN NOSTRAND REINHOLD COMPANY
NEW YORK CINCINNATI TORONTO LONDON MELBOURNE

Library of Congress Catalog Card Number 82-8646

ISBN 0-442-21400-6

Printed in the United States of America

Published by Van Nostrand Reinhold Company Inc.
135 West 50th Street, New York, NY 10020

Van Nostrand Reinhold Publishers
1410 Birchmount Road
Scarborough, Ontario M1P 2E7, Canada

Van Nostrand Reinhold Australia Pty. Ltd.
480 Latrobe Street
Melbourne, Victoria 3000, Australia

Van Nostrand Reinhold Company Limited
Molly Millars Lane
Wokingham, Berkshire, England RG11 2PY

16 15 14 13 12 11 10 9 8 7 6 5 4 3 2 1

Library of Congress Cataloging in Publication Data

Becker, Vivienne, 1953-
    Antique and twentieth century jewellery.

    Bibliography: p.
    Includes index.
    1. Jewelry—Collectors and collecting. 2. Jewelry—
History—18th century. 3. Jewelry—History—19th cen-
tury. 4. Jewelry—History—20th century. I. Title.
NK7304.B38 1982   739.27   82-8646
ISBN 0-442-21400-6   AACR2

Contents

Foreword   7
Acknowledgements   8
Introduction   9

1. Diamond Brooches   11

2. Coral Jewellery   21

3. Nineteenth Century Gold-work   25

4. Piqué   35

5. Silver of the Late Nineteenth Century   45

6. Collecting in Unusual Materials   59

7. Mourning Jewellery   84

8. Scottish Jewellery   111

9. Flowers in Jewellery   118

10. Animals in Jewellery   127

11. Stick-pins   134

12. Cameos and Engraved Gems   139

13. Mosaics in Jewellery   155

14. Egyptian Revival Jewellery   167

15. Signed Jewellery of the Mid-nineteenth Century   177

16. The Famous Jewel Houses   189

17. Signed Art Nouveau Jewellery   199

18. Pendants at the Turn of the Century   214

19. Arts and Crafts Jewellery   223

20. Liberty and his Rivals   244

21. Edwardian and Art Deco Jewellery   267

Bibliography   291
Index   293

Foreword

I very much welcome Vivienne Becker's new book, which with its focal as opposed to chronological sequence, offers the collector a syntax of jewellery, grouping similar objects or stylistic movements together and dealing with each thoroughly under one chapter heading. This approach enables us to dip into the book at any point of interest without the guilty feeling that we have missed a crucial artistic turning point described in an earlier chapter.

It is fascinating to realise that almost all of the beautiful pieces illustrated in this book have been available on the London market during the last three years. It is an index of the enormous wealth of jewellery continually surfacing. These illustrations provide an important yardstick for the collector to measure the quality of his own objects and it is encouraging too, for if this is what was available then surely there must be as good if not better awaiting us in the future.

I am sure that there can be few people engaged in the London trade who do not know Vivienne Becker, she has been looking over our shoulders at everything from the fabulous to the ordinary for many years now, and in so doing has distilled the knowledge gained into this excellent book. For those of us who are expert in only one field we must surely learn something of other fields. For those who are not expert but have a strong interest in the subject, this will be an important and permanent work of reference.

MALCOLM CARR
London, 1980

Acknowledgements

I owe a huge debt of gratitude to all the people who have helped me with this book. In particular, I would like to thank Malcolm Carr, who helped to plan the original series for *Retail Jeweller*, and David Callaghan, both of Hancocks & Co; and David Coombs, Editor of *The Antique Collector*, who gave me the opportunity of first writing about many of these subjects. Chapters 9, 10 and 18 are based on articles which originally appeared in *Art and Antiques Weekly*.

The following have all helped me with specific chapters and I must thank them for sharing their hard-earned specialist knowledge: Victor Arwas; John Benjamin; Richard Digby; Ralph Esmerian, New York; J.F. Ewing; Charlotte Gere; Peter and Debbie Gooday; Nicholas Harris; Tanya Hunter; John Jesse and Irina Laski; Anthony Landsberg; Geoffrey Munn; Nicola Redway; and Gabrielle Ruthven.

In addition I would like to thank Brian and Lynn Holmes and all my friends and colleagues in Grays Antique Market and in the antique jewellery trade who have been so enthusiastic and encouraging, and who have all contributed to the illustrations.

Finally my thanks go to Barnes and Bradford, Fine Art Photographers, for their patience and excellent work, and a special acknowledgement to the staff of *Retail Jeweller* for their help and support.

Introduction

One of the main advantages of collecting antique jewellery, as opposed to other works of art, is the fact that it can still be worn, and so put to its original use of decorating and complimenting fashion and beauty. Some people enjoy collecting jewels for historical and academic interest, but it is also a fascinating challenge to choose jewels from a past age which will still flatter modern clothes and — at the same time — add that inimitable touch of old charm, a glimpse of another society, remote in customs, values, beliefs.

Before I began to study and write about antique jewellery, I worked 'in the trade' for some time. There I met a variety of customers and dealers whose lively enthusiasm and love of jewellery was so contagious that my initial hobby grew to be an absorbing career. With this book, I very much hope that I can share some of that fascination and my own rich experience of jewels, their stories and their collectors. I also hope I might give would-be collectors some confidence to embark on a collection, however modest, by supplying some of the background knowledge to various materials, designs, tastes and jewellers, as they changed through the years.

Buying confidence will develop with knowledge: pleasure, of course, grows considerably with both knowledge and confidence. Different people collect different things, to suit their own pockets, lives and personalities. I have come across jewellery devotees hunting for themes varying from top-hats, hearts, hands, lovers' knots, frogs, serpents, to death jewels, cut-steel, sentimental jewels and stylish or 'kitsch' twentieth century jewellery. Each of them had gradually become an expert to some extent in one small corner of jewellery history. I learnt that styles, revealing and evocative motifs, and craftsmanship were often considered more important by these collectors than intrinsic value. I felt then that what these people needed was information on each collecting area gathered together, and well-illustrated with pieces currently or recently on the market, or from smaller, personal private collections. A series of articles written for the jewellery trade paper, *Retail Jeweller*, on these lines inspired the idea for a book based on the same formula.

This is the reason that the book has been divided into chapters each standing as a short history itself, concentrating on the kind of jewellery handled by dealers and sought by collectors. I have chosen some particular subjects because they are often neglected, due perhaps to their transience as fashions or whims, their low intrinsic value or lack of historical or artistic importance. Silver love brooches, worn by late nineteeth century servants, Scottish pebble jewellery of the 1860s, or the dramatic Egyptian revival jewellery of the 1920s are all relatively inexpensive, plentiful, fun to wear and attractive reflections of past popular tastes and crazes.

There is an emphasis on the late nineteenth century and early twentieth century jewels which corresponds to the growing interest in these periods, their changing decorative styles and attitudes, and their contributions to twentieth century art. The emphasis is also developed because these later jewels are more generally available and because earlier periods have already been extremely well documented. I have tried to lead the reader to recognise and appreciate good style, the pure designs which were very much a part of their age, quality and craftsmanship — however humble the materials may be. Jewellery styles became particularly strong when allied to artistic movements around the turn of the century, under the influence of *avant-garde* designers and brilliant entrepreneurs like Liberty & Co.

Modest budgets have often forced enterprising collectors to explore the full range of materials, which have been so ingeniously translated into jewels or clever imitations through the years. Many of these are described in Chapter 6, Unusual Materials. Marks and signatures, too, are valuable and have been brought more and more to the attention of collectors in recent years. They should be used merely as a guide, because studying the pieces made by the most skilfull and imaginative jewellers should shape your own judgment of quality and style on unmarked — and often less expensive — but no less attractive examples. The chapters on signed jewellery will hopefully also give you the feel of the jewellery scene and ruling artistic atmosphere of each period, against which can be placed your own acquisitions.

The illustrations have been chosen with these guiding principles in mind; some aim to show the kind of jewellery that can be found at most antique shops and markets through the country; while others record the finest and most interesting jewels which have passed through the trade in recent years, rather than the rare never-to-be-seen-again museum pieces which are on public view. Many of the photographs are intended to share with the reader the jewels which dealers themselves collect and treasure.

The themes which colour the history of jewels are endless; I have tried to select a varied group to fit into the limits of a book that I hope will whet your appetite for continuing my own search and exploration into antique and twentieth century jewellery.

VIVIENNE BECKER

1. Diamond Brooches

Against a colourful background of meandering jewellery fashions, the diamond brooch has continued through the centuries, and remains today still as one of the best-loved representations of fine traditional jewellery. Its universal appeal is due to a winning combination of the cherished beauty of the diamond with the freedom of brooch designs. While rings, necklaces and bracelets have to be worked around a basic shape to fit finger, neck or wrist, the brooch imposes the least of these practicalities on the jeweller.

In spite of this, designers seem to have been in awe of diamonds, keeping them in conservative styles throughout the nineteenth century. It was not until the appearance of jewellers such as Cartier and Boucheron, whose respect for the stones did not overwhelm their artistic ideas, that adventurous, high fashion brooches were produced in the most luxurious materials.

It was in fifteenth century Paris that the fashion for diamond jewellery started. The celebrated Court beauty, Agnes Sorel, acted as a model for a diamond merchant called Jacques Coeur. By this time, experiments in cutting had begun and it was really only with the first facets that the huge potential of the diamond as an ornament began slowly to emerge. The table-cut, with one square top facet, was one of the earliest cuts for diamonds. It was popular on European jewellery from the beginning of the sixteenth century until the middle of the next.

It was appropriately the magnificence of the Court of Louis XIV that helped to reveal more of the qualities of light within the diamond. This was the age of the great merchant, Jean Baptiste Tavernier, who journeyed to and from the mines of India, selling his diamonds to the extravagant French Court. Cardinal Mazarin sponsored lapidaries to work on and improve the cutting of these stones. The Mazarin cut was named after the Cardinal and is thought to be the result of his efforts, but it may have originated earlier.

The rose-cut, too, was more widely used after the Cardinal's encouragement. A rose diamond was cut with a flat back and a domed front, faceted in triangles to look like the opening petals of a rosebud. This certainly added to the life seen in the diamond, and was an important factor in establishing the basic jewellery form of the diamond brooch, and of all conventional diamond jewellery.

Work continued and interest in the stones and new techniques grew, and around 1700 the brilliant-cut was developed. Exactly how or by whom it was discovered is doubtful, but the early brilliant-cut is generally attributed to a Venetian lapidary called Vincenzo Peruzzi. The outline was cushion-shaped with 58 facets in all — 33 on the crown and 25 on the pavilion. The brilliant-cut was not extensively used, however, until the nineteenth century.

Progress in diamond cutting during the seventeenth century coincided with the growth of a decorative style that revolved around naturalism, and together they bred the traditional flower brooch. Inspired by the fascinating specimens of a famous Paris garden (later known as the *Jardin des Plantes*), the first flower designs for jewellery appeared in 1602. This, and other gardens, had started a passion for plants, flowers and consequently for botanical jewellery which flourished in eighteenth-century Europe and continued through the nineteenth century.

Improved diamond cutting also led jewellers to concentrate on the stones themselves, and gradually they began to drift away from the statutory enamelling. The designs of Gilles Légaré, published in the 1660s, epitomise the jewellery style of the time, pointing to a new emphasis placed on diamonds. The leading Paris jeweller, Louis de Berquem, stressed the importance of foil-backing stones to enhance colour. At this stage, he still insisted on just a touch of enamel work on the setting.

Out of all these changes, the diamond brooch can be seen gradually developing in the form of 'Brandebourgs', or frogs (ornamental fastenings) of diamonds, worn by both men and women, and also in bow-shaped ornaments. There was a new lightness about these jewels that heralded the arrival of the eighteenth century. This glamorous age set the seal of approval on the future of diamond jewellery: nothing compares to the beauty of faceted diamonds seen by candlelight.

Fig. I. I. (Left) Late 18th century crescent brooch of pavé-set diamonds mounted in silver and gold. About 1780. (Right) The back of the same piece, partly closed but with the largest central stones open-backed. Made during a period of transition in diamond setting. (Harvey & Gore)

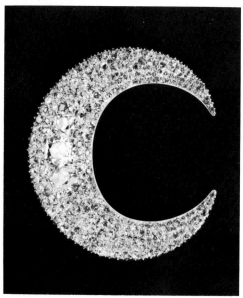

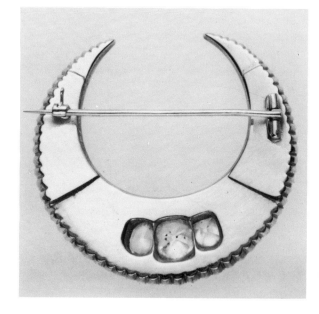

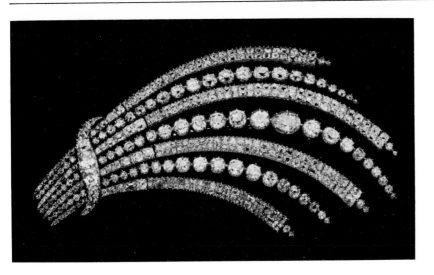

Fig. I. 2. English Georgian diamond spray brooch, about 1800. The strands of the wheatsheaf are all moveable, adding to the overall effect. Made during a period of transition, with some of the stones enclosed and others open-backed. (Landsberg & Son)

The Eighteenth Century

Clothes of the eighteenth century were made of fabrics light in weight and texture; velvets had an almost transparent weave, inviting jewels of delicate bright floral patterns; just as the heavy brocades of the sixteenth and seventeenth centuries had suggested rich enamel work. Brooches took the form of corsage ornaments, bow-shaped brooches, now known as Sévignés and sprays fastened or sewn to the dress. All were made with the practical consideration that after a few years they would be broken up and re-set in the latest fashion.

Jewels were closed in at the back, enabling diamonds to be backed with foils, often of yellow, blue, green or red. The backs of stones were also sometimes covered with paint, or a black spot was painted on the culet; all in an attempt to improve the brilliance and colour of the gem. In the eighteenth century, diamonds were set in silver and usually mounted in gold. The pavé setting was one of the most popular, and effective. The surface of the jewel was literally 'paved' with diamonds, set very close to each other and held by small raised grains of metal. The claw setting was used for larger stones.

Unfortunately, relatively few early diamond brooches survive and their development can best be studied through paste jewellery of the same period. The improved pastes were hardly considered as fakes, and were worn in the most aristocratic and fashionable circles. They were cut, foiled, set and mounted in exactly the same way as precious stones, giving valuable information about their diamond-set counterparts.

The French Revolution deprived fashion-followers on both sides of the Channel of heads that had worn the most lavish jewels, and for some time jewellery in France was reduced to a bare minimum. With the arrival on the scene of the beautiful Empress Josephine, diamonds regained their former popularity by the beginning of the nineteenth century. Taking its lead from Paris, English diamond jewellery continued on the grand scale.

The Early Nineteenth Century

Early nineteenth century diamond brooches appear to be very similar in style to those made in the previous century, and certainly for some time eighteenth-century designs dominated jewellery. Even the seventeenth century taste, in the manner of Légaré, with rose-cut foiled diamonds seemed to linger in the early years of the century.

Further progress improved the appearance and settings of diamonds, if the designs remained stagnant. Some time around 1800, in a gradual process, it was found that the brilliance of diamonds was increased if the back of the setting was opened. More light and life was reflected, and the brilliant-cut was more widely appreciated and used. The late eighteenth century crescent brooch shows the transition, with the largest diamonds left open to the light and others still enclosed. Diamonds were still set in silver to flatter the whiteness of the stone, while the backs were set in gold. This arrangement continued throughout the century until platinum took over from silver.

Fig. I. 3. The back of an early 19th century brooch, showing the open setting. The three drops are detachable, and the diamonds are set in silver and mounted in gold. About 1825. (Harvey & Gore)

The backs of some early nineteenth century diamond brooches are worth studying closely, both for the attractive and intricate designs, and for a guideline to date. The collet setting was favoured at this stage for larger stones, or for small clusters; but pavé setting continued on areas which had to be densely covered with smaller diamonds.

Conservatism set the tone for diamond brooches during the rest of the Victorian era. Developments in the first half of the century centred around a

Fig. 1. 4. Mid-Victorian diamond flower spray; the leaves and petals of the flower are completely pavé-set with stones. (Phillips)

renewed interest in botanical jewels, working on the eighteenth century flower-spray. The main difference between the flower brooches of the eighteenth and nineteenth centuries is realism. The eighteenth century was more concerned with the jewel as a fashion accessory, and was content with an abstract and stylised version. The nineteenth century jewellers, on the other hand, aimed at precision of design and at obtaining exact copies of flowers.

Once again, it was the Parisian jewellers who took the lead in this style. The Restoration of the Monarchy in 1814 had revived a taste for eighteenth century and Louis XVI styles, and the rather formal Napleonic scrollwork had given way to naturalism. By the middle of the century the flower-spray was perfected, principally by Oscar Massin.

Massin had spent some time in London studying English workmanship, before he produced the diamond brooches for which he became famous. These were elaborately realistic in design and immaculately executed. They were characterised by *tremblant* plant stems; and by diamonds in a waterfall setting known as *pampilles*. The stones were arranged to look like sparkling drops of dew dripping from the leaves and petals. This idea added a new movement and finesse to the flowers and captured the imagination of the public. Massin's flower-sprays were widely copied, and remained popular until the 1880s, reaching the height of success around the 1860s.

The Later Nineteenth Century

In England, the second half of the nineteenth century was turning into the age of the Exhibition. Jewellery was always well represented in British and foreign displays, and the new concepts of composition and technique offered by the Exhibitions were quickly followed up in the prosperous years of the 1860s and 1870s. A great number of diamond pieces were shown at the Great Exhibition of 1851, and most brooches were formed as flower bouquets, now heavier and more complicated than those of the early nineteenth century.

J.V. Morel and Co. won a medal for their exhibit of a bouquet brooch of diamonds and rubies which separated into several pieces, each to be worn as a different ornament. The Exhibition catalogue described the brooch as a 'bouquet composed of diamonds and rubies of fine water, representing a rose, a tulip and a volubilis'. The brooch was then described as being separated by an 'ingenious contrivance' to form the stomacher, brooches and bracelet. It contained about 700 carats of diamonds and 200 carats of rubies of even colour, all set in gold. Hunt & Roskell were particularly proud of their huge flower sprays, meticulously copied from nature, and they too could be divided into various pieces, each complete in itself.

The size and quality of the stone, and its setting, were of great importance at this time, and brilliant-cuts are often found mixed with rose-cuts.

The 1860s ushered in some of the most gimmicky and whimsical jewellery

Fig. I. 5. The 19th century move towards naturalism can be seen on this bouquet of violets in diamonds in the manner of Vever of Paris. French, about 1880. (Wartski)

fashions, that left us with a host of diamond brooches dating from this decade until the end of the century. A craze for insect and animal motifs led to successful interpretations in diamonds of the bee (the emblem of the Bonapartes), the butterfly, the lizard, the frog and endless other creatures. The body of the bee is often found banded with rubies or sapphires, and the wing markings of the butterfly are similarly contrasted in coloured stones.

A brief fashion for sporting jewellery introduced yet another range of brooches to the 1880s. Diamond horses, dogs, horseshoes, foxes usually date from this period; although they were made well into the twentieth century.

Another variety of late nineteenth century diamond brooch often found today is the small pin, worn as a fastening for folds of lace or for decorating an evening coiffure. A leading inspiration for these small diamond pins was the much admired figure of the Princess of Wales, later Queen Alexandra. Apart from butterflies and swallows, her favourite shapes were stars, often worn in sets, and crescents. Diamond stars made in 1890s were more complex than those produced in the 1860s. They had between six and 12 points, which would be pavé-set with a mixture of rose- and brilliant-cuts. Between the points, a single diamond might be collet-set at the end of a thin wire.

The latest craze for colourless stones was confirmed first by the introduction of the electric light. Also, the discovery of South African diamonds in the 1870s and increased supplies meant that cutters could afford the wastage essential to reveal maximum optical qualities. More accurate cutting was encouraged. The pavilion was cut deeper; and the culet facet, which previously had been large, was now cut almost to a fine point. Rose diamonds were revived in the last decades of the nineteenth century for smaller, less expensive brooches.

The Turn of the Century

Settings became more open, enabling as much light as possible to pass through the stone. Although platinum had made an appearance earlier in the century, the combination of silver setting and gold backs was still considered the most satisfactory.

Fig. I. 6. Late 19th century diamond brooch designed as a feather. (Phillips)

Fig. I. 7. (Left) This Edwardian diamond brooch uses a mixture of foliate design interspersed with a radial pattern, anticipating Art Deco styles; about 1910. Note the use of fine knife-wires. (Harvey & Gore)

Fig. I. 8. (Right) Edwardian diamond brooch, showing very fine setting, resembling lace work. (Harvey & Gore)

These improvements helped to maintain the popularity of the classic diamond brooch throughout the Arts and Crafts Movement, and Art Nouveau.
It was not completely unaffected by the new ideas, and any late nineteenth
century examples will show a lightness and delicacy which contrasts markedly
with the massive sprays of the 1860s. It also indicates the beginning of an Edwardian style.

One feature of diamond brooches of the turn of the century is the addition
of pale stones, such as amethysts, peridots and opals. These were introduced
during the temporary halt in diamond supplies, which was caused by the Boer
War.

The flowing lines of Art Nouveau lent themselves more to necklaces and
hair ornaments than to brooches, and examples of diamond brooches on pure
Art Nouveau lines are rare now. Most jewellers spurned the idea of using
precious stones, or else were limited by financial considerations. Lalique was
perhaps an exception, and his work and that of Vever and Fouquet have
become the most sought-after collectors' pieces. (See Chapter 17, Signed Art
Nouveau Jewellery.)

*Fig. I. 9. (Left) An
Edwardian butterfly brooch
of diamonds and sapphires,
with an onyx body and wing
markings. (Anne Bloom)
Fig. I. 10. (Right) Platinum,
gold and diamond brooch of
Art Nouveau design, with
whiplash lines and curving
leaves. (Anne Bloom)*

As the short-lived but intense impact of the Art Nouveau waned, a new and
refreshed attitude to diamond jewellery had risen. There was a strong reaction
against the escapism of turn-of-the-century jewels, and their fantastic
creatures and dream-like females with flowing hair. Women were becoming
emancipated and anxious to throw off their image of fragility and
subservience; they looked for stronger colours and outlines in their jewellery.
The era of Edward VII and Queen Alexandra was one of luxury, and society
loved to follow, even from afar, the magnificence of the Court. But Edwardian styles were tinged with a restrained elegance. Moulded by the most
famous jewellers of the century, and falling between the extremes of Art
Nouveau and Art Deco, the combinations of diamonds and brooch designs in
the years between 1900 and 1914 were some of the most successful.

A delicacy and whiteness, like fine lace work, characterised early pieces and
many brooches were made to look realistically like lace bows. Others incorporated eighteenth century styles, baskets of fruit or flowers. Gradually more
solid lines, or an occasional sunburst pattern became mingled on a brooch
with, perhaps, a rococo motif, in a subtle hint of the fashion to come.

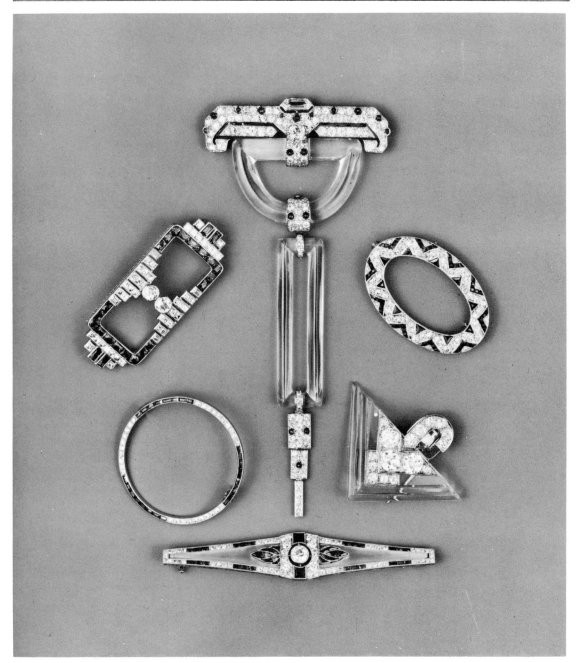

Fig. I. 11. Group of elegant and extremely stylish diamond jewels of the 1920s and 1930s. The combination of crystal with diamonds was popular, while the tapering bar-brooch below uses frosted crystal with diamonds and sapphires. Sapphires and diamonds also created the desired contrasts, used in geometric designs, as on the slim circle brooch, a favourite motif. The umbrella brooch in crystal and diamonds reflects the light-hearted approach to design that altered the look of the traditional diamond brooch in the early 20th century. (Anne Bloom)

Fig. I. 12. Art Deco brooch, showing the use of crystal and onyx with diamonds, to follow the fashion for black and white. The flower is quite realistic for the period, about 1920, and has tiny diamond stamens at its centre. (Harvey & Gore)

The 1920s and Art Deco

The grandeur of this court luxury was dispersed by the harsh reality of war in 1914. The effect of the war was to produce a society more eager than ever to enjoy itself after 1918. The money that had been made during the war was used to buy the best in fashionable accessories, and diamonds, of course, were a priority. The modern lady wanted her jewellery to reflect her recklessness and love of luxury in colour and design. Black and white were favourite colours and were adapted to jewels by the use of diamonds with onyx or black enamel. Other jewellers favoured designs using all the precious stones in their composition: it is not unusual to find the bright colours of rubies, sapphires, emeralds, pearls and diamonds together in a brooch. (See Chapter 21, Edwardian and Art Deco Jewellery.)

The contrast between translucent stones and opaque coral, onyx or jade was also used to great effect. Abstract, geometric lines were the most admired under the influence of Art Deco. Paris became the centre for these frivolous trinkets, perfect in proportions, style and workmanship, and the Paris Exhibition of Decorative Arts in 1925 reaffirmed its superiority. Leading jewellers included Cartier, Boucheron, Lacloche and Fouquet.

Platinum had been used for setting diamonds since the end of the nineteenth century. During these decades, it was used freely and with great versatility before rising prices made white gold a more practical alternative. The baguette- and emerald-cuts, which had been developed in the nineteenth century, were extremely popular in the 1920s because they blended so well with the geometrical lines of brooches. After 1930, the economic crisis and threat of another war put an end to this lightheartedness in diamonds and softness began gradually to creep into jewellery designs.

The early twentieth century helped jewellers to break away from a rather rigid adherence to the grand style. By adding such variety to the displays of today's antique jewellers, the imaginative designs of all ages have stimulated the desire for the most treasured stone in the most beautiful setting.

2. Coral Jewellery

The Victorians seem to have been particularly fickle towards jewellery designs, discarding one fashion after another in favour of the latest craze, and it appears that the most intense fashions suffered the most complete rejections. Coral was one material that was treated in this way. It rode the crest of the fashion wave around the middle of the nineteenth century, and then absolutely disappeared from fashionable wardrobes, making a brief appearance in the 1920s, and then reappearing in modern jewellery.

Coral is the skeleton of a marine animal, the coral polyp *(Corallicum)*. The animal is like a mass of jelly, and attaches itself to the rocks in certain seas. There a hard skeleton-like deposit is formed, mostly of calcium carbonate, on the outer part of the animal's body. Most coral is found off the coasts of the Mediterranean sea, and the deepest colours come from the Spanish coast. The coasts of Algeria, Tunisia, Corsica, Sardinia and Sicily are also homes of the coral polyp.

The deeper in the ocean the coral grows, the less colour it usually has. Red is the most usual colour, but rose-pink or deep blood-red are the most desirable. White and yellow varieties are also possible.

The story of the use of coral in jewellery starts in ancient Rome, where it was worn extensively, and where so many of its superstitions originated. In the ancient world it was considered a very effective antidote to poison, and throughout the Middle Ages the qualities of coral were highly esteemed by pharmacists.

Many beliefs developed at this time, and coral was constantly worn as a talisman against enchantments, witchcraft and Satan. It was thought that when worn by a healthy man coral was dark red, but when worn by a woman it turned paler. It was also pale when worn by a dangerously sick person. Ground coral was even taken internally. Grains of coral put into babies' milk were thought to guard against fits.

Coral, together with silver bells, has always been associated with babies and children, as the best means of warding off evil spirits. In the nineteenth century, coral beads were given as a christening present to a baby girl, and a boy received a silver rattle with a stem of coral for sucking and cutting his teeth.

With such a strong background of ancient beliefs, coral commanded a great

Fig. 2. 1. Gold butterfly
hovering on a coral stalk.
English, about 1860.
(Landsberg & Son)

deal of respect in early nineteenth-century society. It was one of the dominant jewel fashions that continued through the years of the restoration of the French monarchy after 1814. There it was intricately worked and often form-ed as cameos, joined into extensive parures in the 1820s. A leading French fashion magazine of the time stated that coral was still definitely in vogue, but pointed out that when a complete parure was worn, blue, white or lilac flowers for the hair should be replaced by a pomegranate, amaranth or corn-poppy, in fact, anything that matched the coral. Also at that time, rows of small beads, pendants, rings and hair-combs were all worn by young girls, as alternatives to the customary pearls worn with white gowns. The taste con-tinued into the early Victorian period, when coral was considered proper for day wear.

The French court took a keener interest in the material after 1845, when the Duchesse d'Aumale was given some particularly fine pieces by her bridegroom. A little later, Napoleon's Italian campaigns and the consequent mania for everything Italian helped coral to the height of fashion in the 1860s.

Coral ornaments had been made in Italy for some time, especially for children who wore them as prevention against disease and evil. From 1830 to 1860 the trade, which was centred around Naples, increased to such an extent that in 1870 Robert Phillips of Cockspur Street, London, was given a decoration from the King of Italy for his service to the coral trade.

The rose-pink colour was the most sought after at this time, and its bran-ches were painstakingly carved into the most delicate arrangements of flowers, twigs, leaves and fruits. Roses and chrysanthemums with immaculate petals were regular features, while cherubs and classical figures made fre-quent appearances too. Tiny hands as charms or clasps were formed from coral, some wearing tiny gold rings or detailed cuffs set with turquoises.

Fig. 2.2. Brooch and
matching ear-rings of gold
with coral drops, shaped as
arum lilies; a very beautiful
and fluid design, well made
with fine gold-work. About
1860. (Nicolas Harris)

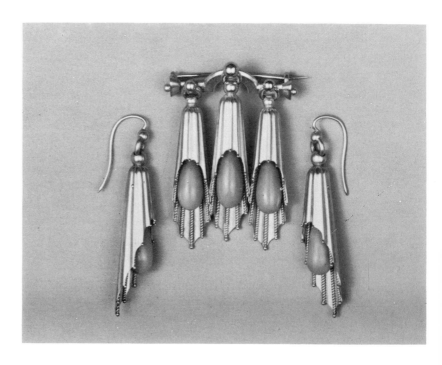

Fig. 2.3. The coral hand was a popular early Victorian jewel, the hand often gripping another part of the jewel or acting as a clasp. As here, there was usually a gold and gem-set bracelet around the wrist.

The clasp, top left, is made of white coral; the hand clasping the anchor, a symbol of hope, with a deeper coral heart for love, the tassels also of white coral. The tiny good luck charms held by two of the hands are immaculately carved, and include a shoe, a boot, a dog and a hat. About 1830-40. (Brian and Lynn Holmes)

Often the coral was left in its natural branches, a style especially suited to tiaras, but generally less decorative. This kind of branch coral now is far less expensive and desirable than the carvings of the same period. Many cameos were carved from coral in the 1850s. Much of this work was done in Rome.

Beads of coral were polished; sometimes they were faceted or 'diamond'-cut like a pineapple skin. In the 1860s, strings of beads were still worn by young girls, as the pale colour combined very well with a white ball gown, and single beads surmounted gold and tortoise-shell hair ornaments.

Apart from intricately carved suites, smooth coral was frequently added to gold brooches of the 1860s, and used in the same manner as pavé-set turquoises. Classicism was a guiding influence, and gold was left plain and lightly coloured to give a delicate 'bloom' that needed no further engraving. Set deep into the centre of the brooch there would be a smooth sphere of coral, with perhaps a border of the fine gold wire-work that was a speciality of the era. In the 1870s, coral was added to brooches with diamonds and emeralds, a combination that usually worked well with a plain, frosted gold background.

Ear-rings, too, were designed in the same style. For longer ear-rings, worn after 1865, coral balls were hung in the centre of gold hoops. Very beautiful, smooth buttons or tear-drops of coral were ideal compliments to the classical gold-work of the 1860s.

Over-use, or misuse of coral ornaments led to the criticism of vulgarity, and by the late 1860s, its popularity was steadily declining. In 1868, George Augustus Sala rudely referred to coral as 'twisted sticks of seeming red sealing wax', obviously with the rather bare branch coral jewellery in mind.

Unfortunately, the delicacy of the carved bracelets, brooches and suites has made perfect examples quite rare and expensive. They move more and more into the realm of the true collector as they are not easy to wear. On the other hand strings of polished coral beads, of a deep colour, are fashionable. Again they are difficult to find.

Apart from the intricate work involved, which could not be repeated today, nineteenth century pieces represent good value in terms of the amount and quality of coral, as the price of the new material is rising all the time.

Fig. 2.4. Coral cameo of Bacchus, about 1780. (Hancocks & Co)

3. Nineteenth Century Gold-work

Of all the influences, novelties and discoveries which transformed jewellery in the nineteenth century, the change in attitude towards gold-work was one of the most important. About the middle of the century, jewellers awakened to the properties and possibilities of the materials with which they worked; then they began to produce the impressive gold jewellery which was so typically Victorian.

Early in the century, gold was mainly used as backing to silver-set stones. The gems themselves still provided the focal point of jewels. The second decade saw the birth of a new gold decoration, a kind of filigree work known as 'cannetille' which was named after the gold embroideries of the Napoleonic years. By 1814, the Bourbon monarchy was restored in France, but Europe was feeling the effects of war, and even the grandeur of the new court had to submit to economies. 'Semi-precious' stones became fashionable, and

Fig. 3.1. and 3.2. Two gold brooches, showing the repoussé early Victorian gold-work, set with semi-precious stones and draped with chains.
Fig. 3.2. (Right) Uses the entwined scrolls or knot motif; the hollow scrolls give an impression of substantial weight. (Ronald Benjamin)

Fig. 3.3. Suite of early 19th century amethyst and 'cannetille' gold-work. Note the floral and shell motifs. (Nicolas Harris)

Fig. 3.4. Messages of sentiment were often associated with the symbolism of floral motifs, here in intricate gold-work with curling tendrils, vine leaves and grapes. The pendant, on its original chain, has a hair locket inside and bears the message 'REGARD'; a favourite sentimental jewel motif throughout the 19th century. About 1820-30. (Asprey)

amethysts, topaz and aquamarines were all set in this skilful filigree that made the most of a small amount of gold.

The style was popular in both England and France during the 1820s. The stones were usually foiled for uniformity of colour, and were set in nests of tightly-curled fine gold wires, with trails of tiny gold granules. Very intricate designs often used floral and seashell motifs to surround massive stones on each piece of a parure.

The taste for cannetille had completely faded by the 1840s; its place was taken by repoussé work, at first stamped from thin sheets of gold, but later improved and refined. With this method, the design was raised in relief by hammering the gold from the back, and machine-made parts were often hand-finished. Designs for this kind of gold jewellery were based on rich scroll-work, strap-work, shells, flowers and leaves. Many of the motifs and patterns established at this time continued more or less throughout the century.

In the 1830s, gold was skilfully wrought into charming sprays of flowers, small brooches with stylised flower-heads of turquoises, pearls or sometimes citrines and amethysts for pansies. Coloured gold, mixed with copper for a red sheen or with silver for a green tint, was used for the stems and leaves; and the matt surface achieved combined well with the satin finish of turquoises or pearls.

Perhaps the best examples of the use of gold decoration in these pre-Victorian years can be seen on gentlemen's seals, which were considered very important items of costume at the time. These accessories attracted endless care and skill in the 1820s and 1830s. Gold on both massive or minute seals was richly chased into flowers, leaves, seashell motifs, animals or coiled serpents.

Fig. 3.5. Heart pendant with coloured gold decoration of grapes and vine leaves, incorporating a gem-set flower. About 1830. (Anne Bloom)

During the 1840s, while the young Queen Victoria's influence on jewel fashions was emerging, patterns for gold-work very much revolved around the natural world. These motifs suited feminine delicacy and the purely ornamental woman who acted as a showcase for her husband's success. In this era of peace and prosperity, wealth was displayed in jewels and especially in a sumptuous spread of gold. Every surface of gold was chased, engraved, pierced or enamelled. Ivy leaves trailed over gold lockets; snake-skin scales were imitated on gold chains; stones were framed by rich scrolls, pierced strapwork, or gold twigs twisted and entwined with foliage. Bracelets were formed of plump chased links in fancy shapes, and fastened with an engraved heart, which might be set with a cabochon garnet.

Fig. 3.6. The lotus flower, from Nineveh and Egypt, was a popular motif on gold jewellery, like this gold brooch with matching earrings. About 1870. (N. Bloom & Son)

Archaeological Influences

Important influences came from North Africa, where the French had been fighting for Algeria, and from the Middle East, where excavations revealed the fascinating remains of Nineveh. The Algerian knot and tassel was incorporated into gold jewels, thus initiating the theme of elaborate knots, bows, entwined boughs and serpents which was so dominant in nineteenth century jewellery. From Nineveh came the simple lotus flower which can be seen again and again on gold-work of this period, and for many years afterwards.

Brooches were large and imposing; many were composed of machine-made parts. Hollow tubes of gold, tortuously twisted, were hung with loops of fine gold chain; from this was suspended a stone, probably a garnet, embedded in more engraved gold. Sometimes flimsy gold stampings were filled to add weight to the jewel.

By the middle of the century, attention was turned to the gold jewellery made in Rome, where an entirely new approach to jewel designs and to gold-work had been developed. The greatest influence on Victorian gold jewellery undoubtedly came from the ancient Etruscans, and recent excavations of their metalwork had bred a new kind of archaeological jewel (see Chapter 15).

It was the Italian Fortunato Pio Castellani, who was first fascinated by these Etruscan ornaments and who tried to recreate classical Greek, Roman

Fig. 3.7. Gold suite, set with garnets, showing the repoussé work with designs of scrolls and feathers. (Christie's)

Fig. 3.8. The Etruscan bulla
was much imitated by 19th
century jewellers. Here the
circular-shaped locket, finely
worked in the Etruscan
manner of gold-work, is set
with a lapis-lazuli. The
necklace is hung with lotus
flower motifs with tiny pearl
centres, which alternate
with lapis-lazuli drops.
(Nicholas Harris)

Fig. 3.9. Excellent gold
bangle with ram's head
motif, decorated with trails
of filigree and granules in
the Italian archaeological
manner. The bangle itself is
designed as a horn, the
width tapering as it meets
the ram's head again. About
1860. (Anne Bloom)

and Etruscan jewellery. In particular, the lost technique of granulation puzzled and captivated Castellani. From about 1826, he began to produce close and successful imitations of these ancient jewels in Rome; although the real secret of granulation was not discovered until the 1930s.

Castellani aimed to produce exact replicas of ancient jewels, so that he copied designs as well as techniques. Because of this, jewels made from gold alone were fashionable in the 1860s and 1880s. The ancient 'bulla' became a well-known shape for lockets and pendants. This was a circular gold ornament, worn by the Etruscan and Roman children of noblemen as an amulet. Brooches took the form of fibulae; others were round with mosaic centres; gold necklaces were fringed with seashells, amphorae, rosettes and rams' heads.

This revival left little room for new, creative jewellery designs during the 1850s and 1860s, but the innovation lay in the attitude and approach to gold-work. The appearance of this gold jewellery is very distinctive: it has a pure, rich and polished look, with more substance than earlier jewels, both in physical materials and in design. Another aspect of this change was the need for more specialised work, which entailed several men with different skills being involved in the production of one piece.

The fashion for serious copies of Etruscan jewels grew in England, where, at the same time, in the 1860s, there was a plague of frivolous novelties in the jewellery trade. Carlo Giuliano, originally from Naples, had come to London to work, and he too produced superb and accurate copies of ancient jewels. Of the English jewellers, Robert Phillips excelled in fine gold jewellery, and John Brogden also worked in a similar style but drew more inspiration from Egypt and the Middle East.

Eventually, the styles spread to less expensive jewels. Ancient motifs were

Fig. 3.10. Georgian gold chain, with typical textured, rounded links and elaborate clasp, about 1820. The quizzing glass has a chased border of flowers and leaves, similar to the work found on seals of the 1820s and 1830s, with a turquoise and emerald flower. (Asprey)

blended with contemporary styles, and granulation and gold wirework in the Etruscan taste can be found on gold bangles, bar-brooches, and tie-clips almost until the end of the century.

The Classical Revival

This influence accounted for the use of gold on its own in nineteenth century jewellery. However a change in the attitude and position of women during the 1860s also introduced stronger, more geometric jewels to assert their new authority. Where before every surface had been covered with fussy but delicate decoration, gold was now left plain and smooth, and the only embellishment might be in an unobtrusive classical style.

Plain gold was often 'coloured' or given a 'bloom'. This process, which had been used since the middle of the century, involved dipping the piece into an acid bath of salt, saltpetre, muriatic acid and water. This dissolved the outer

Fig. 3.11. Archaeological style gold-work frames a mound of pavé-set turquoises, with a star and diamond motif at the centre, on this brooch and matching ear-rings. About 1860. (John Joseph)

layers of alloy, so leaving a film of pure gold on the surface, covered with thousands of minute holes like pinpricks. Jewels coloured in this way have a frosted, creamy sheen, which looks particularly rich and appealing on plain surfaces.

Lockets were now often plain; although they were sometimes relieved by a central motif of pavé-set turquoises or a star set with half-pearls. It is the brooches and ear-rings of this period that provide the most distinctive and interesting examples of gold-work. One kind of brooch was huge and geometric in form and made entirely of gold. This often used the theme of tangled knots or interlacing. The other well-known type of brooch was round, or a horizontal oval in shape, with gold surrounding a central boss. This would be coral, pavé-set turquoises, cabochon garnet or dark blue enamel. The surround of gold and the centre design would be level, with a sunken rim of metal, like a moat, between the two. On others the centre formed a slight mound, but

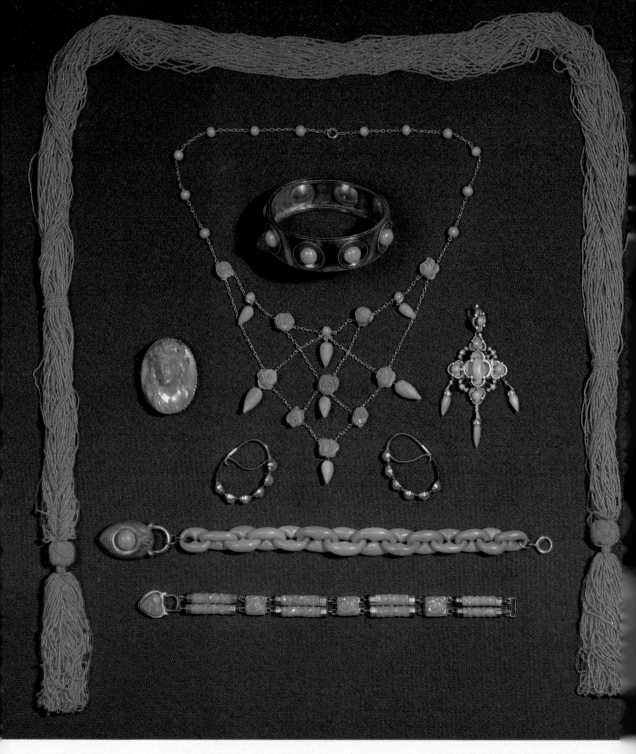

Plate 1. (Previous page) *Transitional Edwardian jewels with an enamel, pearl and diamond plaque brooch, about 1925. The perspective rectangular brooch, in rubies and diamonds is Russian, about 1900. (Sotheby's)*

Plate 2. *Group of coral jewels of various periods: the carved ear-rings are early 19th century; the very fine bead rope is early 20th century; other pieces date around 1850–60. (S. Rogers and M. Ventura)*

Plate 3. Mid-19th century gold-work. Left: two brooches showing a mixture of delicately engraved oak leaves with trails of rope-work and beaded edges; set with rubies and diamonds. Right: the Algerian knot and tassel motif using entwined ribbons. Below: gold locket, about 1860. The flower motifs are traced by Etruscan-style work, set with turquoises and pearls. (John Joseph)

Plate 4. (Overleaf) *A selection of gold desk and fob seals, set with hardstones, which demonstrates the ingenuity of the gold-work. From about 1775 to late 19th century. (Asprey)*

Fig. 3.12. Typical gold jewels of the late 19th century, around the 1870s: pair of Etruscan style bangles, one would be worn on each wrist; 'creole' ear-rings; locket, wound with two straps and buckles and set with pearls and rubies, on necklet of flat gold links; other popular designs for lockets; and a brooch with moving fringe, covered with clusters of granules. (John Joseph; Brian and Lynn Holmes)

generally the border of gold was decorated with very light arrangements of gold granules, wire-work or rope-work. Another feature was the flexible gold fringe, graduated towards the centre, which hung from brooches, pendants and ear-rings, adding movement, gaiety and lightness. The fringing was often made from a kind of snake chain.

Ear-rings of the 1860s and 1870s showed great ingenuity and variety of motif. During the mid-Victorian years, they became high-fashion accessories. Looking at these ear-rings, you can see how the treatment of gold had become uninhibited and adventurous, in the same way that the use of diamonds was to change with the twentieth century. The lightly 'bloomed' or frosted gold was extensively used and decoration was traced with the lightest of filigree, wire-work or granulation, so that it did not detract from the basic, strong shapes. These included triangles, long and slender drops, circles or hoops, pear or tear-shapes, Greek amphorae or vases and bulbous bomb shapes.

Long ear-rings offered great scope for movement, and jewellers lost no time in exploiting this advantage, making good use of fringes. Apart from the usual chain fringing, borders were formed by little rows of drops: round, tear-drop or spindle in shape. Sometimes the fringe alone, or a gold tassel hung from a gold bar. Another way of adding movement was to have loops, or concentric circles, swinging freely inside one another. Shapes were sometimes cut out from an oval or circle of gold, to form pendants hanging within the hollows.

Ideas about the wearing and purpose of jewels changed considerably in late Victorian years, prompted by a decline in standards of design and production. By the 1880s, silver was worn instead of gold, and when this fashion had passed, the approaching influence of the Arts and Crafts Movement and Art Nouveau could be clearly seen. New ideals and priorities moved the emphasis from Victorian gold-work to other aspects of the jeweller's art.

Fig. 3.13. Selection of inventive gold ear-rings of the 1870s. (Anne Bloom)

4. Piqué

'A beautiful minor art' is the way Herbert C. Dent chose to describe his beloved piqué and it still seems a most appropriate title for the objects this man so passionately collected in the 1920s. Piqué is, by definition, gold and silver decoration on tortoise-shell or ivory, sometimes with the addition of mother-of-pearl. This form of decoration was used extensively in the seventeenth and eighteenth centuries for small, personal objects and was then revived in the second half of the nineteenth century for jewellery.

It can be a very beautiful decorative art. Like so many other techniques, the secrets of its production were handed down from generation to generation and have now been almost completely forgotten. This, of course, adds to the appeal of piqué as an interesting area for collectors.

In 1925, Major Dent was persuaded by the high prices paid for piqué at the time, to remove his collection from the Castle Museum, Norwich, and sell it at Sotheby's. There an early Louis XIV tobacco-box sold for £15; a Louis XIV salve-box in blonde tortoise-shell made £28; a Louis XIV spectacle-case realised £9.15s (£9.75); and a very fine Louis XIV ivory fan fetched the high price of £45. Since then early piqué boxes, bonbonnières, étuis and lorgnettes have established for themselves an important place among sought after objets d'art.

By comparison with these trinkets, the nineteenth century piqué jewellery may appear of lower quality in design and workmanship, and it is often dismissed by jewellery dealers as just another late Victorian jewellery craze which played no part in the important artistic movements of the time. But it is just these very reasons that make piqué, and so many other similar minor fashions, interesting clues to popular tastes, techniques and costume of the late nineteenth century. Piqué jewellery is becoming more popular with collectors, as it is still quite inexpensive, very attractive, easy to identify and to appreciate, and there are virtually no modern fakes or reproductions.

It is the type of jewellery that is seen a great deal in the indoor markets in London, and probably passes through the hands of most antique jewellers at some time. Some occasionally keep a few good pieces in their stocks, when they come across them; others find piqué particularly appealing, buy more pieces and therefore attract collectors and also those who want to sell.

The Basic Material

True tortoise-shell, a dark reddish-brown mottled material, is produced by only three species of marine turtles, and the most important of these is the Hawksbill turtle. The tortoise-shell is found orginally as overlapping plates or blades. Those on the back, or carapace, of the turtle come in the deep brown shades; while the plates on the underside, or belly, are a light amber-yellow from which comes 'blonde' tortoise-shell.

The versatility of tortoise-shell, its rich colours and the ease with which it can be worked, have helped to make it one of the most popular, sought after materials to come from the sea. Its natural markings are patches of translucent sherry-gold mingled with cloudy chestnut, and these give a fascinating depth to a smooth flat surface. It is also a material that lasts well, and feels very good to handle, which is why it is a natural choice for small every-day items.

The blades of the turtle-shell are separated from the body or skeleton by heat, and eventually they come to the craftsman who chooses from the separate plates those pieces he needs. To obtain the correct thickness, several blades can be welded together, again using heat, or small pieces can be joined, so that little need be wasted. This quality of softening under the heat — either wet or dry — has helped the craftsman adapt the material to his own ideas.

The tortoise-shell is then moulded and shaped, again using heat. It is immersed in boiling water, with some salt added to prevent any alteration in colour, and then it can be pressed into moulds — for boxes or cigarette-cases perhaps — or used as a veneer. Strips can be joined to make rings, or hoops for ear-rings. It is also when the shell is softened in this way that the gold, silver or mother-of-pearl can be pressed into it as decoration.

Just as these techniques, mastered and refined by seventeenth and eighteenth century craftsmen, were handed down to the next generation of workers, so the methods of polishing have also been cherished in the same way. Simply explained, the shell is scraped, very carefully smoothed and then polished several times with oils and powders. The name 'piqué' comes from the French *piquer*, because in the earliest form of this decoration, the points of metal were actually 'pricked' into the tortoise-shell.

Types of Decoration

There are two distinct types of piqué decoration. 'Piqué point' consists of patterns of stars or dots, in which the pins of metal are level with the surface of the tortoise-shell and polished with it. 'Piqué posé' uses strips of sheet metal to produce ribbons of gold or silver, scalloped or geometrical designs, or flower decoration.

There have been variations of these two methods: sometimes piqué point was extended to include longer points of gold or silver known as 'piqué clouté'. There is also a kind of piqué posé with extremely fine strands of gold or silver which has come to be known as hair-work.

Mother-of-pearl was added in early specimens and then again at different periods. In the seventeenth and eighteenth centuries, the mother-of-pearl was finely engraved, whereas a little later it was always left plain.

The exact origins of piqué are obscure but it seems certain that the art was born and bred in France. A great deal of credit for this work has been given to

Fig. 4.1. (Opposite page) Tortoise-shell is traditionally an attractive and suitable material for hair ornaments, being light, easy to wear, and especially attractive when the light shines through to show the mottled markings. This group shows the variations in piqué combs, mid to late 19th century. (Galérie 360; Private Collection)

Fig. 4.2. Above: link bracelet with piqué posé. Below: the sections of this bracelet are bordered in gold, enclosing a floral design. (Brian and Lynn Holmes)

André Charles Boulle (1642-1732), the most famous cabinet-maker of the Louis XIV period, who often worked for the King himself. Boulle perfected a style of marquetry in tortoise-shell, using thin sheets of brass, and the name of this *premier ébéniste du roi* was given to this particular kind of work. It is more usually known today as 'buhl'.

According to Major Dent, in his book on the subject, the moulding and inlay of tortoise-shell was done as early as the 1620s; about 50 years before Boulle reached the height of his success and was given an apartment in the Louvre in 1672. It is possible that an older member of the Boulle family might have originated the craft.

Whatever the origin of the work, it was developed and improved in this second half of the seventeenth century, and it was just at a peak of perfection when the Revocation of the Edict of Nantes, in 1685, forced thousands of Huguenots to leave France.

Among some 40,000 families who fled to England were many craftsmen who specialised in piqué and brought this art form with them. For this reason it is often difficult to distinguish between French and English piqué-work dating from the late seventeenth century.

Over a long period of time, these Huguenot craftsmen naturally absorbed the influences of their new surroundings and very gradually the delicate French refinement was replaced by more stolid English ideas of design. However, the high standard of workmanship was maintained throughout the next century.

Dutch craftsmen who came to England, particularly at the time of William and Mary, also contributed to this art, and as they had been used to moulding horn into beautiful boxes, they very easily picked up piqué techniques.

Another link with the Dutch lies in the actual trade in tortoise-shell. At the end of the seventeenth century, a great deal of the material was imported from Asia. As the Dutch had strong trading ties with the East, they probably transported and handled most of the tortoise-shell in Europe at that time.

The majority of items produced in this medium are small, partly because of the materials involved, and partly because of the customs and habits of a luxury-loving society.

Early piqué appears on boxes, mostly tobacco or snuff boxes, patch-boxes, scent-bottles, bonbonnières, carnets de bal, étuis, bodkin-cases, fan sticks, lorgnettes and cane heads. Jewellery was not made in piqué until the nineteenth century. The size of these pieces also explains how the craft and the objects travelled from their country of origin, as refugees from political or religious persecution could easily carry these trinkets with them, when they had to leave most other valuables behind.

The expert will be able to recognise the different periods of piqué, and the difference between English and French work. This only comes with experience, but there are a few basic distinguishing features of each age.

Fig. 4.3. Very unusual piqué ring, with a circular bezel decorated with a solid patch of silver. (Brian and Lynn Holmes)

The Seventeenth Century

In the early part of the Louis XIV period (reigned 1643-1715), very little strip-work or piqué posé was done. Most of the patterns were exquisitely formed by points or dots of gold or silver. These dots were grouped to form favourite motifs, exclusive to piqué design, such as flies, cornucopia, vine-leaves and bunches of grapes, fleur-de-lis, birds, and the symbolic sunflower and peacock, the emblems of Louis XIV, the Sun-King.

Designs used on other art forms of the time are also to be found on piqué items. During the middle of the reign, piqué point and posé are found used together; while towards the end, either one or the other was used on each piece. This was perhaps one of the best periods of French piqué. Under Louis XV (reigned 1715-74), the style tended towards more elaborate piqué posé with scroll designs, pastoral scenes and some classical figures.

The star is the chief characteristic of piqué made during the Louis XVI period (reigned 1774-92), and it was produced in the same way as the dot of piqué point. The stars are usually evenly spaced out over the whole surface, as a decoration in their own right, instead of being grouped to form a pattern.

Fig. 4.4. Piqué bangle formed of two semi-circles and linked by elastic. Decorated with geometric patterns and bordered with the popular honeycomb pattern. (Brian and Lynn Holmes)

Fig. 4.5. Group of late 18th century/early 19th century piqué boxes. Note the piqué point star and dot decoration on the large Italian box, combined with a mother-of-pearl inlaid cross, about 1800; and the woven ivory with gold points or nails, about 1810. The plain round box for 'cachous' is about 1800; and the baroque style toilet box is about 1730. (Galérie 360)

Flowers also appear at this time, in sprigs, sprays or as a luxuriant basket of flowers. Later eighteenth century work also includes the extra-fine hair strands of piqué posé.

Toward the end of Louis XVI's reign, and during the Napoleonic years, piqué was more often worked on ivory. On the whole, ivory has been used less as a background to this work, as tortoise-shell is more easily moulded and it also provides a more effective contrast and background for the delicate inlays. You can trace the use of piqué on ivory through beautiful, small boxes (rectangular, oblong, oval or shuttle-shaped) needle-cases, cane heads, toothpick cases and other objets d'art.

The one major characteristic feature of English seventeenth century piqué decoration is the tiny circle or ring. The effect of this design can be seen most-ly on large tobacco-boxes of the period. The circles are usually neatly arrang-ed around the edge of the lid, grouped as little triangles or pyramids of three rings. Sometimes the circles form lines or designs around the body of the box. As the customs of snuff-taking had not yet been widely accepted in this coun-try in the seventeenth century, these larger tortoise-shell boxes were made for tobacco; but from the early years of the next century, boxes were made smaller in order to hold snuff. These new trinkets again found their in-spiration for shape and design among the French, who had adopted the habit far earlier.

The Eighteenth Century

Several different influences worked together to make the eighteenth century, and particularly the years from 1740 to 1760, the high point in English piqué production. Both French and Dutch craftsmen had established themselves in this country, perfected their technique and introduced elements of their native designs. All aspects of fashion and costume accessories took their lead from Paris, while in England furniture and architectural design was dominated by the brilliance of Chippendale, Sheraton, Hepplewhite and Adam. Yet another influence on design came from the East and was expressed in delicate 'Chinoiserie' scenes. All these influences, which shaped current tastes and fashions, can be found, in piqué, on the beautiful boxes and luxurious trinkets of this glittering and frivolous age.

Early eighteenth century boxes were usually oval-shaped, with elaborate lids, and a great deal of mother-of-pearl was incorporated. The fine silver strand piqué is also a feature of this period, but it was not as popular as the broader piqué posé and was consequently not as common. A little later, boxes became round, often with Sheffield plate bodies and tortoise-shell lids.

From the last quarter of the eighteenth century, the Adam influence is very noticeable. Neo-classical urns, honeysuckle, festoons and garlands, and swags of drapery all cover a variety of objects, such as bodkin-cases, étuis and patch-boxes. From the 1780s, the Sheraton style appears in piqué work on shuttle-shaped boxes. The lids are set with a marquise-shaped panel of engraved silver or gold, a miniature, or an oval floral design, all echoing the shape of the box.

One variation on eighteenth century piqué comes in the shape of tortoise-shell (sometimes ivory) boxes made with a basket-weave design. Oblong or rectangular in shape, the woven squares were nailed with metal pins, and panels for monograms were set into the lids.

The Nineteenth Century

After reaching the height of its glory, piqué-work began to decline with the close of the eighteenth century. Workmanship continued to be very careful, conscientious and fine through the nineteenth century, but as far as boxes were concerned, designs became clumsy and less stylish. The eclecticism of the Victorian period diluted the strength of eighteenth century characteristics and tastes, and piqué design was left with no particular guiding influence.

By the mid-century, this beautiful minor art had found a new direction, and was revived as a decoration for jewellery. It proved to be a very popular and effective idea for secondary, day-time jewellery. These piqué jewels seems to bear little resemblance to their aristocratic ancestors and should not perhaps be compared to seventeenth and eighteenth century boxes. They have a charm and interest of their own and an important place in the jewellery story of the mid-nineteenth century.

Fig. 4.6. Group of piqué ear-rings, showing the various designs and their similarity to gold ear-rings of the same period: loops that move freely inside each other, torpedo shapes decorated with geometric squares and star design, shorter ball ear-rings with piqué point star motif, and Creole shaped hoop ear-rings decorated with silver piqué. (S. Rogers and M. Ventura; Claire and Ingeborg)

Fig. 4.7. Two piqué crosses.
Left: a Maltese cross with
rich flower and tendril
decoration. Right: a plainer
cross outlined in gold.
(Anne Bloom)

The piqué jewel fashion seems to have followed the popularity of tortoise-shell, especially worn to decorate the hair. In the 1830s and 1840s, the wave of naturalism and romance saw tortoise-shell coaxed into shapes resembling wood, branches and twigs. However by the 1850s and 1860s, the material had resumed its most suitable rôle as a hair ornament. In 1862, it was fashionable to wear a tortoise-shell hair-comb studded with steel.

In the 1860s piqué jewels were selling extremely well. Dress buckles of slim rectangular shapes looked very pretty for day wear and were often matched with a set of piqué buttons. Brooches were very popular: they were usually circular, smoothly rounded with scalloped or patterned borders enclosing a delicate flower and leaf design, sometimes with added mother-of-pearl. This always complemented the technique with very fine, curling tendrils. A honeycomb design at the centre was also common, together with key pattern borders. More unusual shapes, such as a butterfly or Maltese cross were worn. The piqué is very skilfully worked on such pieces.

Strings of piqué beads looked attractive, and bangles too were adapted to the fashion, sometimes with a pendant heart to hang on to the back of the hand. Other bracelets were formed by threading various shaped discs together. Large chain bracelets, very well carved and joined, were light and easy to wear. The lightness of the material also lent itself well to ear-rings which, by the 1870s, had reached extraordinary proportions and outrageous shapes. Piqué ear-rings of this period tended to follow current gold styles. Small ball drops, Latin or Maltese crosses, butterflies, torpedo-shapes either smoothly rounded or with flat, tapering triangular sides and Creole shapes with loops or circles which moved inside each other, were all made in tortoise-shell with the gold and silver inlay. The form of decorative inlay varied. It could be flowery and naturalistic or consist of bolder, plain swirls of piqué posé in gold, creating a dramatic contrast with the dark tortoise-shell.

In the 1860s, piqué-work was still done entirely by hand, but the ambitious Birmingham jewellery industry soon exploited its possibilities. By the mid 1870s, piqué jewellery was being mass-produced with the aid of machines.

The shapes for inlay were pressed out mechanically from sheet metal, and then into the softened tortoise-shell. This meant that designs became more geometrical, with formalised, scalloped borders; circles inside squares; and the honeycomb design. These more abstract styles were also considered preferable to the earlier naturalistic, flower motifs. Crosses became a speciality of these Birmingham firms, who sold exclusive designs to London retailers.

Tortoise-shell and piqué remained very popular in this kind of jewellery from the 1860s until about 1885. After that it again disappeared; perhaps because silver jewellery with its lighter colours and colourless stones became fashionable around this time. It is very likely that tortoise-shell had been worn as part of mourning dress; as soon as Queen Victoria relaxed her rigid mourning rules, society ladies completely rejected anything which reminded them of the long years of dark and sombre jewels.

The piqué fashion was not revived and remains a peculiarly Victorian phenomenon. It is now far enough in the past to look attractive and dramatic in wear today.

5. Silver of the Late Nineteenth Century

Silver as a material for jewels had been very much at the mercy of the dictates of fashion and economical fluctuations throughout the nineteenth century. It was raised to the heights of popularity and then equally swiftly rejected and despised. In the early part of the nineteenth century, silver was used to make cheaper jewels as a substitute for gold, along with alloys such as pinchbeck. In the 1870s, it developed a style of its own, when the popularity of silver coincided with a new and strong artistic influence. Examples of this style have survived very well, because their relatively low value have saved them from the melting pot and from alteration. Many new collectors have found these silver jewels to be authentic and decorative reflections of the era.

During the prosperous mid Victorian years, impressive gold suites were worn, very brightly coloured with blue enamel or rich red cabochon garnets against the coloured or 'bloomed' gold. But, by the 1870s, colours were becoming softer and ornamental contrasts less marked. By the 1880s, the vogue was for colourless stones and jewels, like pearls and diamonds. This may have been largely due to the widespread use of electric light which flattered diamonds but made bright gold and enamels look cheap and vulgar. It was also due to the discovery of diamonds in South Africa in 1867, making the stones more plentiful.

Silver was obviously an important part of this vogue, but there were other reasons for its sudden rise in popularity. The main factor involved was the discovery of the Comstock Lode in Nevada, U.S.A. about 1860 which meant an enormous increase in the world's supplies of silver. It was some time before the benefits of this discovery were felt by the jewellery trade but, by the 1870s, silver jewellery had received the seal of approval from the leaders of fashion.

Large lockets were the favourite items, some followed the earlier designs of gold lockets, but were now worn on huge silver chains with bulky links, or on very wide flat collars. Most of the lockets were oval, although occasionally they were rectangular in shape. They all bore a large repertoire of ornamental designs, being elaborately chased all over, or decorated with a wide panel of engraved flowers and ivy leaves, or bearing alternate stripes of plain silver and engraving. Some very plump, smoothly finished lockets were topped with raised, interlocked Gothic-style initials, a raised motif of an oak leaf, or a spray of flowers. Anchor motifs, silver rope-work and fluted edges were all features offered in endless permutations. Technical improvements in photography eventually led to small prints. This meant that lockets had to be large enough to accommodate the picture. This was particularly convenient and rewarding for manufacturers with large amounts of silver at their disposal. From jewellers' catalogues and contemporary fashion magazines, it would seem that 1878 was the best year for the silver locket.

The Japonaiserie Craze

Bangles, another feature of mid-Victorian attire, were worn several at a time. These now appeared in silver, along with brooches and ear-rings, at first all in styles reminiscent of grand gold jewels. Designs were again similar to those of lockets: wide expanses of engraved, scrolled or foliate patterns, or heavy Gothic-style borders and beaded edges. However it was the most fashionable design influence of this period which best suited these silver jewels and gave them their distinctive and unusual character. This influence came from the hither-to unknown art of Japan. In 1854, Commander Perry of the U.S. Navy was successful in signing a treaty of trading rights between America and Japan. Other countries soon followed and this opened up an unknown culture to Europe and the United States. A treasure-house, full of the wonders of exotic arts and crafts, was now seen and examined for the first time. They had an amazing effect on all decorative design, creating a mania for all things Japanese.

Previous historical influences had been fully exploited. As ideas were fast becoming stale and overworked, it was with huge delight that designers greeted this completely fresh and picturesque form of artistic expression. They were first introduced to the contemporary folk art of Japan through the coloured prints, which gave an overall impression of exoticism. These were followed by the ceramics which far surpassed current European standards. These too expressed the basic elements of Far Eastern design. Colourful lacquer-work and textiles continued to enchant the Western world, and great interest was shown in the legendary Japanese metal-work.

These wonderful metal-working skills had developed from the tradition of sword-making, one of the most highly respected of all crafts. Sword fittings, guards and shields had become highly decorative and some swords were made solely for decorative wear or ceremonial use. The chief features of the craft were the exquisite inlays and alloys, such as 'shibuichi' (silver and copper) and 'shakudo' (gold and copper). The wearing of the ritualistic Samurai sword was prohibited by the Japanese government in 1877. Soon afterwards, many of the craftsmen began to supply the West with pieces of metal-work decorated in the traditional fashion. Also the Samurai were in many cases forced to sell their swords, which were family heirlooms; many of these eventually reached Europe where they served as fine examples for study and imitation.

The qualities of design revealed in all these crafts appealed immediately to the followers of the Aesthetic Movement. They admired the rich imagery and symbolism of prints and paintings, the totally alien but charming attitudes of

Fig. 5.1. (Opposite page) The popular massive locket was often hung from a wide necklet of flat links. This chain is decorated in the aesthetic manner. Note the asymmetrical division of the design on each link and Japanese motifs; the bangle and matching brooch are decorated with coloured gold, and a hovering insect amongst the flowers. The lockets remain resolutely Victorian in design. (John Joseph; Brian and Lynn Holmes)

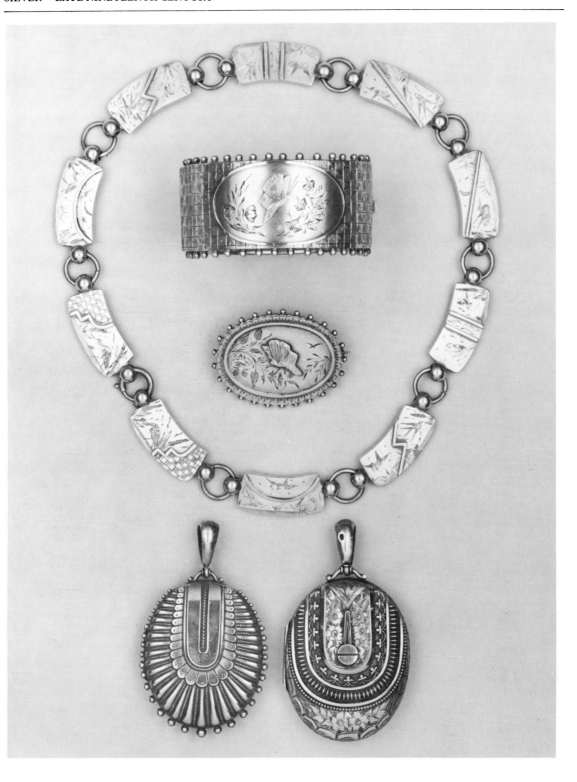

Fig. 5.2. Two bracelets from a 'Shakudo' suite. Japanese shakudo work in English gold mounts, about 1850. (Landsberg & Son)

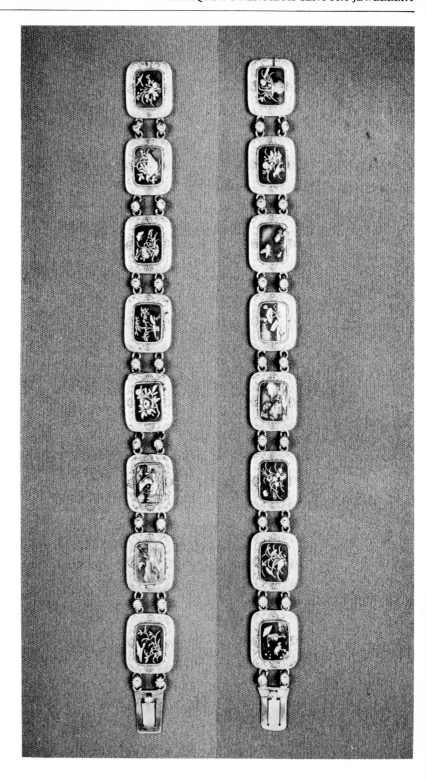

Plate 5. (Previous page, top) *Gold, diamond and emerald suite, showing the cannetille work popular around 1800, English. (Landsberg & Son)*

Plate 6. (Previous page, below) *Bracelet, showing delicate filigree work and chased oak leaves. Probably by Petiteau le Père in 1820. (Wartski)*

Plate 7. (Above) *Two silver and enamel brooches of the late 19th century. Above: showing the Romantic mood. Below: a Japanese fan with a scene after Japanese prints; with the diamond registration mark. (Ewing)*

Plate 8. (Below) *Tortoise-shell piqué butterfly brooch, gold filigree work body. Set with pearls, rubies and a turquoise, about 1870. (Anne Bloom)*

Plate 9. (Above) *Two crosses by John Brogden, showing his particular style of archaeological gold-work, which was influenced by Byzantine art. Left: set with a cameo of Christ, and edged with blue and white enamel. Right: set with a cameo of the Byzantine symbol for Christ (PX). (Consolidated Gem Co)*

Plate 10. (Left) *Gold suite of brooch and ear-rings with real bird of paradise feathers. An English novelty of about 1860, illustrating an unusual material used for jewellery. (Landsberg & Son)*

Plate 11. (Above) *Pair of Art Nouveau horn hair-combs, illustrating the decorative effect and versatility of horn. The veined and curved leaves are scattered with glistening moonstone dewdrops. (Brian and Lynn Holmes)*

Plate 12. (Left) *Plastics from the 1920s and 1930s: pendant of carved plastic with a central Art Deco enamel plaque; ring with a strong geometric design; red box, signed by Lalique, with a stylised design of cherries on the lid; very well made and stylishly carved perfume bottle, simulating amber; and an amusing cigarette-case in a swirl of colours resembling 'hundreds and thousands', the clasp formed as a jewelled hand. (John Jesse)*

Fig. 5.3. Brooch from the same 'shakudo' suite.

the East, their customs and beliefs, their inscrutable faces and colourful clothes, and finally their awareness of their heritage and the pride in their past. Above all, their sincere and enthusiastic love of nature was reflected in all forms of art. They took delight in its simplicity: a majestic mountain, a single blade of grass, a swaying bamboo, birds, flowers and plants, and the sun, of course. In particular they used the sixteen-petalled chrysanthemum, which was the Imperial Crest, and the prunus blossom, the emblem of the Empress. All these symbols and the geometrical patterns were drawn from ancient legends upon which the whole Japanese culture was built. Emperors were believed to be descendents of the sun goddess, and the religion of Shintoism revolved around the worship of nature and the changing seasons. So it was hardly surprising that this deep understanding and reverence of nature became the central theme of their art, and even after so many years it was beautifully and sensitively represented.

The Aesthetic Movement

Simplicity was the keynote to all design: an economy of line, perfectly spaced and proportioned asymmetrical compositions, and just one carefully observed individual characteristic of each leaf, flower, bird were all the elements needed to create the atmosphere and aesthetic beauty that so intoxicated Europe and the West. William Morris and his followers drew inspiration from the Japanese stand at the Paris Exposition Universelle in 1867; and Arthur Lazenby Liberty devoted his shop to the crafts of the East. In Paris, Samuel Bing collected Japanese objects for his salon and published a monthly periodical called *Le Japon Artistique;* and in New York, Tiffany was already a leading exponent of the fashion.

The influence spread of course to jewellery design. The French tended to concentrate on reproducing enamel-work and fine carving on unusual materials such as horn, while in England and America designers were captivated by the beautiful mixed metal-work. In France, the firm of Falize was best known for the superb cloisonné enamels in the Japanese taste. Lucien Falize had been so enthusiastic that he wanted to visit Japan and bring back Japanese craftsmen; an audacious plan in those early days of world travel. He was restrained by his parents and fervently studied enamels in France, collaborating with the enamellist Tard.

In America, Louis Comfort Tiffany was one of the earliest to sense the growing trend towards 'Japonaiserie'. He himself, like his father, had been an early admirer and avid collector of Japanese objects. The firm's chief designer and silversmith, Edward C. Moore, had also long been passionately involved in the study of Japanese arts and crafts. His wealth of knowledge was particularly valuable to the firm, and he had experimented with metal-working techniques, possibly employing Japanese craftsmen in his workshops. The Americans had one advantage over the English in that they were allowed to combine precious metals with materials of lower value, whereas in England this practice was forbidden by the Assay Offices. Nevertheless, similar work was carried out in England, mostly on silver using gold for decoration, this may also have been done by Japanese craftsmen.

Commercial Success of Japonaiserie

This new mania coincided with the rise of popularity of silver in English jewellery. During the 1870s and 1880s, huge quantities of lockets, bangles and brooches were covered with Western interpretations of Japanese design, using inlays of pink gold (or copper and less valuable materials if manufacturers could get away with it). Commercial Birmingham manufacturers seized the new trend and adapted it successfully for mass consumption. It is interesting to see that, although the Japanese style was always rendered as faithfully as possible, the jewels themselves are still very firmly placed in Victorian England.

You will find the same Japanese motifs occur again and again — motifs taken from original metalwork, or from prints and paintings. In charming and peaceful scenes, set in oriental gardens among reeds, bamboos and palm trees stand patient storks; a solitary kingfisher or a butterfly hovers in the sky, and the sun disappears behind calm waters in which might float a placid fish.

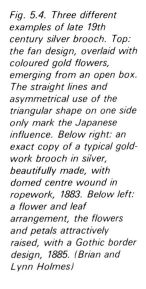

Fig. 5.4. Three different examples of late 19th century silver brooch. Top: the fan design, overlaid with coloured gold flowers, emerging from an open box. The straight lines and asymmetrical use of the triangular shape on one side only mark the Japanese influence. Below right: an exact copy of a typical gold-work brooch in silver, beautifully made, with domed centre wound in ropework, 1883. Below left: a flower and leaf arrangement, the flowers and petals attractively raised, with a Gothic border design, 1885. (Brian and Lynn Holmes)

Geometrical patterns were also an important part of these pictures. The scene was engraved on the silver to give a very delicate effect, and was often overlaid with pale coloured gold, usually pink.

The Japanese fan had become almost a status symbol among the avant-garde. It was an integral part of fashionable costume or interior design, and so became a favourite motif for jewellery. Either a fan would be incorporated into the design; or a brooch itself, perhaps with matching ear-rings, would be formed as a fan, with a tiny bamboo handle. This was also very popular for gold jewels with delicate metal-work designs, and Tiffany made some very fine versions. Occasionally a double fan brooch was made out of silver, usually the shapes stamped out of the metal and the standard scene engraved on the fans. Even on such small items of cheap jewellery, the Japanese techniques were very carefully followed.

Brooches, as always, allowed the most freedom of line, and they demonstrated the new use of compact, basic outlines. A circle, square or oblong shape replaced earlier beaded or flowery edges. On some brooches, there is a startling use of a jagged edge, a kind of geometric bite out of one side of an oblong or square. This reversal of the symmetry and balance marked another change in design; the axis of the design now ran along a diagonal and the focal point was off-centre. This was thought to be more aesthetically pleasing than the laboured symmetry and fondness for sets of matching jewels which was characteristic of the earlier years of the century. Naturally tastes could not be changed overnight, and it is always amusing to discover remnants of past styles mingled with a modern Japanese motif. You might, for instance, come across a very plain round brooch with engraved bamboo and butterflies, on which the maker could not resist a flourish of Gothic, in a diagonal band across the brooch.

Fig. 5.5. Silver bangle showing open-work with a floral design overlaid in pink and yellow gold. The sides are textured with a pattern of crosses and little squares. (Brian and Lynn Holmes)

Another technique borrowed from the East and used to great effect on the silver of the 1880s was that of pierced metal-work. Silver brooches, or wide bangles, were delicately pierced into an open-work design of flowers and leaves and then decorated with coloured golds. Traditional engraved jewels were still being made and worn throughout this craze, but the use of coloured gold on silver pieces in traditional or Japanese designs seems to be quite widespread at this time. More conservative tastes might still prefer an English romantic design of flowers and ivy leaves between heavily patterned borders or beaded edges on lockets and bangles; but very often the flowers were overlaid in gold. Just a slight concession to 'Japonaiserie'. It was a technique that remained in favour for some time.

The Aesthetic Movement style silver jewels were also produced in America, where mass-production methods were more advanced. They are usually found to be marked 'STERLING' or 'STANDARD' or with some indication of the quality of silver used. Some American pieces do seem to show a more developed appreciation of Japanese taste, probably influenced by the early accomplishments in this area by the Tiffany workshops.

Collapse of the Silver Jewellery Market

By the late 1880s and certainly by the 1890s, silver was entirely out of favour again in fashionable circles. This was because silver jewellery had become cheap enough to tempt even working girls with very little money to spend on luxuries: so, of course, any hint of silver in high society was seen as sheer vulgarity and bad taste. This was one of the factors which led to the precarious situation of the Birmingham jewellery trade in 1885 and 1886. They themselves had caused this inevitable reaction against silver jewellery. Manufacturers had been overeager to exploit cheaper and more plentiful supplies of silver; they had gone too far in cutting costs, and therefore the quality of production and design had suffered. There were other economical factors involved too, plus the fact that Victoria's strict rules about mourning had limited the choice of jewels for so long. Also, in the mid 1880s, the ladies of the Aesthetic Movement asserted their position in the world, refused to be regarded as ornamental displays and rejected jewels altogether. For some years very little or no jewellery whatever was worn during the day.

The Birmingham jewellery trade became desperate and in 1885 a meeting was held to discuss an appeal for Royal patronage. The idea was to ask the Princess of Wales to wear day jewellery and so encourage a revival of interest in jewels. It is not certain exactly when the petition was sent, but two years later, at another meeting in May 1887, a letter in reply from the Princess was read aloud. She expressed her sympathy with the condition of the trade, and agreed to view some new samples of jewellery. After a committee had been formed and jewellery selected from leading firms, Mr J. Jacobs and Councillor Charles Green visited the Queen at Marlborough House. Luckily for the committee, 1887 was the year of Queen Victoria's Golden Jubilee marking her 50 years as monarch; this festive event may have softened her attitude for she bought some of the ornaments and wore them on public occasions. This had the desired effect of arousing public attention and a little more jewellery was then worn during the day.

By this stage the Birmingham manufacturers realised that they would need to make a joint effort to revitalise their trade. In 1887 they formed the Birmingham Jewellers' and Silversmiths' Association. Their trade began to pick up again very slowly and the new Association planned to strengthen its position in several ways. One aim was to offer better training opportunities and

Fig. 5.6. Selection of late 19th century silver brooches. These include love brooches with their repertoire of symbols, often overlaid in pink gold; name brooches and message brooches; a double heart 'Mizpah' brooch; and several of the 'aesthetic' style brooches, showing Japanese influence in simple lines, geometric outlines, the fan motif and peaceful garden scenes. (Massada Antiques, Scalpay, Ewing, Claire and Ingeborg, Pierrot, Cleall)

Fig. 5.7. A selection of silver bangles. Note a 'Mizpah' bangle with beaded edge; and in the centre, showing the move towards the simple art of Japan, a single plant stem, but with very English and Victorian leaves and flowers overlaid in coloured gold. (Brian and Lynn Holmes)

technical education, to try to improve the standards of design and manufacture. In 1890, a tax on silverware was removed and this step paved the way for the growth of a new kind of jewel trade in Birmingham. Still lower-priced silver enabled manufacturers to produce a range of small articles, such as boxes, picture-frames, dressing-table accessories, match-cases and various novelties. It also brought mass-produced silver jewellery within reach of a far wider public — the workers and servants, all but the very poorest — and they were delighted at this new opportunity of purchasing jewellery. Their unsophisticated tastes were also less fickle and less demanding for the trade. Designs were adapted accordingly to suit the new customers and the whole force of Victorian sentimentality was unleashed through these silver trinkets.

Birmingham began to thrive again on vast orders for inexpensive silver jewels and undoubtedly the most successful was the silver 'love brooch'. These were most popular in the 1890s, when workshops were producing huge quantities made by machine. The brooches were assembled from separate parts cut to shape by presses from thin sheets of silver. Decoration was added by a stamping process, while any plain areas could then be engraved by hand, or left blank for the wishes of the individual customer. Minute details were never skimped even on the smallest, flimsiest brooch and, although machine-made, there was a great deal of hand-finishing.

Symbols on Cheap Jewellery

Perhaps the most intriguing aspect of these brooches is the elaborate symbolism used and the meaningful motifs which were heaped on to each piece. Endless variations were produced from a small selection of the most popular motifs, but occasionally you may find a more unusual motif and symbol.

The study of flower lore was taken very seriously in the second half of the nineteenth century. The translation of the language of flowers, in particular, had become a fashionable pastime in the 1850s, and several small volumes had been published as guides to the various meanings of flowers. They also delved into the exotic associations of flowers with ancient and Eastern tales. In 1856 Mrs A.C. Burke compiled a dictionary of flowers and their meanings: this followed an even more learned study by Thomas Miller called the *Poetical Language of Flowers or The Pilgrimage of Love*. In his preface, the author claimed that his was the first original work in the English language on the subject, all others having been 'mere translations' from the French work of Aimé Martin. Mr Miller calls flowers the 'messengers of friendship and love' and this was exactly the function they fulfilled on jewellery.

One year later, in 1857, another small book appeared entitled *The Language of Flowers, an alphabet of floral emblems*. Here the author also explains that messages of nature were simple and attractive enough for even the most 'illiterate rustic' wishing to express his love. In 1866, another version called the *Language and Sentiment of Flowers,* was compiled and edited by 'LV'. This included floral records and selected poetry with very beautiful colour illustrations. After retellings of the ancient stories associated with flowers, came the 'vocabulary' list — both from flowers into words and words into flowers — for sending and deciphering messages, and then examples of seasonal bouquets and how flowers and words could be put together. For instance, if you wished to say 'Your humility and amiability have won my love', you would send a bouquet of broom (humility), white jasmine (amiability) and myrtle (love). Yet another volume in 1871, called the *Language and Poetry of Flowers,* arranged on similar lines, stressed that 'flowers are calculated to raise generous and tender emotions in the heart'.

It was only a small step for jewels, traditionally love tokens, to be embellished by these expressive emblems. Items of sentiment and mourning always enforced their meanings with a flower motif (see Chapter 9, Flowers in Jewellery). By the time they appeared on almost every one of the stamped-out silver brooches of the 1890s, the various species of plant could barely be recognised, and the flowers and leaves became very stylised. The ivy leaf, meaning friendship, fidelity and marriage; the forget-me-not for true love; the fern symbolising fascination, magic and sincerity; and the bluebell for constancy were amongst the most popular. The rose had a different meaning for each variety: a cabbage rose meant 'ambassador of love', and a thornless rose, 'early attachment'. The little round five- or six-petalled stylised flowers which appear most often on love brooches, almost always represent forget-me-nots. The flowers were usually overlaid with pink, and their leaves with yellow gold.

Fig. 5.8. Silver love brooch formed as an artist's palette, with paint brushes overlaid with pink flowers. (Author)

Apart from this foliage, several other symbols were used on brooches: love birds with an obvious meaning; the anchor of hope; the heart alone or with a cross and anchor for faith, hope and charity; a lovers' knot or buckle; and a horseshoe for good luck. Of course, the heart was particularly significant. You can often find it pierced with an arrow, as two hearts united by Cupid's arrow, or in the form of a heart padlock perhaps tied with a pink-gilt bow and resting on a key. The love bird was often perched on a crescent.

The confusing etiquette associated with the visiting card ritual was occasionally interpreted so that the brooch resembled a card with one corner turned down, but these are quite hard to find. Less common also are the clasped hands of friendship, an artist's palette or brooches showing a raised, woven basket of flowers. Patriotism was expressed through nationalistic emblems quite often found on these brooches in the form of thistles, harps and shamrocks.

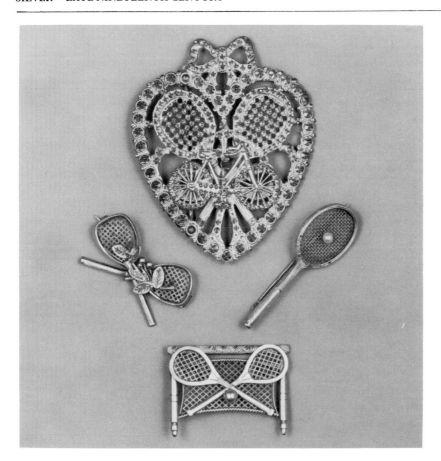

Fig. 5.9. The sporting craze of the 1890s coincided with the fashion for silver, producing these variations of the silver brooch. Above: a belt buckle in faceted metal, the bicycle emphasised in gilt. (Ewing)

Name brooches were another extension of this fashion and they too were enormously popular and turned out very quickly and profusely. Surprisingly, although they appear very similar, it is a challenge to match any two exactly. These were sentimental tokens, worn by daughters of working-class families, by maids or seamstresses who were called Maud, Jennie, Alice, Nellie, Lilian, or Emily. The engraved names were surrounded by the same stylised flowers and leaves. Very simple, bold and often crude lettering was used; and sometimes the name was made of open silverwork in a beaded border. These must have been a welcome addition to the uniforms and drudgery of many a life in service. Even plainer name brooches were added to the range, and these look almost like labels reading 'Mother' or 'Baby'.

Message Brooches

The third group of brooches you may come across consists of 'message' brooches. The most common of these was the 'Mizpah' brooch, which would be given by a lover about to be parted from his beloved. The word comes from the Old Testament, from Genesis 31:49, which tells of a pillar set up by Jacob as a witness to a covenant made between himself and Laban: 'And Mizpah; for he said, The Lord watch between me and thee, when we are absent

Fig. 5.10. (Right) Silver and
silver gilt brooch designed
as a cuffed and gloved hand
holding a flower and a
message 'Souvenir'. A gilt
heart hangs from the
bracelet around the wrist.
Fig. 5.11. (Far right)
Japanese style brooch
shaped as a mandolin, silver
inlaid with gold Oriental
motifs. (Both: Brian and
Lynn Holmes)

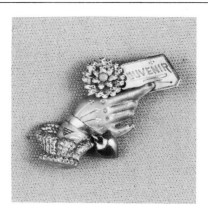 

one from another.' The word had appeared slightly earlier on fashionable lockets, where it might be spelt in rose diamonds, or on bangles or rings. Mizpah rings in gold were usually made as plain bands; sometimes the front section unhinged to reveal a name and some decoration. Twin hearts were the most popular and appropriate shape for these silver brooches and this itself signified united love. One heart would carry the relevant quotation, and the other was stamped 'Mizpah'. Added to this could be flowers, an anchor or bird motif, or coloured gold decoration.

Other cheerful messages were added to the range, such as 'Best Wishes', 'Merry Thoughts', 'Ever Thine', 'Seasons Greetings'. A lucky horseshoe or wishbone might accompany these mottoes. Finally, in 1897, at the height of this fashion, brooches were made to commemorate the Queen's Diamond Jubilee, celebrating 60 years of her reign. These can be recognised by the letters V.R., and the dates 1837-97. The word 'Jubilee' might be draped with ribbon and perhaps joined by two hearts and a crown, or the national emblems of rose, shamrock and thistle.

This trinket trade revitalised the Birmingham jewellers and they were able to continue successfully, expanding steadily up to the First World War, even after this particular craze gradually faded in the early years of the twentieth century.

For some time, the excessive sentimentality of these brooches was despised as well as the commercial mass-production and unsophisticated designs which they represented. Now it seems they are attracting more and well-deserved attention from collectors who can view such jewellery with a fresh outlook. The fact that they were inexpensive ornaments turned out by the thousands and worn by working girls even adds to their interest for some people. They are still easy to find, usually in good condition, relatively inexpensive and therefore available for study. Even more important they are amusing to collect and to wear.

The silver jewels of the 1880s are now widely appreciated. Jewellery lovers enjoy the Japanese and Aesthetic influences, and their delicate coloured gold decoration, all within a typically Victorian framework. The richly varied assortment of designs that have been left to us adds to the fun of learning about these late nineteenth century accessories.

6. Collecting in Unusual Materials

Ideas for collections of antique jewellery are as varied and colourful as the lives and personalities of the people who explore them. Collectors may not have the dealer's opportunity to view, at first hand, the entire spectrum of the antique jewellery market, but they can concentrate on one small corner of jewellery history and, in time, even become specialists. Of course your own particular preferences and growing ideas of what you would like to collect will also be largely influenced by the amount of money you have to spend. The very word 'jewel' has always implied a treasured and valuable possession conjuring up visions of precious stones, sumptuous and rare. But in fact the most basic function of jewellery, of complimenting natural beauty, has often been fulfilled by humble materials: the rare and costly materials have inspired ingenious and beautiful fakes, while time-consuming and highly individual skills have been imitated by commercial techniques, using short-cuts and compromises.

Some very fine collections have been based on one or more of the most unusual materials, or on fakes and imitations. An exhibition called 'Synthetic Jewellery', compiled by East Midlands Arts in 1979, and shown throughout the country and at Goldsmiths' Hall, demonstrated the wealth of unusual or fake materials through the centuries, including the modern introduction of synthetic stones.

Cheaper substitutes have been used in jewellery for thousands of years: the ancient Egyptians perfected sophisticated techniques for effectively imitating the colours and appearances of stones by using inlays of coloured compounds, glazed soapstone, faïence, glass and rich enamels (see Chapter 14, Egyptian Revival Jewellery). Since then imitations have always been developed to cater for a demand that far outweighs supply, and to reproduce at lower cost and in quantity the effect of rare and treasured materials.

Paste

The best known of all jewel simulants is almost certainly paste, used to copy the most desirable and precious gemstones at a time when they were in huge demand. The great age of paste jewellery was the eighteenth century — an era of glamour, extravagance and glittering beauty — when the rose-cut diamond was enormously popular and cried out for a suitable substitute. Rock crystal was sometimes used but was not entirely satisfactory. Techniques for producing colourless glass had been rediscovered in the fourteenth century, and it was the Venetians who had taken over the traditions of glass-making from the Egyptians and Romans. In the fifteenth century, they were manufacturing a clear glass, but there was no real demand for a gem-substitute as diamonds were not fashionable during this period. Any Renaissance pastes were deeply coloured to suit the rich enamelling of the settings. The next step can be traced to England, to George Ravenscroft, the owner of the Savoy Glass House in London. He discovered flint glass in the 1670s by using English flints instead of marble pebbles from the River Po. This was shortly followed by the invention of lead glass in 1681. The brilliance and clarity of this glass provided the answer to the problem of a diamond substitute.

The invention of paste as used in jewellery, is attributed to Georges Frédéric Strass (1702-1773), whose name has since been used as a synonym for paste. He was born in Strasbourg, but came to work in Paris as a jeweller on the Quai des Orfèvres in 1724. By the 1730s Strass was using lead crystal to create beautiful jewels which looked like the fashionable diamond ornaments of the day. His shop became famous, his wares enormously popular, and in 1734 Strass was appointed jeweller to the King of France. These jewels were admired for their own merits, and were not considered merely as imitations. It was certainly no social disgrace to be seen wearing paste jewellery — in fact quite the opposite when they were at the height of their popularity.

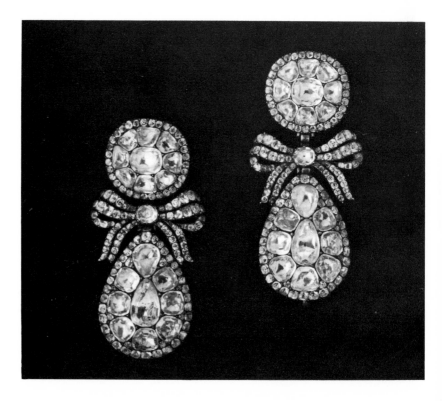

Fig. 6.1. Pair of French paste and aquamarine earrings, about 1760. (Landsberg & Son)

Fig. 6.2. Group of 18th century paste jewellery, including buckles, ear-rings, brooch and buttons. (Christie's)

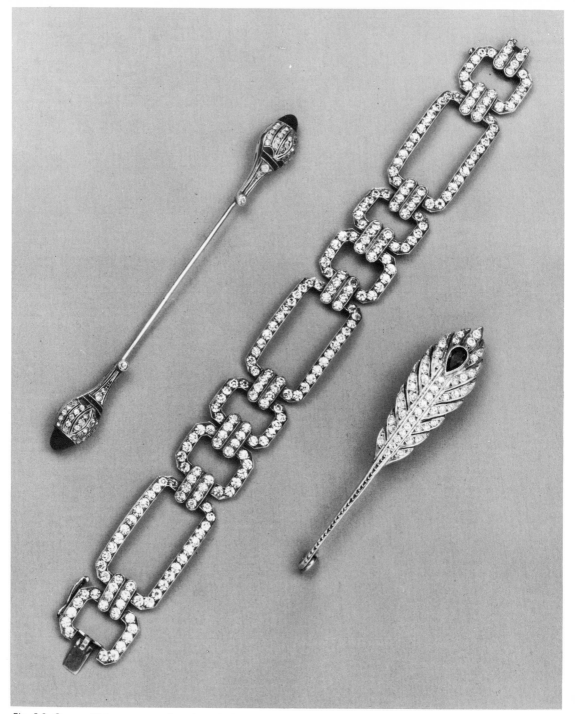

Fig. 6.3. Group of later pastes, well made and of good design, from the 1920s and 1930s. Bracelet with open links, jabot pin of paste and black onyx, and feather brooch, set with green paste teardrop. (Brian and Lynn Holmes)

Wearing paste was also a financial safeguard against street robbery, which was a very real danger at that time. Strass was an accomplished jeweller and his paste-set items were exquisitely made, with as much care and attention given to design and finish as for expensive jewels. The simulated gems could be more adventurously cut than diamonds, as the cost of the latter's wastage was prohibitive, and this added a wide range of designs to the appearance of paste jewellery.

Early paste was often rose-cut, like the diamonds it imitated, and eighteenth century paste jewels closely follow the styles and closed settings of contemporary diamond jewellery. Bow-brooches, aigrettes, tiaras, and shoe-buckles were among the most popular items. Paste diamonds were by far the most popular, but coloured pastes appeared too, and these were backed with foil to strengthen and enhance their colours.

Opal pastes were very pretty adaptations, more popular in France than England. They did not look exactly like opals, but had an opalescent, pinkish tint; they were cut 'en cabochon' and set over rose-coloured foil to deepen their colours. Paste jewels were very popular in England and the firm of Wickes and Netherton proudly advertised their range of so-called 'Falsework'.

The quality of paste deteriorated in the mid nineteenth century, partly because the Victorians regarded it purely as an imitation and partly because the open settings of the nineteenth century were not flattering to pastes. A method was developed of 'silvering' the back facets of pastes, in an effort to create an effect similar to that of foiling, but the grace and charm of the eighteenth century had been lost.

The designs of paste jewellery were gradually reduced to rather uninteresting copies of traditional diamond jewels. These simulated jewels seem to come into their own again in the 1920s when a new approach to the use of diamonds and precious stones revived the fashion for glamorous and extravagant jewels. A similar situation to the eighteenth century then arose when there was a demand for effective copies. Again, at this period, paste jewellery was often very well made in the best Art Deco style: firms such as Cartier made fine diamond paste 'high-fashion' jewels. Nowadays, antique paste jewellery has become very much sought after and is increasingly hard to find. However later paste jewellery, particularly that of the early twentieth century, is still quite plentiful and can be found in very stylish designs. For further information on the history of paste jewellery, read *Antique Paste Jewellery* by M. D. S. Lewis.

Glass

Glass has appeared in various other forms through the centuries and there are a few particularly interesting collecting areas. The moulded paste cameos and intaglios by James Tassie and the glass-encrusted cameos of Apsley Pellatt will be discussed in Chapter 12, Cameos and Engraved Gems; but an earlier decorative use of glass was found by the second Duke of Buckingham in his plate-glass factory at Vauxhall, set up in 1663. This glass house became famous for the production of mirrors, but to jewellery collectors, the term 'Vauxhall glass' means the small glass-set jewels of the late eighteenth and

Fig. 6.4. Heart brooch of clear Vauxhall glass, about 1770. (Private Collection)

early nineteenth century. They were mostly made around 1800, and are quite rare nowadays.

In the nineteenth century, Roman mosaics were made of tiny fragments of coloured glass (see Chapter 13, Mosaics in Jewellery) and there was a vogue for French jet, explained in Chapter 7, Mourning Jewellery, which was really a glass imitation of black Whitby jet.

The end of the nineteenth century marked a change in jewellers' attitudes to the materials they worked and the emphasis was placed more on colour, textures and decorative qualities than upon rarity or value. Glass began to make a new appearance in jewellery. Some of the Arts and Crafts jewellers used glass or paste; May Morris, daughter of William Morris, in particular made strings of beads in unusual colours and materials including Venetian glass. René Lalique, the greatest of the Art Nouveau jewellers, was also passionately interested in glass-making and created many very attractive glass pendants in the early twentieth century.

In the 1920s, very pretty, amusing and very stylish necklaces were made using glass of different colours. Flowers or fruit in pale pastel shades were strung as short necklaces; stunning contrasts of black and clear glass, or glass beads moulded or sculpted in highly stylised shapes, were achieved.

Fig. 6.5. Necklace of clear, cut and frosted blue glass, 1920s. (Merseyside County Museums)

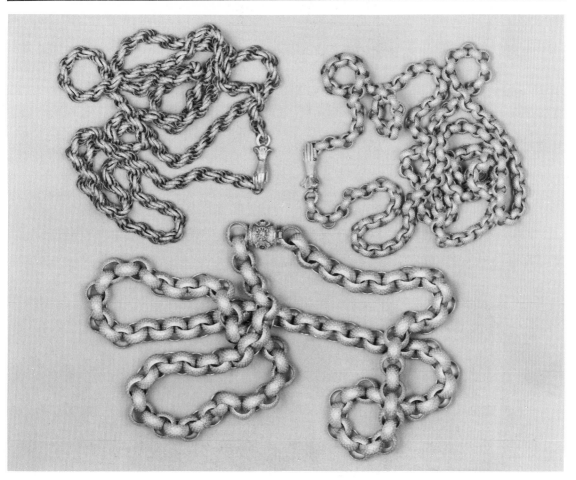

Fig. 6.6. Long chains about 1820-30, or muff chains (on which a muff would be hung), were often made in pinchbeck, closely following the styles of gold chains. They have finely made rounded and textured links, giving an impression of weight, and intricate clasps, often in the form of a gloved hand. (Brian and Lynn Holmes)

Pinchbeck

Christopher Pinchbeck (1672-1732) was a Fleet Street watchmaker who invented an alloy of zinc and copper that very closely resembled gold. The famous metal was named after its inventor, but now the term 'pinchbeck' is often loosely applied to any gold-coloured metal which appears in nineteenth century jewellery. There were however many other similar alloys produced by competitors which were not as good as the true pinchbeck. Pinchbeck's son continued the business after his father's death and in 1733 he was forced to place an advertisement in a daily newspaper to warn customers about cheap imitations of his father's invention.

Real pinchbeck (a contradiction in terms?) has become quite hard to find. It certainly looks much richer in colour than other alloys, seems to wear better and tarnishes less. The actual proportions of the alloy were never disclosed although there have been many speculations. It was very beautifully worked, again receiving the same skill and attention as real gold jewels, and was often used to set fine eighteenth century pastes; the combination of the two substitutes is particularly successful. It is a good idea to look at a piece known

to be made from pinchbeck — examine the style, workmanship, the feel and colour of the materials — before testing your judgement on other gold-coloured metals.

In the eighteenth century, cheaper jewellery of various kinds was made from pinchbeck. Buckles, hair-ornaments and chains were especially effective and some are extremely attractive. Tiaras were often set with pastes in floral designs, sometimes with stones set *en tremblant*, from the middle of the century; then in more classical forms towards the end of the century. These would be set perhaps with faceted coral paste beads, typical of the Napoleonic style. This kind of fine work was often French and, according to Dora Jane Jansen in *From Slave to Siren*, about 1729, Renty of Lille, and later Leblanc of Paris, were producing alloys that were very good copies of Pinchbeck's metal. Obviously, as with paste jewellery, designs followed current styles of gold-work, which at that time was regarded mostly as a complementary setting to the all-important gemstones.

Real pinchbeck jewels continued to be popular in the early part of the nineteenth century, particularly in the 1830s and 1840s. In this period, it is seen at its best on wide mesh bracelets fastened at the front with a miniature, a decorative oval or oblong gem-set clasp. The mesh chains of the bracelets are often beautifully wrought, following the early nineteenth century 'cannetille' style of gold-work (see Chapter 3, Nineteenth Century Gold-work). This period of 1830s and 1840s was essentially romantic, and the clasps of the bracelets might be set with stones or pastes whose initials spelt a sentimental message such as 'Regard' or 'Dearest'.

Early nineteenth century long chains, a very fashionable item of jewellery, were often made in pinchbeck and looked exactly like their gold counterparts. The most desirable now are those made of plump rounded links, textured with dots or stars, and fastened by a clasp shaped as a gloved hand. Bracelets were also made from this kind of chain. Pinchbeck seals of the period were just as beautifully fashioned as gold examples, with flowers and shell motifs and set with pretty and interesting intaglios. Other gold jewellery was cleverly imitated by cheaper alloys and by pinchbeck; for example, the die-stamped suites of the 1840s of scroll and foliate design with matching pendant ear-rings set with rich garnets perhaps, were effective. Work in pinchbeck virtually disappeared after 1854 when it became legal to use lower carat gold. There after 15, 12 or 9 carat was most often used for secondary jewellery.

Pottery and Porcelain

It was the ancient Egyptians who first searched for substitutes and simulants to replace rarer materials in their jewels. They developed techniques for working in coloured glass, and also used a faïence, which they found particularly suitable for imitating the beloved lapis-lazuli that could not be found in Egypt.

Pottery and porcelain have been used in jewellery at different times, mostly following the Egyptians' examples, as imitations or substitutes. Wedgwood's stoneware trinkets were inspired by classical art. In 1724 Josiah Wedgwood introduced a stoneware called 'Jasper', which could be stained in pale colours: blue, green, lilac, and yellow-blue is the best known. He used Jasper to create

Fig. 6.7. (Opposite page) Three hair ornaments of pinchbeck set with pastes. French, early 19th century. (Birmingham City Museum)

the effect of a cameo with the relief sculpted in the classical style from white stoneware and fixed to the coloured Jasper background (see Chapter 12, Cameos and Engraved Gems).

Various kinds of porcelain jewels were made at different times, and their forms naturally progressed alongside the development of major porcelain factories: the porcelain was usually enamelled. In England during the mid nineteenth century, the Worcester Porcelain Company produced enamelled plaques, decorated in the Limoges styles, depicting well-known romantic paintings. Thomas Bott was an artist who specialised in decorating porcelain plaques to be set in jewels, some of these were mounted by Robert Phillips into a gold necklace which was exhibited at the International Fair of 1862.

Parian was a white porcelain, occasionally found in jewellery, but most often used for small figures, based on famous sculptures. It lent itself to jewellery as an imitation of ivory and for a short time, around 1850, it was moulded into flower brooches and bracelet clasps that looked just like carved ivory but were far cheaper. Unfortunately it was fragile and rather impractical: very little survives today. Belleek was another white and pearly porcelain that was finely worked and could stand in for ivory.

The appearance and form of ceramics changed drastically towards the end of the nineteenth century with the arrival of Oriental wares in Europe, the growth of the Arts and Crafts Movement and a new interest in materials and glazes. A decorative use of ceramics in jewellery can be found in 'Ruskin pottery' brooches. John Ruskin was the major force and inspiration behind the Arts and Crafts Movement (see Chapter 19, Arts and Crafts Jewellery), and the British pottery workshop at West Smethwick was named after him. It was established in 1898 by W. Howson Taylor, who was the son of the headmaster of the Birmingham School of Art, where many leading figures of the movement studied or taught. W.H. Taylor concentrated his efforts on achieving new glazes, and these glaze effects are the chief decorative characteristics of all Ruskin pottery. He was particularly noted for experimenting with high firing and used small round or oval pottery plaques to test the new glaze effects. These plaques were then mounted as brooches or buttons by a firm called A.E. Jones. They are recognisable by the mark 'Ruskin' or 'Ruskin pottery' and by mottled spotted glazes and deep swirling colours. Some look very attractive, others are slightly murky in tone, but all are very different and individual. Settings were usually very plain silver or silver-gilt rims; occasionally the plaques were set in pewter or beaten copper. The brooches cannot really be classed as Arts and Crafts, although made by an art pottery. Most of them were quite late, early twentieth century, and, as they were sent away to be mounted by a different firm, they did not really comply with Arts and Crafts requirements.

Unusual Stones

Victorian Scottish pebbles illustrate an interesting nineteenth century passion for Scotland and romance (see Chapter 8), and also a skilful technique of cutting and setting coloured agates. The greenish Connemara marble was cut and worked in a similar way on jewels with Irish associations; most typically in brooches. shaped as shamrocks and harps.

Fig. 6.8. Two pâte de verre *pendants made by Argy-Rousseau, 1920s. Pâte de verre, an ancient technique, was revived towards the end of the 19th century, and produced a mouldable substance which was a cross between pottery and glass. These pendants were sculpted on very pale, subtly coloured backgrounds. (Lewis M. Kaplan Associates)*

For a time, new interest in science and Nature influenced jewellery; ladies were proud to display their education and self-improvement by wearing jewels set with the deep blue or purple fluorspar found in Derbyshire, known as 'Blue John', or with curled fossils or ammonites. These were mounted in gold, silver or jet as brooches, or ear-rings, and were popular during the 1850s.

The moonstone is a variety of feldspar which is very light and delicate in appearance. It is nearly colourless, but with a milky depth that often takes on a bluish tint. This is another stone which came into fashion in the 1880s with the vogue for colourless gems; it was generally cut en cabochon and almost always set in silver. Moonstones seem to have been most popular in the 1890s when they were used on little lace brooches which were pinned to bonnet strings, scarves or frills of lace around the neckline. These even merited a mention in the ladies' fashion magazines of the time. The moonstone is often surrounded by diamonds and pearls but perhaps it is most appealing when it is carved into a flower, or as the smiling face of the man in the moon, often perched on a gold crescent. English craft jewellers were very fond of moonstone (see Chapter 19, Arts and Crafts Jewellery), as were the Art Nouveau jewellers of the turn of the century.

Dramatically Victorian are the jewels set with deep blood-red Bohemian (pyrope) garnets. This jewellery was made in large quantities in Bohemia towards the end of the nineteenth century. The stones were usually rose-cut, set in large quantities clustered close together, and often with a large cabochon garnet at the centre. They were most often set on very low grade gold or gilt metal and were made in a small variety of basic designs, such as flower-like clusters linked as necklaces, or stars and crescents which were used for brooches, ear-rings, hair-ornaments or as a central design on a bangle.

Organic Jewellery

If the metallic sheen of steel and iron (page 74) or the darkness of Bohemian garnets seem to demand a rather special taste, there is a lighter and brighter

Fig. 6.9. Mid-19th century
ivory: a heavy cross carved
with flowers and a ring of
twisted thorny boughs, very
often seen on carved ivory;
and a cameo, showing a
classical head, vines and
grapes in her hair.
(Jacqueline)

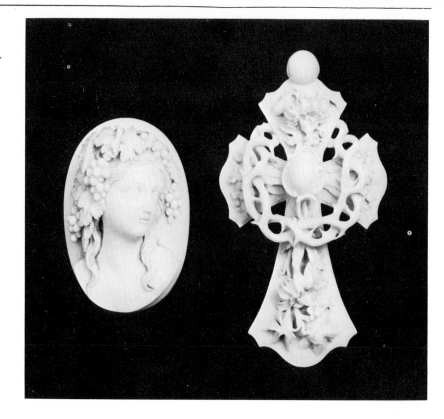

Fig. 6.10. The art of carving
ivory reached great heights
in the late 19th century: a
perfect rose; grapes and
vines; and a pendant with a
female figure crouching
inside a flowered border.
(Ewing)

group of materials and substitutes to study. Ivory alone can make a fascinating and attractive collection, as it was used in a wide variety of styles through many different eras. It was beautifully transformed into piqué decoration (see Chapter 4, Piqué) in the seventeenth and eighteenth centuries. However it enjoyed great popularity in jewellery during the latter part of the nineteenth century, particularly in the 1880s when colourless jewels became the vogue.

One of the main points of Victorian Romanticism to look for is the botanical motif which found a perfect expression in carved ivory (see Chapter 9, Flowers in Jewellery). Bouquets of flowers were carved as brooches, pendants and ear-rings. Sprays of lily of the valley, crosses and brooches in the form of twigs and branches wound with ivy leaves, curling tendrils and flowers or matching sets of brooch and ear-rings carved with bunches of grapes and vine leaves, were all very characteristic of early and mid-Victorian jewellery. Romantic messages were conveyed by carved hands holding bouquets of flowers. Bracelets were made of polished or carved ivory plaques, threaded on elastic; in the 1860s ivory flowers set into a jet background made

Fig. 6.11. Finely carved ivory; the symbolic hand holds a basket of grapes. Early 19th century. (Galérie 360)

popular jewels. Some of the most skilful work can be seen on ivory chains, where all the links have been carved from a single piece of ivory, without any joins; these very often have crosses attached. Much of the finest carving was brought back as tourist souvenirs from France, from Switzerland and from Dieppe, where the tradition of ivory carving had been revived in the early nineteenth century.

For something special, look for very fine, delicate carving on brooches that look like miniature sculptures in which a stag with antlers is seated in a wooded landscape, or is leaping, pursued, through the forest, the whole scene enclosed by a garland of branches. For something attractive to wear, look for very large pendants and brooches carved as single roses with full curling petals. These particularly were imitated in bone, which can be carved effectively and less expensively. Bone does not have the creamy and glossy finish of ivory; it tends to look more yellow and have a dull surface, but it was very often stained to give excellent floral effects.

Seed-pearl jewellery is quite hard to find in good condition, as it is very fragile and usually quite early in date; the early Victorian era saw the end of the fashion. These tiny pearls came mainly from China or Madras, and were threaded, on white horsehair, on to a base of pierced mother-of-pearl. The styles were always very elaborately romantic, again incorporating the favourite flower or vine motifs.

One light and unusual material became inextricably linked with Art Nouveau and that was horn. Searching for horn ornaments will involve the collector in a study of the period; while any representative group of Art Nouveau jewels must include some horn. The attraction of horn to the turn of the century craftsmen, was its light and subtle natural markings in patches of dense clouds, which drifted across translucent surfaces. It was also easy to work, strong and light to wear. Lalique was captivated by the possibilities of horn and created some beautiful jewels, but probably Lucien Gaillard (see Chapter 17, Signed Art Nouveau Jewellery) was the finest master of this material, supremely sensitive to its natural colourings. Designs were greatly influenced by Japanese art, and much of the best work produced in Paris about 1900, was done by Japanese craftsmen.

The favourite organic motifs taken from nature were expressed in horn,

Fig. 6.12. (Right) Seed pearl necklace, about 1840. (Jean Bateman)

Fig. 6.13. Art Nouveau haircomb in carved and stained horn, set with moonstones. Found in its original box, bearing the name of Hall & Co., 5 Hatton Garden, London. The sycamore leaf was a very effective turn-of-the-century motif. (The Purple Shop)

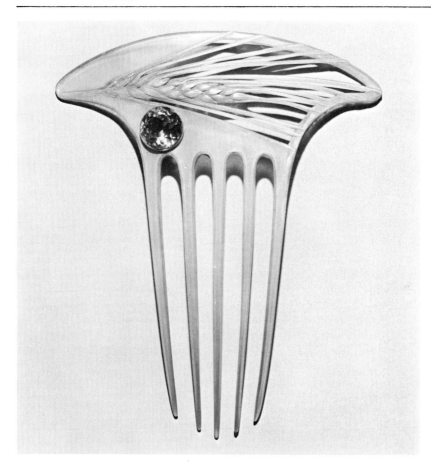

Fig. 6.14. Horn hair-comb
by Lucien Gaillard, with a
wheatsheaf motif, set with
brown citrine. About 1900.
(Bellamy)

Fig. 6.15. Hat-pin by Lucien
Gaillard, carved from horn,
with wheatsheaf and
'shrimp' design. (Lewis M.
Kaplan Associates)

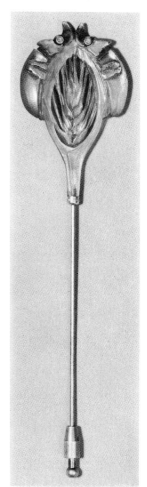

which could be lightly stained to add to the effect. The wings of insects, butterflies and dragonflies were interpreted in the veined translucency — in the
same way appeared delicately carved flowers, the fragility of sycamore leaves
and round, flat Japanese style leaves, the windblown sadness of full flowers,
writhing fronds of ferns and seaweed. Horn lent itself particularly to hair-
combs and ornaments as the light could shine through and flatter its
translucency, texture and carving in flowing outlines. Lalique and Gaillard
made some exquisite examples which fully explored the qualities of the
material, sometimes adding jewels or enamels. Pendants were also very
popular, hung on silk chains with some coloured beads. Insects and flowers
were the favourite pendant motifs, very often lightly stained. The quality of
these pieces can vary tremendously (and there are many reproductions); it is
important to look closely at the carving which should be very fine and with a
natural effect. Look, too, for subtle colouring, the kind of sensitivity which
matched, for instance, a pinkish sheen of the horn to pink beads on the chain.

Unusual Mourning Jewellery

Jet and black glass imitation French jet are fully described later, in Chapter 7, but less well-known perhaps is Vulcanite, a peculiarly Victorian artificial substance.

Vulcanite, or ebonite, was in fact a type of india-rubber, which was combined with sulphur and 'vulcanised' by heating to produce a hard inflexible rubber. It was then worked in exactly the same ways as jet for jewels. It is usually found as pendants, medallions, cameos, and wide bracelets. It feels lighter than jet and has a slight brownish tinge and shiny rubbery surface. Vulcanite jewels were moulded instead of carved, and this is easy to detect. Vulcanite was also used as a simulant for bog-oak, which is another unusual Victorian material to consider.

Bog-oak was also worn during mourning and in its turn served as a substitute for jet. Like jet it was a kind of fossilised wood, found in peat-bogs in Ireland. Its Irish associations meant that it was favoured for Celtic style ornaments and it was often shown in exhibitions set with Irish pearls. It is most frequently found very heavily carved with flowers, particularly in the shape of a cross, or as a hand holding a wreath of flowers. It can be distinguished from jet by its brownish, matt surface.

Hair jewellery (see Chapter 7, Mourning Jewellery) makes a very interesting collection which could span many years and expresses the extremes to which Victorian taste stretched in its search for novelty.

Iron and Steel Jewellery

Ornamental qualities of jewels traditionally require them to have the rich, bright colours of sparkling gems or the polish of precious metals. However at various periods and for different reasons, dark or sombre materials have been worn as adornments, and today they can look elegant and effective. The mourning ritual was the main reason for darkly coloured jewels, and this inspired the use of several unusual materials and substitutes which are widely collected today.

Fig. 6.16. Berlin iron brooch, showing the Virgin and Child. Early 19th century. (Jacqueline)

Berlin iron jewellery was considered suitable for mourning wear but its interest now lies in the highly decorative use which was made of a cheap and basically unglamorous material. Made of cast iron, lacquered black, the more elaborate pieces are decorated with gold. A factory for such iron-work jewellery was set up in Berlin in 1804, but most iron jewellery was made during the Prussian rebellion against France, around 1813-15. The wealthy were asked to donate their jewels to the war effort and in return were given cast-iron jewels inscribed *'Gold gab ich für Eisen'*. The work was very attractive, looking like delicate, miniature wrought iron. Originally it followed Neo-classical styles; then a little later about the middle of the century, it is found in open foliate designs with some Gothic influence. Unfortunately, it is rare now and not easily available to collectors; a fuller account can be read in Ann Clifford's book, *Cut Steel and Berlin Iron Jewellery*.

Far easier to collect and to wear is the matt, black-coated iron jewellery of the later nineteenth century, mistakenly known as 'gunmetal'. In fact this is delicate lightweight iron jewellery and usually very well wrought into good decorative styles and with a very smooth, silky surface. Nineteenth century long chains or long guards from which would hang keys or a watch, were made from this material. They look most attractive, especially if you can find them set with tiny crystals, varied with interesting long flattened links, or spaced with tiny balls. Lockets were often completely plain and slim, or self-

Fig. 6.17. Two lockets and a fob brooch of the smooth, matt, blackened steel known as gunmetal. Late 19th or early 20th century. (Brian and Lynn Holmes; Private Collection)

patterned with ridges, as were watches cased in this material. Small brooches emphasised the smooth curves obtainable from the metal; they were often shaped as flowers — perhaps as a sprig of lily of the valley with dangling pearl flowers. Purses or chain bags were very popular as well. In the early twentieth century, trinkets such as watch-cases or vestas (match-cases) were made of gunmetal; these are particularly acceptable when studded with tiny turquoises or with a turquoise flower set in one corner.

This group of materials includes cut-steel jewellery which played an important rôle in cheaper, secondary jewellery, principally in the late eighteenth century. For some time the accent had been on gemstones, especially diamonds, which reflected flickering candlelight in every facet. It was then

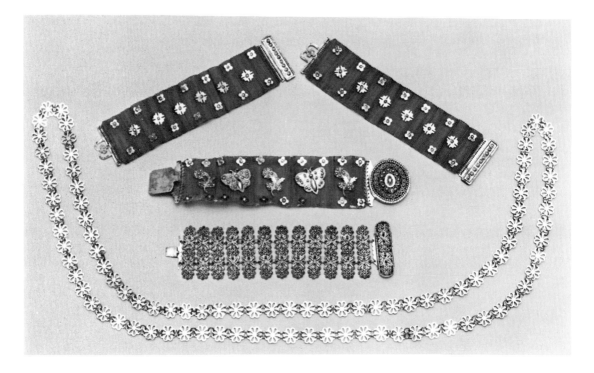

Fig. 6.18. Steel jewellery: the intricacies and exceptional craftsmanship of cut-steel jewellery at its best, in the late 18th century. These are probably all English. The lower of centre two bracelets shows the kind of work perfected at Woodstock, the upper is very unusual with butterfly and flower motifs attached to a mesh bracelet. (Private Collection)

discovered that faceted steel could produce a similar and very impressive effect at a fraction of the price; it was therefore being used extensively for jewellery around the 1770s. Tiny studs of steel were cut with as many facets as possible and then riveted to a plate of steel or another metal. There were important centres for the manufacture of cut-steel jewellery at Woodstock in Oxfordshire and at Birmingham. There the leading manufacturer was Matthew Boulton, and he set up his famous factory at Soho, London, in 1762.

Every kind of jewel was produced in cut steel; the all-important item of attire and status symbol of the eighteenth century — the shoe-buckle — was produced in enormous quantities and varieties in this material. When Wedgwood began producing his Jasper cameos in the 1770s, many were set in cut-steel.

Fig. 6.19. Hair ornaments of cut-steel were popular as they very effectively caught the light in their many facets as does diamond. The butterfly and flower coronet is early 19th century; the fleur-de-lys tiara is French, about 1810. (Private Collection)

For a time Wedgwood worked in conjunction with Matthew Boulton. Buttons, brooches, belt-buckles, aigrettes and hair-ornaments of flowers, stars or butterflies were worn, and whole châtelaines were carefully made from steel.

If you look at necklaces and bracelets, you can appreciate all the time and detail that was devoted to this jewellery, which was also produced and widely worn in France at the end of the eighteenth and beginning of the nineteenth centuries. The fashion continued for a few decades of the nineteenth century, but standards of production declined, and by the middle of the century it was no longer popular. By this time, instead of the studs being cut and fixed individually, they were stamped out in strips. If you can detect this difference, it is one way of telling how early a cut-steel piece may be.

The enormous popularity of the diamond in the eighteenth century brought yet another substitute into fashion; marcasites, made from iron pyrites, which look very much like cut steel. Iron pyrites has a very high metallic sheen, which when cut, provides a suitably reflective surface. It was pavé-set, in silver or metal and used in very much the same way as cut-steel.

Fig. 6.20. Slightly later cut-steel jewellery, still individually riveted. The charming brooch is designed as the key to the heart. Both items around 1835. (Private Collection, Brian and Lynn Holmes)

Fig. 6.21. Group of niello jewels, late 19th and early 20th century, including a match-case, bird brooch, and lockets with chains in stylish 20th century designs. (Jacqueline; Brian and Lynn Holmes)

During the nineteenth century, it was worn as very cheap jewellery and appeared again in the 1920s, 1930s and 1940s when it was effectively incorporated into some highly stylised designs.

If you like this category of dark colouring, your eye might well be attracted to some jewels or trinkets, products of the late nineteenth century, in which silver has a dark greyish, metallic inlay. This work is called niello, a name that derives from a diminutive form of the Latin *niger,* meaning black. Niello was an ancient technique for decorating silver, which was revived in the early nineteenth century by a German jeweller working in Paris, and particularly suited the later neo-Renaissance style. The design was engraved on the silver, whereupon the engraved recesses were filled with an alloy of silver, copper, lead and sulphur. The technique was usually employed to create very elegant, restrained designs: very often geometric patterns, stripes or squares, which are occasionally augmented by pink gold inlay. Niello appears on Russian works of art, but most of the trinket work was done by Parisian firms. In London, the technique was adopted by S. H. & D. Gass who exhibited two bracelets at the Great Exhibition of 1851.

Plastics in Jewellery

The word 'plastic' tends to connote unreal, expressionless, devoid of any artistic merit or individuality; this association is therefore obscuring a very amusing and stylish range of collectors' items. Just a quick look at some of these early twentieth century accessories should put all the expression, life and individuality back into plastic. As far as collecting is concerned, 1920 to 1950 is the best period; the time when plastic artefacts started coming on to the market, and the novelty of the material — its great imitative possibilities and versatility — was welcomed by imaginative and talented designers.

Plastic jewellery and objects were very much a product of their era, and for a greater appreciation it is important to study the period: the social and political attitudes; the changing rôle of women; the effect of travel in motorcar, aeroplane, ocean-liner; the film industry and jazz music all contributed to the great strength of style which is so concentrated in the cheapest of materials as well as the most extravagant (see Chapter 21, Edwardian and Art Deco Jewellery).

It was an Englishman, Alexander Parkes, who invented the first kind of plastic, a cellulose nitrate, to be used commercially. This was as early as 1855. Specimens of this new substance, named Parkesine, were exhibited in 1862 at the London International Exhibition by Parkes who was awarded a medal. This success led him to set up a firm called Parksine Co. and Parkes was called upon to read a paper on his invention to the Society of Arts in 1865. In this he explained how he had recognised the need for a new material to be used in the arts and in industry; and he listed numerous applications for his invention in the future.

It seems that, at this early stage, plastics were regarded, even by Parkes himself, as just a valuable substitute for natural materials. It received relatively little appreciation for its own individual properties and virtues and it took some time before it was seen as a new material offering a wide range of colours which had varying transparency, as well as lightness and malleability, and which in return demanded appropriately new ideas.

Parkes immediately used his new plastics to manufacture items which imitated the popular ivory, amber, tortoise-shell, horn, agate, malachite and coral. The Parkesine Company remained remained in business until 1868; then the development of plastics was taken over by Daniel Spill, a former manager for Parkes. He called his version of the material 'Xylonite'. Production continued mainly on the same lines, turning out substitutes, but adding slight variations on new plastics. One of Spill's most successful specialities was imitation coral jewellery. In America similar work in plastics was being carried out by John Wesley Hyatt, who had also discovered cellulose nitrate, which he called 'Celluloid'. His discovery was urged by a need for a cheaper substitute for ivory billiard balls.

The next important step in the story was taken by Leo Hendrick Baekeland, a Belgian chemist living in America. His discovery has become well-known by its trade name 'Bakelite', patented in 1909.

New kinds of plastics were then developed in the early part of the twentieth century, all with descriptive and amusing names. One used extensively for small decorative objects was casein, discovered in Germany and produced in England from 1919, under several different names such as 'Dorcasine', 'Erinoid', 'Keronyx' and 'Lactoid'. Catalin was another kind produced in Britain from 1928, while from the United States came plastics called, among other names, 'Gemstone Marblette', 'Opalon' and 'Prystal'. These plastics had a far-reaching effect on design. During the 1920s and 1930s, coinciding with the height of the Art Deco style, they were transformed into a vast

Fig. 6.22. Unusual materials turned into elegant hair-ornaments in the jeweller's hands suggest another idea for collecting: hair-combs. Top and centre: plastic imitating ivory, set with jet or painted. Right: finely carved tortoise-shell, about 1860. Left: tortoise-shell painted with gold and silver birds, French, about 1890. Below right and left: two Art Nouveau hair-combs. Bottom: French jet. (Galérie 360; Private Collection)

Fig. 6.23. Seals made of steel, all around 1745-75. The seal on the left is a rare Jacobite silver-mounted revolving seal, engraved on one side with the portrait of Bonnie Prince Charlie, the other with the Matthew coat-of-arms. This was presented by Bonnie Prince Charlie to the son of one of his supporters, named Matthew, who had given his life to the Loyalist cause. The seal on the right bears the inscription 'L' amour nous unis' around a motif of twin hearts. (Private Collection)

number of items, ranging from decorative trinkets to useful, everyday objects. The combination of new materials and lively artistic design produced the kind of plastics jewellery and objects that are, or should be, collectors' items.

It was an era of great extravagance, pleasure-seeking and frivolity for the rich, who enjoyed everything money could buy (while they still had their money). It was also an age of uncertainty and insecurity, with financial crises and the prospect of another World War looming: this led to a recklessness and an indulgence of fantasy in design. Jewels and objects were produced in the most luxurious materials, with daring combinations of precious stones, in *avant-garde* styles. The nouveau-riche, who had appeared after World War I, aimed to copy high society and follow their fashion and extravagance. Where the real jewels and objets d'art were out of their reach, plastics imitations provided the required degree of 'chic', the latest outrageous whims, at the right price. The two extremes of materials — the precious stones and the obvious fakes — were equally fashionable; plastics were fun, and fun was 'in'.

During this period, plastics became more accepted as a material in its own right. Much of this jewellery makes the most of plastics' qualities to achieve highly decorative and stylish effects. Many excellent and respected designers appreciated the special virtues of plastics, and even Lalique designed for the material. One example of his work in plastics is the small red box, the lid carved with bunches of cherries, and signed Lalique. Candlesticks, lamps, boxes and clocks were all manufactured in plastics, as well as small personal accessories, particularly cigarette-boxes, evening handbags or minaudières and scent-bottles, all of which should appeal to the jewel collector.

Jewellery followed current designs, often closely imitating ivory, amber and onyx jewels. Flat beads on necklaces, bracelets, carved bangles and pendants in these imitation materials can be very stylish and attractive and, at the same time, are unashamedly plastic. Brooches or buckles could be conceived as women's heads, a glamorous Hollywood star, an ocean liner like the *Normandie* which was launched in 1932, a cactus in its pot, a palm tree or an elephant's head. Carved pieces are often very good, because plastics allowed a great deal of scope. There was no need to be concerned about wastage, mistakes, or expense which had to be considered when working with natural materials, so that the finished effect on plastics could be even more luxurious and extravagant than on the real item.

The pieces illustrated here come from a major collection, and show the decorative possibilities of collecting plastics. It is particularly important to be discriminating in your choice, to apply the same criteria to plastics as you would use when judging other jewellery or objects. Good style and design is essential and the pieces should be well made, of good quality, and of sound materials however modest. Successful imitations look impressive and, at first, have more appeal to the eye trained to appreciate the originals. However do try also to choose pieces that are obviously and proudly plastic, pieces that explore the qualities of the material in the adventurous artistic styles of the day. As the period and its characteristics become more familiar, it may be more fun to concentrate on particularly zany, or 'funky' pieces, which so perfectly express the uninhibited atmosphere of an era which was ruled by 'style'.

❦7. Mourning Jewellery

The wearing of a special kind of jewel as part of mourning dress seems to have its roots in a custom, most common in the seventeenth century, of bequeathing rings to friends and relatives. The rings would be worn by the mourners in memory of the departed. This practice had originated some time before, in the Middle Ages, when jewels that had once belonged to the dead person were left to members of the family or friends as sentimental tokens or as more financially substantial gifts.

A problem developed with the increasing numbers of mourners who deserved such an honour, as there was bound to be a vast difference in the values of the jewellery available for distribution. So, instead of giving existing items, it became customary to leave instructions in a will, for several identical rings to be made specifically for the mourners; thus avoiding any jealousy or embarrassment. It is due to this custom, and perhaps because the ring itself is a symbol of eternity in its very shape, that rings have always had a special significance in the history of mourning jewellery.

Early Mourning Rings

Fig. 7.1. Gold signet ring with swivel bevel reversing to show this Memento Mori *skull motif. (Fortnum Collection, Ashmolean Museum, Oxford)*

There are some early and interesting examples of such provisions in wills. King Richard II left one gold ring to each of the five bishops and four nobles he chose as his executors.[1] Some two centuries later in 1616, by a provision in William Shakespeare's will, rings were bequeathed to a group of friends from Stratford and to three of his actors: Burbage, Heming and Condell. During the sixteenth century, the fashion had gathered support. As the numbers of rings increased, the sentimental value became far greater than the intrinsic worth. Samuel Pepys tells us in his famous diaries of several such gifts left to him, probably in his official capacity. On his own death in 1703 he left 123 rings to be given out to his friends.

The rapid growth of this custom is generally attributed to one very significant death, mourned by a wide public. This was the execution of Charles I in 1649, a crime that could not be forgotten by the Royalists. These loyal supporters wore slides, rings, pendants, and lockets enclosing enamelled portraits of Charles I, to commemorate the loss. Slides were worn on ribbons around

Fig. 7.2. Top: this slide is in memory of Caroline Eyles, dated 1708 on the reverse. It is unusual to find a full inscription on this kind of slide. The enamelled skeleton is accompanied by the words 'I rest'. Left: woven hair forms the background for gold initials, a skull and cross-bones, and the date 1687. Right: This is in memory of Mary II, wife of William III of Orange; it bears the royal cipher and the date 1694. (Private Collection)

the neck or wrist, and had the initials 'CR' in gold wire on a silk background, under crystal. This added fuel to the mourning fashion or perhaps, as some say, it marked the beginning of true memorial rings. The event certainly launched a series of commemorative jewels, many of which were worn secretly to prove loyalty to the Stuarts. Other events to inspire commemorative rings include the Jacobite uprising of 1745, and the deaths of Napoleon and Nelson.

The appearance and form of these rings changed markedly over the centuries, and to trace their decorative development it is important to look at another ancestor of mourning jewellery — the *Memento Mori* jewel. These 'death' jewels became particularly fashionable during the sixteenth century and served as reminders of the wearer's own inevitable death. At this stage, death jewels did not necessarily have commemorative associations, but were more the manifestation of a current preoccupation with death. Wars, plague, lack of sanitation and poor medical treatment made Death a well-known visitor who might knock unexpectedly at any time. Constant reminders of mortality in art, literature and then in jewels, helped people to come to terms with the ever-present idea of death, and to prepare spiritually for the serious and unknown prospect awaiting them. The *Memento Mori* had a rather grim appearance, but they have fascinated collectors with their intricate workmanship on the most macabre designs. The usual motifs were the skull and cross-bones, coffin and skeleton. Late sixteenth and seventeenth century rings often had an enamelled skull on the flat bezel or, as on one late seventeenth or early eighteenth century German example,[2] a fully-shaped, enamelled and jewelled skull bezel which swivelled to show a plump lady's face, rather fleshy and full of life on the other side. A very stark and chastening reminder to any vain eighteenth century beauty!

The theme of passing time also played an important part in *Memento Mori* ornament, introducing such symbols as the scythe and hour-glass to recall the fact that time could run out at any moment. Some sixteenth century watches were made as *Memento Mori* pendants to emphasise the importance of time,

Fig. 7.3. Group of early to mid 18th century mourning rings. Some are enamelled around in black with the symbols of death and a skeleton; others have a crystal bezel, some coffin-shaped, containing skeleton or skull and cross-bones, mounted on silk. (Private Collection)

and these were shaped as skulls. In his engravings published in 1559 Pierre Woeiriot included a pendant incorporating a skull in the pattern. Other pendants were designed as miniature enamelled coffins, opening to reveal a detailed corpse or skeleton inside.

During the sixteenth century, the death's head symbol was worn extensively by widows as a part of mourning attire. Gradually death jewels were adapted to the purpose of commemorating a specific loss. The motifs and styles of *Memento Mori* jewellery therefore largely influenced and shaped the appearance of early mourning jewellery and the memorial rings designated in wills. From the introduction to the Catalogue of the Crisp collection of memorial rings we learn that in 1648, Jaspar Despotin, a foreign physician living in Bury St Edmunds, left instructions for ten gold rings to be made, each to the value of twenty shillings, some bearing a death's head. These were to be distributed one month after his departure to friends, unnamed, to be selected by his executors. This shows that the early gruesome symbols often continued to characterise the mourning rings and jewels of the seventeenth and early eighteenth centuries.

At first, memorial rings distributed according to mid seventeenth century wills, were either plain gold or a band of gold enamelled all the way round with a black or white skeleton, cross-bones, hour-glass, crossed pick and shovel — in fact, all the emblems of death and burial. Any inscription would be engraved inside, and usually consisted of dates and initials or a name. During this period, some rings, as mentioned earlier, would have the bezel shaped as a skull. This form was popular until approximately the end of Queen Anne's reign (1714); although the bands enamelled with skeletons often date from the 1720s. Of course, as with all jewel fashions, the styles changed gradually.

Next came the romantic influences of French design, which brought the inscription on to the outside of the band in raised letters of gold against black and white enamel. This was the main feature of mourning rings until the wave of Neo-classical designs in the last quarter of the eighteenth century.

These enamelled bands have a beautiful delicacy that marks a move away from the grim portrayal of one's own death to a more easily acceptable focus on mourning and its close associations with eternal love and sentiment. As more people died at an early age, young love was often an integral part of this sorrow. The early enamelled bands of this kind were thought to have been the work of French craftsmen. A very pretty variation was obtained when the band was divided into small scrolled sections; each bearing a portion of the inscription.

Fig. 7.4. Late 17th century slide with gold wire initials on a woven hair background, set in gold. (Eleanor Hutton)

Early Mourning Pendants

The use of crystal, often faceted, is another major decorative feature of this period. This again had been encouraged by the jewels made to commemorate Charles I, when the slides were made with gold wire initials on silk, under faceted crystal. Around this time, too, in memory of lesser beings, gold wire initials were set on backgrounds of woven hair, sometimes edged with silk of bright royal blue or turquoise, which perhaps denoted social rank. Gold wire was also sometimes looped into designs on these borders, and initials on the hair might be joined by motifs such as the white enamelled skull and crossbones, or enamelled skeleton flanked by angels or cherubs. The work is fascinating for its intricacy and detail, if rather sombre in theme. In the early eighteenth century, rings very often had bezels of similar faceted crystal, a single stone, or occasionally in a coffin shape. The back of the crystal bezel

Fig. 7.5. 17th century slides and pins were worn on ribbons at the neck or wrist, often holding macabre decoration under a faceted crystal. These date from about 1690 to 1710. (Diana Foley)

might be ribbed with black or white enamel, and such rings had chased foliate shoulders.

Small and delicate heart-shaped mourning pendants of the mid eighteenth century follow the same style of ornament as rings. Scrolled sections with gold lettering on enamel form the border to a heart-shaped crystal compartment for a lock of hair. Alternatively, in anticipation of later styles, a classical scene painted on ivory or enamel is sometimes found. Often the pendant is surmounted by an arc of pale garnets, or some tiny stones are folded into the scrolls. Another style of pendant has an enamelled and lettered bow — a symbol of love — with a central rose diamond, above the crystal locket. You might also come across brooches with a heart-shaped outline in pale garnets and with a tiny oval miniature made of hair, inserted at the top. A variation has a crystal heart-shaped compartment encircled by a serpent, tail in mouth — the symbol of eternity — in gold and cross-hatched in black enamel. In these jewels the heart is very often misshapen, with the point curving to the left side. This shape occurs in Scottish jewels, and is found on the crowned Luckenbooth brooches and on jewels associated with Mary Queen of Scots. It was probably derived from an old Celtic design for brooches. It is sometimes known as a 'Witch's heart'.

Fig. 7.6. Gold, hair, amethyst and diamond mourning brooch. This conscientious collector found an entry in The Gentleman's Magazine *of 1792 to correspond to the inscription on the back of this brooch. Under the notices for August came this sad story:*

'At Cirencester, Co. Gloucester, Mrs Pitt, wife of Jos. P. Esq. She rose, as usual, in good health and spirits, and was cleaning her teeth with a brush, some of the hairs of which, being loose, it is imagined, slipped into her throat, and, by the irritation they caused, brought on a violent fit of coughing and vomiting, which, in her advanced state of pregnancy, produced the most dismal consequences, and she survived the accident but one day. This should operate as a caution, and make people careful to examine the state of their toothbrushes before they use them.' (Private Collection)

Neo-classical Influences in the Eighteenth Century

The use of white enamel to represent the virginal, unmarried state seems also to stem mainly from this period. By the second half of the eighteenth century, this kind of more romantic interpretation had created a strong partiality for memorial jewels. As interest in them was roused, they became gradually more influenced by prevailing fashions, especially Neo-classicism. The successful publication in 1742 of Edward Young's *Night Thoughts on Life, Death and Immortality* had also helped to arouse enthusiasm, strengthened also by Young's earlier *Elegy on the Death of Queen Anne*, and finally Gray's *Elegy in a Country Churchyard*, completed in 1750, reawoke the sentimentality surrounding death. These fine works added to the charm of wearing jewels to commemorate a lost loved one.

By this time, too, the shocking reality of the death's head or skull motif had been replaced by gentle allegorical scenes in which an atmosphere of death

Fig. 7.7. Collection of late 18th century mourning miniatures in typical Neoclassical taste, many incorporating hairwork. (Eleanor Hutton)

and grief was suggested by various symbols. This is an interesting reflection of the age, as it seems that the light-hearted eighteenth century society no longer wished to look death directly in the face. People preferred to stand on this side of death and contemplate the sorrow of those left behind. The large numbers of memorial jewels and particularly rings, made in the last twenty-five years of the eighteenth century, have had a special appeal to collectors in recent years; and their prices have risen dramatically with the new demand. The decoration on rings moved from the band on to the bezel, which became far larger than before and was usually found in an oval, a marquise or shuttle shape, an oblong, or an elongated octagonal shape. Clasps, brooches and pendants were formed in the same shapes.

Following the style of Charles I's memorials, the simplest of these jewels had plaited hair under crystal, sometimes surmounted with gold initials, or an urn in gold. The urn might then be further decorated with enamel and/or seed pearls; so these pictures under glass became more and more elaborate and detailed. The most distinctive are the large miniature scenes, painted on

ivory or on enamel, in water-colours as pale as tears or more often in sepia, with some hairwork.

This fashion of incorporating hair into the picture originated in the practice of enclosing a lock of hair under crystal as a memento. You can trace the transformation of this lock of hair through the heart-shaped pendants of the mid century mentioned earlier, or the larger oval brooches or rings with circular bezels. These often had a garnet surround, with the hair spread out and fixed to the background so as to look like a tree. Perhaps at first it was supposed to be the Tree of Life, but, more often than not, in these late eighteenth century miniatures, the tree represented by wisps of hair was the picturesque weeping willow. The colour of the hair was matched by the brown sepia used to draw the rest of the picture. Under the willow was usually placed a suitably grief-stricken young widow, perhaps leaning wistfully on a tomb. There was invariably an urn, and quite often a brook — another symbol of eternity.

There were numerous variations on this basic theme, using the highly emotive symbols of grief. For instance, the tomb might have opened to release the soul, which would be accompanied on its journey to heaven by cherubs or angels. The desolate female might be leaning on a spade, or an anchor of hope, or looking out to sea from a hilltop or cliff. She might be with some children, so innocently sad; or if alone, seated on the banks of a stream, cradling a spaniel in her lap, for comfort. At first the figure was always female, but later a male appeared in the pictures.

All the scenes showed the very strong Neo-classical influence of the time; particularly in the preference for pastoral scenes and costumes, or classically draped robes. The urn itself was a popular decorative motif, again with draperies and swags; broken columns of Roman or Greek ruins were added to complete the sense of desolation and to recall the ancient world. The artist Angelica Kauffman was an important guiding influence on these scenes, although she herself was not a miniaturist. She epitomised the Neo-classical style in art, and encouraged the classical figure and sentimental scenes.

In a further elaboration, seed pearls, enamels and gold wire could be sprinkled in appropriate places in some of these pictures. A small selection of spiritual, if hypocritical, mottoes were used; the most common was 'Not lost but gone before'. Other examples often written on the tomb, included 'Fate snatched her early to the pitying skies', or 'I have your portrait strongly'. Specialist painters were employed to turn out these miniatures in huge quantities and, although they all appear very similar, it is hard, if ever possible, to find two exactly alike. A great deal of imagination was used in varying the arrangements of symbols.

The frames were mostly classically plain, perhaps of beaded gold. Borders of pearls (the symbols of tears), pastes, rose diamonds or enamels were also favoured. Enamels appeared in black, blue, red, occasionally green or purple. They often had spots or zig-zags of white enamel, or self-patterned 'guilloché' enamels with dotted or wavy backgrounds. Bright-cutting, another feature of Neo-classical decoration, was particularly used on silver, as well as in decorative pink gold borders of rings or brooches. This decoration was often continued on to the back of the miniature.

Apart from these intricate scenes, the large marquise heads of rings took some other forms. You may see some completely covered in enamel, with an

Fig. 7.8. (Opposite page) Examples of the Neo-classical, late 18th century, mourning miniatures with elaborate scenes. (Sotheby's)

urn made of rose diamonds, or the bezel of the ring itself shaped as an urn, usually again in diamonds. A very good effect was obtained by using an opaline enamel background for the motifs. A shield enclosing initials, and surrounded by garlands and swags, could also fill the crystal case. In rather larger compartments, delicate and three-dimensional floral arrangements of tiny, lustrous seed pearls were complemented by backgrounds of deep royal-blue enamel.

Inscriptions are to be found on the backs of these jewels, mostly on rings, and are useful because they give dates of birth and death, or the date of death and the age, as well as the name of the deceased. One interesting point about these late eighteenth century mourning jewels is that they represented a particularly English style of jewel; an idea nurtured, developed and loved by English society.

Fig. 7.9. Diamond memorial pendant with a miniature of a young child, the back with a hair compartment, the winged shoulders set with diamonds. About 1800. (Private Collection)

As a contrast to these large memorial scenes, another style of ring was worn towards the end of the century, and this was more European in appeal. It was a plain gold band, enamelled all the way round in black or white, with gold edges, and with gold copper-plate lettering in Roman capitals. One such ring, described in the Crisp collection and now in the Victoria and Albert Museum, had the words inscribed on intertwined ribbons of blue enamel, with white between the ribbons, on a pale blue background. It commemorated Henry and Betty Savory. Another double mourning ring discovered in this plain style, with black enamel and gold lettering, mourned the deaths of Louix XVI and Marie Antoinette. Rings enclosing portrait miniatures also date from this period.

The Early Nineteenth Century

From the early years of the nineteenth century, the preoccupation with death and sorrowful reminiscing gathered momentum, and gradually turned into an obsession during Queen Victoria's reign. Her unbending attitude towards the correct and respectful appearance of widows and mourners had the gradual effect of destroying public support for the fashion of memorial jewels. This eventually spoilt the delicacy and imagination previously devoted to their design.

Perhaps a word is necessary here to explain the strict rules of etiquette which governed the behaviour of society, and particularly the rules of the mourning code. The example set by the court was closely followed; in polite circles it was imperative to conform to the customs of the day. It was vital to do, wear, and say the right things at the right times. Outward appearances were all important. Only a few yards of black silk, mourning jewels, and a black-edged handkerchief were required to give the appropriate impression — so often false — of sorrow and grief. This hypocrisy was inevitable. Court ladies were obliged to go into mourning for every death in the Royal Family, however distant; although the period of mourning differed in length according to the relationship. It was only natural that young ladies would eventually resent these all-too-frequent commands to discard their pretty clothes and flattering jewels for sombre and subdued costume and behaviour.

When the Duke of York died in 1827, an order was issued saying that it was 'expected that all persons do put themselves into deep mourning'. On such occasions, the fashion magazines would be full of illustrations, suggesting ideas for dresses and accessories. With such a high mortality rate — particularly for young children and babies — obviously some women spent most of their lives in full or half mourning. This morbid behaviour was linked to the Victorian attitude to religion. Lavish funerals were also considered most important and became almost a status symbol, even among the poorer people who might spend all their savings on giving the deceased the best possible start in the next life.

During the opening years of the century, styles remained very similar to those of the late eighteenth century, but there are some features that can be identified as distinctly belonging to the early decades of the nineteenth century. It was perhaps the last period of truly elegant and restrained mourning jewels. There is a far sharper contrast to eighteenth century styles at the start of Victoria's reign than at the turn of the century.

Fig. 7.10. The plainer variety of 18th and early 19th century mourning ring. The three wide rings at the back are early 19th century; the front rings are mid 18th century. Note the bands divided into scrolls (left) and the white enamel ring, commemorating the death of an unmarried person. (Private Collection)

Fig. 7.11. Late 18th and early
19th century mourning
rings at their most elegant.
Note the Neo-classical urn
motif and the ring set with
an amethyst, a stone
permitted for mourning.
(Private Collection)

Ring bezels became slightly smaller, flatter and widened into a rectangle, a curved oblong or a flat circle. The shanks were often plain and flat, wide where they joined the bezel. Pink gold was very commonly used around the period 1810 to 1820. Sometimes the shank consisted of several gold strands brought close together, joined at the back and spreading out towards the centre. Hair under a crystal was still popular, but in a far plainer style now. Usually it was just plaited. It was often replaced by a flat enamel bezel, with gold lettering. Another change can be seen in rings with round bezels — the hair-filled centres are surrounded by borders of blue and white enamel. The most characteristic and interesting style of mourning ring has a swivel bezel. On one side is black enamel with gold lettered inscription; the other side shows plaited hair under crystal. These bezels are rectangular in shape.

One historically interesting example, again in the Crisp collection originally and now in the Victoria and Albert Museum, commemorates the death of Princess Amelia, the youngest and favourite daughter of George III, who died on 2 November 1810. The initial 'A', surmounted by a crown on black enamel, is bordered by white enamel bearing the inscription 'Remember me'. The story says that the dying Princess ordered the ring to be made with a lock of her hair. In her last moments, she slipped the ring on to her father's finger, murmuring the words 'Remember me'. This sad loss was said to have contributed to the madness of the King.

Pearls had always been associated with tears; now they were reintroduced with great success. On many rings of this period, the central lock of hair under crystal is bordered by pearls in the typical 'pinched' gold settings. The crystal compartment could be ringed with black enamel.

Another very charming and popular innovation at this stage is the serpent motif, usually in the form of a snake coiled with its tail in its mouth; an ancient symbol of eternity. This was beautifully interpreted in gold with scales textured in a cross-hatching design; the fluid lines added softness to the plain circles and rectangles popular at the time. The serpent was often enamelled in black, perhaps with tiny ruby eyes. It occurs around the bezels of rings, or on the small mourning brooches which are another well-known feature of the early nineteenth century. They too have survived in large numbers.

Mostly oblong or rectangular, these brooches were pinned on to black ribbon, and worn around the neck or wrist. They had a tiny crystal compartment with a lock of hair, and seem to be directly descended from the Charles I slides, which were worn in the same way. The lock of hair could either be beautifully woven or very simply inserted. They were usually bordered with half-pearls, almandine garnets, coral, amethyst, faceted jet, or with the curled serpent. Early examples have very plain gold borders. They are either a slanting oval crystal in a rectangular gold frame, or as a curved heart. Particularly

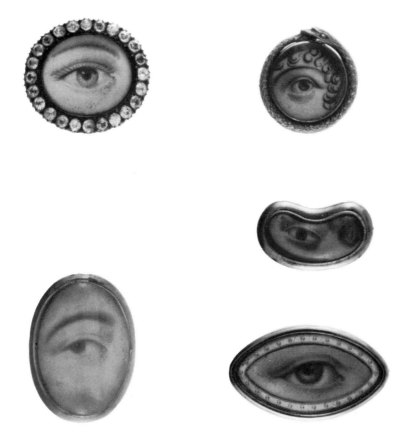

Fig. 7.12. Five examples of the painted eye miniature, one kidney shaped, another encircled by a gold serpent. From the Heckett Collection. (Sotheby's)

romantic are those shaped like teardrops or a fallen leaf. The most unusual were the swan or shell shapes, often set with half-pearls.[3] Small flat pendants, round or oblong in shape, were also worn in very similar styles.

'Tear' Jewellery

There is one extraordinary fashion which slots into the account at this point, because it was very often combined with the serpent motif. I think it is one of the most beautiful by-products of the English passion for memorabilia. It is a single eye, perhaps with a glistening teardrop, which was painted in perfect detail on ivory or enamel and enclosed in a gold frame. It was usually mounted as a brooch or a clasp. The leading miniaturists of the day lent their hand to these eye miniatures, including Richard Cosway (?1791-1821) and George Engleheart, whose work bridged the two centuries.

One of the best collections of these miniatures was sold by Sotheby's in July 1977 as part of the Heckett collection. Many had gold borders in the form of a curled serpent with finely textured scales. Others were in horizontal marquise- or navette-shaped frames, echoing the shape of the eye, in plain gold or with blue and white enamel; one was in a kidney-shaped frame. Occasionally the miniature might be bordered with pastes or with tiny diamond chips or sparks. Both female and male eyes were painted, with great sensitivity to the meaning of the eye, and its expression of the soul. Detailed eyebrows added to the individuality of each painting, and some examples include a glimpse of fashionable, wispy curls lying flat on the forehead and the temples. The skin tones are always exquisitely copied.

The Romantic Revival

Perhaps the greatest attraction of mourning jewels to collectors has been its comprehensive documentation in the form of inscriptions and, especially, dates. The dates are sometimes not quite as helpful as might at first be imagined, as mourning jewels often had their own very individual style, which could not be readily compared to other jewellery. However, in the nineteenth century, mourning pieces shared the favourite decoration of other jewels, whereupon dates and inscriptions then became of greater value. For example, in the 1830s, a typical mourning ring consisted of a wide band of black enamel, usually with gold Gothic letters spelling 'In memory of', and gold borders brimming with flowers, scrolls and shells.

Another type had heavy chasing forming the band; this was rimmed with thin enamel edges, and perhaps a central crystal compartment. These rings are typical of the William IV period; the same elaborate gold-work is found on seals of the period. This change in style corresponded to a more general trend in jewel ornament, strongly influenced by Romanticism, and characterised by the extensive use of flower motifs, sentimental symbols, and intricate chasing of all gold surfaces.

The forget-me-not carried an appropriate message and was widely used on mourning jewellery from the 1830s, especially in carved black and white onyx set in rings and brooches. By the time Queen Victoria came to the throne in 1837, this fever of romance was in full flourish, encouraging the sentimentality which impinged on almost every aspect of Victorian life. Since widowhood and lost love played such an important part in Victoria's later life, it is perhaps significant that her accession was accompanied by a long period of mourning for William IV.

Of course there was no immediate change in the styles of mourning jewels to coincide with the start of Queen Victoria's reign. The style which is now termed 'Victorian', was a steady accumulation of different influences over many years. By the 1840s for example, rings were still being made in gold and black enamel, but the simple elegant lines of the earlier wide band were considered severe and were replaced by more decorative bezels. They often had a shield-shaped centre with a coloured forget-me-not on black enamel; a heart-shaped centre with a similar motif but set with pearls; or a cross in pearls or rose diamonds. The hair compartment in many cases was moved from the outside of rings to the inside, just behind the bezel. Shoulders and bands of rings were heavily chased with flowers and shells. This deep and elaborate chasing, typical of William IV rings, appears also on early Victorian brooches and pendants.

Fig. 7.13. Cross-shaped pendant of gold, black enamel, garnets and woven hair of two different colours. The pendant commemorates two deaths, one in 1838 and one in 1868, as inscribed on the back. The jewel itself seems to date from the 1830s; perhaps the inscription was added later. (Private Collection)

By this time, it seemed that almost every jewel wherever possible was fitted with a compartment to contain a lock of hair. This in no way meant that they were all memorial pieces: the wearing of a lock of hair was just part of exaggerated Victorian Romanticism, built around the image of the young Queen. Romantic novels of the day encouraged the craze, coming to life as they did with the story of Queen Victoria's own great love for Prince Albert, the perfect match and a magnificent Royal wedding.

The Queen herself was fond of jewellery and used it, as well as decoration, to express her love for Albert, her loyalty, her devotion to her family, and her passion for Scotland (see Chapter 8, Scottish Jewellery). She admired sincere and sentimental inscriptions, symbols of love, and where this perfect young Queen led, her subjects slavishly followed. Her love for Prince Albert did not sway her strict approach to morals, religion and etiquette, and particularly her insistence on respect for the dead. The right adornments had to be worn in

Fig. 7.14. Brooch of carved jet. Fig. 7.19 shows the matching bracelet. (Whitby Museum)

her presence at times of mourning by all who craved social standing.

Jet was the most favoured mourning gemstone at court; but equally respectful were the black enamel and onyx which crop up over and over in jewel fashions for the rest of the century. Heavy brooches and lockets began to take over from rings as the principal items of mourning jewellery. Some of the most typical mid century examples are the large, oval brooches with arrangements of hair under glass in the centre, bordered with gold cartouche-shaped frames which were filled with black enamel. After a while, this scroll and feather outline tended to become plainer as did the inscription, so that Gothic letters disappeared in favour of straight, plain, upright capitals. So many of these brooches, and small oval lockets were produced that they became very impersonal; the earlier long inscriptions and mottoes were reduced to a mechanised and meaningless 'In memory of'.

Nevertheless, these later nineteenth century mourning jewels are still plentiful, and are often in excellent condition. Although they follow a distinct pattern, there was a surprising variety in their design, and all were well made. As accurate reflections of their age and of the changing attitude to the mourning ritual, they do have a certain charm and value to recommend them to collectors. No study of Victorian jewellery would be complete without them.

The perfect wedded bliss enjoyed by the monarch and shared by her people was unfortunately to be short-lived. When Prince Albert died in 1861, the intense happiness changed dramatically to equal depths of morbid misery. Victoria determined to continue to show her respect for her husband by plunging herself into the deepest mourning, from which she never emerged. Her marriage continued to be as sacred to her as it had been in Albert's lifetime, and she expected all widows to feel and behave in the same way. Her mourning and widowhood became an obsession which her subjects reluctantly had to humour. Another remarkable lady of this period, Lady Gregory (Isabella Augusta Perse, 1852-1932) was always pictured in unrelieved black with jet jewellery after the death of her husband. Lady Gregory was an important Irish playwright, and a leading figure in the development of the Irish literary movement. The fact that a character with such progressive ideas about the theatre should conform to this fashion shows the strength and importance of mourning in Victoria's reign.

This obsession accounts for the enormous amount of memorial jewellery produced in the second half of the nineteenth century; and because so many women were forced to wear it against their will, it also explains the violent reaction against mourning when Victoria at last showed some leniency in the rules towards the end of the century. During the eighteenth century, there had been a lightness and prettiness about mourning jewellery, which was helped by the frequent use of white enamel. The ponderous Victorian atmosphere imposed its own character on its jewels, and they were heavy, sombre and usually dark.

Those who profited most from the Queen's grief were the workers in the Whitby jet industry. Jet was the most appropriate and popular material for mourning jewellery and was often the only material permitted during full mourning, starting with the death of George IV. The fashion really came into its own in the 1850s when Queen Victoria, in mourning for a cousin, wore jet jewellery to a banquet.

Fig. 7.15. Cross carved in jet and decorated with gold paint by Godfrey Hurst. Unusual because the design is in the Art Nouveau style. (Whitby Museum)

Jet

Jeat stone almost a gemme the Libyans find;
But fruitful Britain sends a wondrous kind;
'Tis black and shining, smooth and even light,
'Twill draw up straws if rubbed till hot and bright.'
(from an old treatise on jewels)

Jet was used for mourning jewellery in the sixteenth century and perhaps even earlier, but it was the nineteenth century that fully explored its decorative possibilities. It is so important in the story of Victorian jewellery that it deserves special attention from collectors. However, it is often neglected and therefore is relatively inexpensive. The history of Whitby jet, details of mining, tools and manufacturers is best told in an excellent booklet, *The Story of Whitby Jet*, by Hugh P. Kendall. It is distributed by the Whitby Museum which houses a good collection of jet ornaments.

Jet is, in fact, a kind of fossilised driftwood, found in certain strata of rocks along the Yorkshire coast near the fishing village of Whitby. There is evidence through archeological finds to prove that it was used by early man, during the Bronze Age, for small personal ornaments. There have also been many interesting historical references to jet by early writers, including Pliny who called this substance, or something similar, *gagates*. This name came from Gagae, a town in the Mediterranean coastal area of Lycia, which was the original source of the material. It is probably from this name that the word 'jet' is derived. Jet was believed to ward off evil spirits, and to be a cure for certain ailments. In the Middle Ages, crosses of jet were thought to counteract the effects of witchcraft.

The start of the nineteenth century jet industry is attributed to Captain

Fig. 7.16. Unmounted jet carvings, very delicately carved with flowers and leaves. (Whitby Museum)

Fig. 7.17. Group of jet jewellery showing the wide range of items, decoration and designs: carved beads, rather plainer turned work on crosses and brooches; and the intricate and romantic carving again on a heart pendant and the hand holding a flower. (Ingeborg)

Fig. 7.18. Flexible serpent bracelet of carved jet. (Ingeborg)

Tremlett, a naval pensioner living in Whitby. He is supposed to have invented the first machine for working jet, and as he shared his discoveries and success the industry grew. Soon after 1800, he first taught John Carter and Robert Jefferson, again local residents; and they then employed Matthew Hall, who helped with the turning of jet beads. In 1832, as this trade was slowly getting off the ground, there were two workshops in Whitby, employing about twenty-five workers altogether. By 1850 there were seven workshops. One of these belonged to Thomas Andrews of New Quay, famous because he became 'jet ornament-maker to H.M. Queen Victoria'.

Some twenty years later, around 1870, the number of employees in the trade had grown to 1400, including men and boys; and there were over 100 shops and manufacturers in Whitby. Workshops had also spread to Scarborough. At the peak of its popularity, every shop window in the town was filled with these awesome black ornaments. The demand for jet grew rapidly after the death of the Prince Consort in 1861, but the trade had been steadily expanding since 1851 when jet was displayed at the Great Exhibition in London, and brought extensive orders from both home and abroad. In 1854, the Queen of Bavaria placed an order with Mr Isaac Greenbury of Baxtergate for a jet cable chain, 4ft 6in (1.37m) long.

While the fashion was still fresh and growing, there was some extremely fine work done in Whitby, with the craftsmen developing their own particular skills, such as cameo and flower carving, turning beads, or engraving designs. Often one piece would be worked by several different specialists. Whole chains were carved out of one piece of jet, without a break or join (the same skill is found in ivory work). Wide bangles were made with a central cameo or medallion; other bracelets were formed as a strap and buckle or as a serpent,

and separate pieces for them were threaded on elastic. Brooches could be carved with delicately detailed flowers — a hand holding a bouquet was especially
popular — or they would imitate entwined branches. Smooth knots or twists
are often found as well. Beads were smooth, round and polished, or faceted
and glittering. Several rows of graduated beads were worn together. Cameos
were well carved: very appropriately, one of the most usual subjects was the
veiled widow. Ear-rings followed the current fashions and were made in great
variety. The jet could be polished to give a high shine, or left with a matt surface.

It was not usual for craftsmen to sign their work but research done at Whitby has identified some of the best manufacturers of the period. E.H. Greenbury was apparently one of the most successful and skilful workers; he won
the medal and Freedom of the Worshipful Company of Turners. He specialised in carving cameo heads, busts and profiles, and exhibited two fine jet
caskets at the Philadelphia International Exhibition in 1876. H. Barraclough,
conductor of the Whitby saloon band, was famous for carving flowers and
fruit; other well-known makers include W.H. Crane, Thomas Tose, T.
Knaggs, and W. Lund. Amongst the best engravers were Edward Kingston,
William Cummins, Thomas Simpson, and R. Simpson.

Most men worked for one master or owner of the manufacturing business.
The foremen gave out pieces of rough jet to the workers, and it was their job
to open and close the workshops. They also had to keep an eye open for possible fires, which were a great hazard in the trade, with the large amounts of jet
dust in the workrooms. Workers mostly used treadle wheels, except in Mr
William Wright's business, where the wheels were driven by a gas engine.
The tools used were also made by the workers themselves, because each
specialist needed a different kind of instrument.

Smaller workshops were also set up in attics of tenement buildings, built
into the cliffside, and in other unusual and unexpected places. These men
were able to make a good living at the height of the industry, in spite of enor-

*Fig. 7.19. Bracelet of carved
jet; the matching brooch is
shown in Fig. 7.14. (Whitby
Museum)*

Fig. 7.20. Jet and French jet: the twist brooch and cameo are of Whitby jet; the arrow brooch and necklace are of faceted French jet. All late 19th century. (Ingeborg)

mous competition. The hours for workers were long and arduous, from 6.00 a.m. to 6.00 p.m., and young boys were brought into the business for training. It is interesting that apprentices were encouraged to take drawing lessons as the best engravers used drawings as foundations to their skill.

The enormous activity that hit the tiny village of Whitby was dwindling by the 1880s. The trade fell victim to the Victorian whims of fashion, which decreed that bulky jewels should be exchanged for lighter, more delicate pieces. Trade was also worn down by competition from cheaper substitutes which could be more easily mass-produced. This led to a decline in standards of design and workmanship. These substitutes had been developed to cope with the enormous demand which could hardly be satisfied by the Whitby jet industry alone. About 1870, jet was imported from Spain. Soft Whitby jet was also used, again lending to a loss of quality, as these jewels soon lost their polish and broke far more easily than those made of hard Whitby jet.

Imitations of Jet

One of Whitby's main competitors was French jet, a black glass which shows purple tinges, especially around the edges. Like glass it is brittle, and takes a very shiny polish. Usually French jet was cut into facets to make full use of this shiny quality and was always backed with steel. It is more likely to chip than real jet, but can still be very effective and dramatic if worn today. A greater delicacy could be obtained with French jet, as seen on the necklaces with faceted buttons and pendant flowers. Hair ornaments, pendants and brooches made as flowers with finely pointed petals were also very successful.

Bog-oak was another imitation, a dark brown wood with a matt finish, which is found in the peat bogs of Ireland. Jewels of this material were often very well made, using similar designs to jet work. Popular pieces were the crosses, heavily carved with flowers, or brooches shaped like a hand holding a bouquet. Quite often the piece has been set with Irish pearls. These jewels were exhibited by Irish firms at the 1851 Exhibition; they achieved their greatest popularity between 1850 and 1855.

Apart from these substances, a great many imitation jet jewels were made from composition materials. Usually a wood powder was coloured and compressed into a mould; most 'jet' cameos found today are, in fact, made of this type of composition, with a rather dull, sometimes brownish surface. Vulcanite, one of these materials, was formed by vulcanising india-rubber with sulphur. (See Chapter 6, Collecting in Unusual Materials.)

Other materials were considered suitable for mourning wear, or for half-mourning; this was a transition period which followed a period of full mourning, immediately after the death. Tortoise-shell and piqué could certainly be worn. Florentine mosaics with their black backgrounds are often found depicting funereal white lilies, suggesting that this style was acceptable too. Black onyx was made into oval lockets — the front bore a cross or star set with half-pearls and there was a hair compartment at the back — or into a very plain angular cross pendant, sometimes with an applied gold filigree pattern or pearls. Clothes in discreet shades of grey and lavender were permitted in half-mourning. Amethysts could then be worn and, perhaps, niello or jewels made from banded agates.

Hairwork

The lock of hair has played a very important part all through the history of mourning jewellery. It has always signified a romantic remembrance, the lasting, physical link with a lost loved one. In early memorial jewels, the hair was mingled with spiritual emblems but, as popular tastes emphasised the sentimental aspects of mourning, so the lock of hair itself became more important, and was appreciated for its versatility in decorative and romantic interpretations.

Considering the Georgian preoccupation with material matters of life, it is not surprising that the first artistic arrangements of the lock of hair came in the mid eighteenth century. Strands were carefully spread out to represent a tree and enclosed in a locket, brooch or ring. Taking this idea a little further, the elaborate sepia miniatures of the late eighteenth century incorporated a weeping willow made of hair. The hair became more compact, and was tightly woven or plaited, in the rings and small brooches of the early nineteenth century. However it was the Victorian era and its excessive sentimentalism which turned hairwork into a jewel fashion in its own right.

This craze reached enormous proportions in the 1850s. From the tiny pearl-rimmed brooches enclosing plaited hair, there next developed the fashion of wearing large brooches which displayed complicated patterns com-

Fig. 7.21. Selection of mid 19th century mourning brooches, showing hairwork arrangements. (Bonhams)

posed of hair. Favourite designs — and those most commonly found today — are the nosegay, wheatsheaf or the Prince of Wales feathers. Against a white or opal glass background, wisps of hair were curled, coiled and crimped; then they were adorned with minute spirals of gold wire, and threaded with rows of tiny seed pearls. Many of them look like fountains springing from a tight ring of pearls, and tumbling in orderly curls around the side of the brooch.

Professional hairworkers could obtain the best results in this painstaking task, but many manufacturers were believed to be unscrupulous. When given an order and the precious lock of hair, it was often said that they were careless and might use the hair of a stranger instead or — worse still — use horsehair which was easier to handle and to keep in place and gave a crisper finish. To safeguard against such ruthless practices, young ladies were advised to tackle

Fig. 7.22. Pair of gold mounted hair bracelets, found with the original accompanying message:
  'These bracelets my dear Mary have been made for you of your own tenderly loved mother's hair, who died 20th May 1842. Your Affecte. Aunt, Elizabeth Grissell. York Road 1843.'
(Landsberg & Son)

their own hairwork. For instructions they could consult several manuals such as Alexanna Speight's *Lock of Hair* (1871) and *A Jeweller's Book of Patterns in Hairwork* by William Halford and Charles Young (1864). The ladies would equip themselves with kits which included tweezers, knife, curling iron, a background plaque, and glue to stiffen and to fix the hair. They could also buy ready-made frames to take the hair picture, many printed with 'In memory of' on black enamel borders. However a great deal of patience and dexterity was required and it is usually easy to tell which pieces were arranged by amateurs.

Horsehair itself was made into jewels, particularly between 1840 and 1845. It was used in its natural colours — usually whitish, black, or dyed red — and was tightly coiled and wound into flat discs which were then built up into the design. Quite often long chains were made of horsehair with alternate links of black and white woven hair.

By the 1860s and 1870s, when these manuals were published, another kind of hairwork had arrived. This went one step further, so that the whole piece of jewellery was constructed from woven hair. Retailers advertised ear-rings of balloon or long pendant shapes, bracelets fastened with chased gold clasps or with miniatures, watch chains, whole necklaces with pendant or crosses, brooches formed as lovers' knots, rings centred with a tiny gold shield or rectangle, or rings of gold open-work design, which allowed glimpses of the spiralling hair. Nowadays it seems a rather distasteful fashion and unpleasant to wear; but like every other novelty, the Victorians welcomed it wholeheartedly.

Hair was sometimes plaited, usually for bracelets. In woven ear-rings and some bracelets, it appeared as a kind of hollow open-work, rather like a net. When used for ear-rings it had the additional advantage of being very light to

Fig. 7.23. Bracelet of woven hair of different colours, with gold clasp. About 1840. (Landsberg & Son)

wear. Serpent brooches or stick-pins are sometimes found with the body of the serpent tightly woven in hair, while the head and heart-shaped drop are finished in enamel.

A glance at the list of jewellers who exhibited at the Great Exhibition and their specialities shows how popular and seriously taken this fashion was at that time. London jewellers W. Cleal, 53 Poland Street, showed specimens of working in hair; W. Bakewell, 25 Red Lion Street, Clerkenwell, called himself an 'Artist in Hair', and offered specimens for lockets and brooches, using Prince of Wales feathers design and inscriptions and initials in pearls. B. Lee, 41 Rathbone Place, exhibited bracelets, brooches and guard chains of human hair. A. Forrer, Regent Street, was another specialist in this area; this firm showed ornaments worked in hair and gold. This included one ornamental frame containing miniatures of Her Majesty, H.R.H. Prince Albert, and other members of the Royal Family which were mounted in hair and gold. Other impressive items included the large vase composed of human

Fig. 7.24. Examples of the delicate hairwork in which the hair was woven to form the jewel itself: acorn ear-rings decorated with gold, and a bow-brooch with tassels and an engraved gold heart. About 1840. (Private Collection)

hair, exhibited by S.H. & D. Gass but executed by J. Woodley, Cursitor Street; and bouquets of various coloured hair, shown by A. Hermann, The Haymarket.

One of the best contemporary descriptions of hairwork comes from the French fashion magazine, *La Belle Assemblée*, in 1858. There is an article which describes the sentimental jewellery of Limmonier. This Parisian jeweller had been an exhibitor at the Great Exhibition of 1851, and had obviously taken the idea of hair jewellery and worked on it. The magazine told its readers that Limmonier had converted a fashion which was once only a memento of the dead, into an ornament to be worn at all times. The writer describes a broad ribbon woven as a bracelet and fastened with a turquoise and diamond forget-me-not. Limmonier apparently also made charms for the neck or for a fan, and medallions with leaves and flowers. He used the pure white hair of the elderly for white roses and lilies of the valley with an excellent effect.

This shows that the fashion was popular in France, and also raises another point about hairwork. Although it developed from a custom favoured in mourning jewellery, hairwork was a purely sentimental fashion, not necessarily with any memorial connotations. In fact, the hair jewels were probably love tokens more often than not. Unless there is an inscription, or obvious use of black enamel, it is not safe to assume these examples of hairwork were worn as mourning jewels. It was however a welcome novelty that would have been acceptable within Victoria's framework of rules.

Mourning Miniatures and Photographs

Queen Victoria popularised the wearing of miniatures; from the time of her marriage to Albert, she was almost always seen wearing his portrait, very often as a massive bracelet clasp. Miniatures of deceased relatives were obviously frequently worn during mourning. With developments in photography in the 1880s, the role of hair as a favourite personal memento was taken over by the photograph. Photographs were mounted in brooches and lockets, which became larger to accommodate the picture. Again these were not only used as mourning jewels; the locket might contain a photograph of a living friend, relative or fiancé. When used on mourning jewels, it was usual for the photograph to be mounted on one side of a brooch, while the other side was covered with plaited hair under glass. The brooch might swivel inside a heavy gold or gilt metal frame.

By the end of the century, the trade in mourning jewellery had become stale. Women were thoroughly disenchanted with dark, sombre jewels and hair jewellery, and had exhausted every possibility of novelty allowed by the mourning code. There was enormous relief felt by the public and by the jewel trade, when Queen Victoria relaxed her rules after the Silver Jubilee of 1887. Anything vaguely memorial or funereal in character was totally rejected, and mourning jewellery was itself sent to eternal rest.

This distaste remained for a long time afterwards, along with a general disapproval of Victorian jewels, perhaps because of the preponderance of mourning jewellery. It is only fairly recently that interest in them has been reawakened; at first that interest was still confined to early examples. It remains a specialised collectors' field. Although seventeenth and eighteenth century jewels are now widely appreciated, Victorian mourning pieces have been neglected. They do have value as social documents, especially if they carry inscriptions, and they reflect the attitudes and fashions of their day. Hair jewellery, for example, is a curious concept; and includes a technique which could not easily be reproduced or faked today. Because of their low intrinsic worth, specimens have remained in excellent condition and unaltered. Along with so many other facets and by-products of mourning jewellery, hairwork remains a fascinating and peculiarly Victorian phenomenon.

Notes

1. Much information has been gathered from the Catalogue of the Memorial Rings, collected by Frederick Arthur Crisp and privately printed in 1908.

2. In the Fortnum collection at the Ashmolean Museum, Oxford; and included in an article in *The Connoisseur*, October 1978, by Diana Scarisbrick. Also in the catalogue, *Finger Rings from Ancient Egypt to the Present Day* by Gerald Taylor and Diana Scarisbrick.

3. Look at the beautiful examples of these in the Hull Grundy gift of jewellery at the British Museum.

8. Scottish Jewellery

The craze for traditional Scottish folk jewels was bred by the early Victorian atmosphere, and it was a fashion enclosed on either side by Gothic and Celtic revivals. The Gothic style, which seemed to become widespread around 1830, was now considered superior to classicism. In jewellery, its virtues were best explored by François Désiré Froment-Meurice. He incorporated the so-called *style cathédrale* into designs for jewels which were like three-dimensional scenes depicting romantic or saintly figures against Gothic architectural backgrounds. Similar pieces were produced by Rudolphi. A little later, between 1844 and 1850, A.W.N. Pugin (1812-52) designed a famous group of Gothic jewels for Hardman & Co. of Birmingham.

Everyone was preoccupied with England's past, stories of the Middle Ages, chivalry and — the underlying reason for it all — with romance. The effects of the Industrial Revolution had left little romance or artistic beauty in the lives of the early Victorians, and it was not surprising that they longed to bring a slightly glamorised past back to life. Famous historical novels of the time, especially those by Sir Walter Scott, stirred the imagination and had far-reaching effects on fashions and jewels.

Victoria became Queen of England when this romantic movement was at its most powerful, and it was perhaps her own love of Scotland that transferred attention to the romantic possibilities of that country's history. George IV had made a state visit to Scotland in 1822, and his appearance in full Highland dress had created a ripple of interest in the Scottish jewels that played a major part in the splendour of the costume.

When Queen Victoria bought Balmoral in 1848, the seal of approval was set on all things Scottish. Scotland became a favourite resort for tourists, especially for honeymooners; the Queen's children wore tartans, and her guests at a ball to mark the opening of the 1851 Exhibition were all required to dress in Scottish outfits. The heart of English society was entirely captivated by the subtle colours of moss and heather, the mysteries of high grey castle walls, and the strict heraldry which still ruled the clans.

All these images were eventually expressed in the huge fashion for Scottish jewels that swept both England and France in the 1860s.

Mid nineteenth century pebble jewellery was based on the traditional

Fig. 8.1. Large Scottish plaid brooch. The central raised boss is set with a crystal, and the surrounding spikes are applied with pearls or pearl-like stones. Twisted wirework and rope border recall ancient designs. Edinburgh, 1852. (Sotheby's Belgravia)

Fig. 8.2. Large silver mounted witch's heart, edged with grey, green and rust agates, filled with a silver thistle. (Brian and Lynn Holmes)

shapes of folk jewellery, sometimes copying them exactly, or just adapting them slightly. Several well-known shapes are seen most frequently.

Ring or annular brooches had been worn in Scotland as early as the second century B.C., and the ancient style remained in use as late as the eighteenth century. After the finding of the Tara brooch in Ireland (dated about 900), and the Hunterston brooch in Scotland (dated seventh-eighth century), the ancient ring brooch once again became a leading inspiration for nineteenth century designs. These annular brooches were formed as a ring of metal with a central pin. This crossed from one side of the circle, passed through the fabric and rested on the opposite side of the ring. If there is a break in the ring, the brooch should, strictly speaking, be described as penannular. Sixteenth century examples, like the Loch Buy brooch, were often set with crystals and river pearls, and sometimes the centre of the ring would be completely filled in by a crystal; both styles that can be seen in nineteenth century copies.

Heart shapes followed the same annular style as early as the fourteenth century; but hearts became most popular in Scotland at the beginning of the eighteenth century, when the crowned Luckenbooth brooches were given as love tokens and as protections against evil spirits. So called because they were sold in locked booths around St Giles' Kirk, Edinburgh, many early examples were made in copper and silver by tinkers. When two hearts were entwined, they often looked like the letter 'M' and were sometimes referred to as Queen Mary brooches. Again, this pattern was imitated in the mid nineteenth century.

Plate 13. (Previous page, above) *The most ornate period of mourning jewels, the late 18th century, produced these* pieces. *The coloured picture on the bracelet clasp, showing the sad figure leaning on the anchor of hope, is unusual.* (*Brian and Lynn Holmes; Jean Bateman*)

Plate 14. (Previous page, below; clockwise from top right) *Gold brooch with black enamel cross. The front opens to show a Polish inscription in black on white enamel, with the dates 1819–1891. (Resners) Enamel serpent encloses a heart filled with hair, bordered with half-pearls, 1845. (Hancocks & Co) Eternity symbol of a snake surrounds a diamond forget-me-not and the usual wording. (Simeon) Hairwork in the form of a tree, arranged on ivory and bordered with garnets. (Simeon)*

Plate 15. Group of Scottish jewels: some set in gold with baronial crests, thistle motif and the basket-hilted sword. Others set in silver with agates, cairngorms and the geometrically-set granites. (Anne Tan)

Plate 16. (Top) *Enamel lilac spray brooch, believed to have belonged to the Empress Eugénie. French, mid-19th century. The flowers have diamond centres, while the leaves are sprinkled with moonstone dewdrops.* (Landsberg & Son)

Plate 17. (Above left) *Two delicate flower sprays, about 1825. Above: set with rubies, emeralds and a turquoise. Below: coral flowers have garnet centres, the butterfly is of gold and silver.* (Harvey & Gore; Brian and Lynn Holmes)

Plate 18. (Above right) *Art Deco flower jewel, in the form of a dress clip, with a very stylised interpretation. The flowers are of cornelian, yellow onyx and stained chalcedony, with diamond centres, mounted in gold.* (Bellamy)

Plate 19. (Overleaf) *Amber glass and diamond pendant on a gold and enamel chain. Designed by Lalique, about 1900.* (Sotheby's)

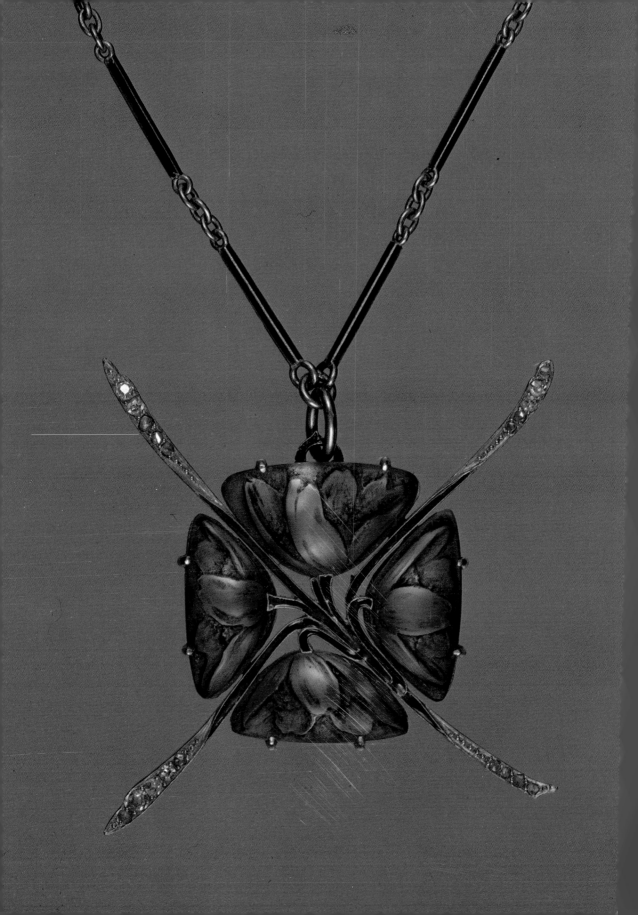

Plaid and kilt pins were, of course, vital to the fashion. Plaid pins were usually circular and kilt pins were often made as dirks or miniature daggers. The dirk was actually a hunting knife worn at the waist, but the knife worn in the stocking was called a skean-dhu. Both were reproduced in exact detail, mounted in silver or gold, and were usually set with thistle-shaped citrines. Another kind of kilt pin can be found in the shape of stag's leg, with a foot of carved cairngorms. In some cases, a real animal's foot is used as an ornament.

The cross of St Andrew was a common emblem. All Scots were entitled to wear this cross, but when it was surmounted by a crown, a royal crest was indicated and the Queen's permission was needed to wear it. These can sometimes be seen in gold with intricate designs in white enamel.

The strap and buckle was one of the most popular motifs, partly because Queen Victoria was head of the Order of the Garter. In Scottish brooches, however, it often surrounded the emblem of the Chief of a clan: this might be an eagle or shield. The emblem encircled by a buckle and strap, could be worn by all the Chief's clansmen. This kind of brooch is usually large and heavy, and was worn as a plaid pin or possibly in the hat. It was reproduced in quantity for fashionable society.

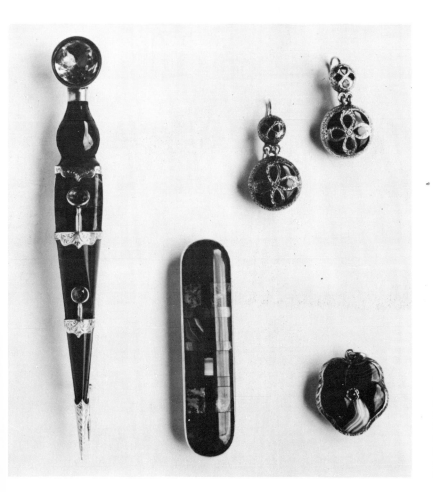

Fig. 8.3. Large dirk kilt-pin with combination of rust and moss green agates, set with citrines. Later bar-brooch in a simple silver mount. Gold mounted ear-rings and small pendant shaped as a pansy. (Brian and Lynn Holmes)

Fig. 8.4. Traditional or purely Victorian motifs occurred in Scottish jewels. Left: the cross of St Andrew surmounted by a crown denoted a high rank. Bottom: the fishing boat is an unusual brooch, again a typically Scottish and romantic emblem. The bracelet with cable links, the sword and shield of the Highland regalia and the anchor are all common Victorian motifs. Top: a traditional Scottish jewel in attractive design. (James Robinson, New York)

The curved shield or 'targe' was just one of the many heraldic symbols considered important features of these jewels. Others will gradually become more familiar — baronial crests, thistle motifs, basket-hilted swords, arrows.

A rather different kind of Scottish pebble jewel was made mainly with pale pink Corennie and grey Aberdeen granites. These stones were arranged in plainer, geometrical styles, using orderly designs which fitted into the limited area of a circular brooch. They are often found with an elongated figure-of-eight pattern crossing through the circle. The grey agates also appeared in a 'lace' design, set in chased silver, again in well-proportioned, precise patterns.

Some pieces were more obviously made as part of the English fashion. These include bracelets, bangles, ear-rings and pendants — not traditionally part of the Highland costume. Bracelets were made of links of agates in all colours, set in silver or gold and joined by a padlock, or sometimes fastened with a buckle. Ear-rings are less common, but are found in typical 1860s styles, in chased silver or gold with agates. Necklaces are rare, as ladies wore plaids over high-necked long white dresses and necklaces could not be seen.

Fig. 8.5. Gold mounted striated grey agate bracelet, with padlock. About 1870. (Landsberg & Son)

Small personal accessories did not escape this romantic craze, and pen-knives, napkin rings, vinaigrettes, perfume bottles, dog whistles and many other items can be found with Scottish decoration.

Pebble jewellery was set with different coloured agates, quarried in different parts of Scotland, and it is the combination of the warm colours of these stones that gives the jewels their own distinctive character. Bloodstone, cornelian, jasper, granite, moss agate, sometimes malachite, and countless variations of agates in mellow shades and patterned with natural striations, were all used. The mount could be either silver or gold.

The production of these brooches demanded a high standard of workmanship and a precise skill in gem stone-cutting. The remarkable feature of this Victorian vogue is the perfection achieved in the technique; even the cheaper pieces are very well made. The stones were sliced thinly, cut into the required shape and then set into a mount already prepared. Very often the stones were sent to Idar-Oberstein in Germany to be cut, mounted and polished.

The jewels were often further decorated with the amber-coloured or brown citrine which was also called a cairngorm. This is sometimes accompanied by the amethyst, when both might be carved into thistle shapes. Rock crystals were widely used, sometimes as very large centre stones in a plaid brooch, or a very pale amethyst might be used in the same way.

The mounts were usually elaborately chased in foliate or scroll designs, or more intricate patterns reminiscent of the Middle Ages. Silver could also be pierced in Gothic styles. The deep colours of the agates required strong,

*Fig. 8.6. Further examples
of different designs and
settings for Scottish
jewellery, all agate set, in
chased silver settings and
adorned with citrines or
amethysts. (James
Robinson, James II
Galleries, New York)*

*Fig. 8.7. Some of the later
pieces emphasised the
excellent stone cutting
without the chased silver or
gold settings, producing a
simplicity and elegance very
different from earlier
Scottish jewels. The arrow,
shell, leaf and butterfly rely
on fine cutting and the
subtle colours of the agates
for their beauty; the lyre,
centre, is more traditional
with chased settings. (Brian
and Lynn Holmes)*

imposing settings, always kept in perfect proportion to the shape and size of the jewel and stones.

Some later pieces made about 1880 to 1890 are marked by the absence of these chased settings. They were not made in traditional Scottish designs, but in plainer shapes with very simple, clear cut outlines, looking almost like silhouettes. Agates, in softer colours, were set so precisely next to each other with their surfaces exactly level, that they gave the impression of a single piece of stone. The bar-shaped brooch in the colour illustration is a perfect example, and others might be found in the form of a ribbon-bow, a stylised thistle or an anchor. Naturally, Edinburgh jewellers made Scottish jewels a speciality, but Birmingham workshops also turned out quantities of jewellery in the Scottish taste.

Today, there is a vast range of prices and styles in this area of antique jewellery. Small plain silver brooches, set with an amethyst perhaps, and hat or shawl pins may be found on market stalls at reasonable prices, while superb gold-mounted suites add to the appeal of many expensive window displays.

The traditional, distinctive styles are usually the most popular and, for some, the simpler later brooches may be an acquired taste. Scottish jewellery is sought after by many specialist collectors, and it is one aspect of antique jewellery that customers can handle with confidence, knowing that each piece is made well and the stones are well cut. Gold-mounted examples are always in demand and the registration mark that occurs on many Scottish jewels especially recommends them to the customer. This was a diamond-shaped mark, divided into sections for particular details such as date, category and pattern number. It functioned as a kind of patent mark, showing that the design had been registered.

9. Flowers in Jewellery

Flowers and jewellery have always made the most romantic of gifts. Few treasures could rival the effect of a single, perfect red rose, and only perhaps the gift of a finger-ring could convey similar hopes of eternal love. From a decorative point of view too, a bouquet of natural flowers was, and often still is, considered the most suitable embellishment for young beauty. It is for all these reasons, and others, that the flower motif has played such an important part in the message as well as the decoration of jewels.

Many beliefs and superstitions about the natural world had foundations in ancient civilisations. For example, the theme of the acorn, which appeared everywhere in mid Victorian jewellery, stemmed from a Roman reverence for the oak tree; while ancient Greek stories linked every flower with a tale of love, tragedy or triumph. The tale of Narcissus is perhaps the best-known.

The English origins of floral patterns in jewellery can be traced to the naturalistic flowers painted in the margins of medieval illustrated manuscripts. This tradition was gradually transferred to another, later art form, enamelling, which formed the basis of most seventeenth century jewel design. Renaissance styles did not tend towards naturalistic floral patterns, and it was the seventeenth century which witnessed the return and develop-

Fig. 9.1. Pair of shoe buckles set with early cut diamonds, based on the theme of the vase of flowers. About 1680. (Wartski)

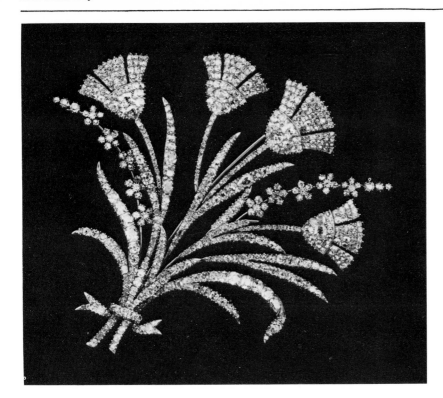

Fig. 9.2. Early diamond flower spray, about 1750, mounted in silver and set in gold. The flowers have the characteristic flat, two-dimensional look that is so charming in 18th century flower jewels. (Wartski)

ment of flower forms in jewellery, mainly due to enthusiastic European interest in plants, flowers and horticulture generally.

At the end of the sixteenth century, a French gardener called Jean Robin opened a garden in Paris, where he cultivated plants, intended mainly to act as models for embroidery designs. Shortly afterwards, the garden was bought by Henry IV, renamed *Jardin du Roi* (later known as *Jardin des Plantes)*, and its new and intriguing specimens inspired and stimulated the growth of horticultural study.

The first signs of floral influence on jewels appeared in engraved designs by Jean Vovert as early as 1602. The goldsmith Jean Toutin of Châteaudun (1578-1644) also published designs in 1618 and 1619 for watch-cases and lockets that incorporated trailing leaves and tendrils. Gradually, engraved patterns for miniature cases and cameo-frames also followed this new form of ornament, and by 1663 the most famous seventeenth century jewel designer, Gilles Légaré, demonstrated his approval of the style in a book of designs published that year.

Early in the seventeenth century, flowers were painted on enamel backgrounds of pale blue, yellow or black on small plaques. Around 1640, the flowers were engraved and shown in more relief, still painted in their natural colours. By the middle of the century, the background was pierced so that each flower stood out in perfect detail. For a while around 1634 the tulip had dominated enamelled bouquets, but other favourites included sunflowers, roses, hyacinths, lilies, mostly arranged in garlands or festoons, and many reminiscent of wood-carvings by Grinling Gibbons.

The passion for flower ornament continued into the eighteenth century, where it fell under the glittering influence of the age, and was transformed by the great progress in diamond-cutting. Jewellers had been breaking away from the previous statutory enamelling to concentrate on the stones themselves, and from this new emphasis on diamonds emerged the ever popular traditional diamond flower-spray.

The partnership of diamonds and flowers suited the mood of the eighteenth century and offered the right scope for the jewellers of the day to demonstrate their exquisite craftsmanship. Small sprays were sewn to the dress, or worn in elaborate coiffures; and all jewels were made with the consideration that, after a few years, they would be broken up and reset in the latest fashion (see Chapter 1, Diamond Brooches).

Although flowers and leaves provided the main inspiration for eighteenth century jewels, no great attempt at realism was felt necessary, and this is the basic difference between the eighteenth and nineteenth century flower-sprays. The early jewellery gives an overall, stylised impression of flowers and leaves. Flower-heads are flat and represent no known species. The stems are wide and gem-set, and the leaves curled to suit the shape and symmetry of the brooch or spray, rather than to follow the rules of nature. The attraction of these pieces lies in this stylisation and in the charm of early stones and settings, as well as in the high standard of workmanship.

Fig. 9.3. Georgian diamond 'tremblant' flower spray brooch. About 1800. (Wartski)

The first half of the eighteenth century also saw the production of the finest paste jewels, with the same amount of care and skill lavished on their beautiful floral patterns. One favourite French motif, used extensively with paste, was the cornucopia or 'horn of plenty', which took the form of a basket of fruit. Another was the flower-basket, making full use of foiled stones in the arrangements of colourful bouquets. French designs were far more elaborate and intricate while English early eighteenth century jewels are marked with a simplicity and lack of unnecessary detail.

Towards the end of the eighteenth century, there was a gentle revival of naturalism, and, with this, came the introduction once again of coloured stones into flower bouquets. However as the nineteenth century approached, the move towards naturalism was halted while classicism adapted foliate designs to the formal arrangements of coronets shaped as laurel wreaths and garlands of wheat-ears.

The restoration of the Bourbon monarchy in France in 1814 heralded an important and revitalised wave of floral naturalism in jewellery that was to last right through the century, on both sides of the Channel.

At first designs were predominantly eighteenth century in feeling, but the profusion of jewelled blossoms shone with new life, optimism and freshness. Improved cutting and setting techniques strengthened the effect of massed diamonds. The brilliant-cut, developed around 1700, was now in more general use. Settings were left open at the back to increase the brilliance of the stone, by allowing more life and light to be reflected.

Horticultural designs were encouraged by a passionate and widespread interest in gardens and flowers; new species, gathered on expeditions to the East, were eagerly greeted in Europe and quickly incorporated into artistic designs. Jewellers concentrated on precision of settings and exact representations of individual flowers.

By the middle of the century, the flower-spray had been perfected, principally by Oscar Massin, a leading Parisian jeweller. Curiously Massin had decided to come to London to study English workmanship before he accomplished the finest sprays for which he became famous. His flowers were immaculate in their realism, exquisite in their workmanship. They were characterised by *tremblant* plant stems that set the flower-heads quivering, and an arrangement of diamonds, set *en pampilles,* that dropped in seemingly careless cascades from leaves and petals. This new idea was especially popular, lending movement and romance to conventional diamond jewellery. Massin's sprays were widely imitated, and remained popular until the 1880s, enjoying their greatest success in the 1860s.

Jewel displays at the Exhibitions of the Grand Victorian period pointed to the next developments of botanical jewellery. Styles were heavier than with early nineteenth century examples, and more elaborate. Firms at the 1851 Exhibition, such as J.V. Morel and Hunt & Roskell, demonstrated the remarkable features of these diamond bouquets. Meticulously copied from nature, and interpreted in diamonds and rubies, the jewel could be divided into several pieces, each of which was a complete ornament in itself.

The height of botanical naturalism was expressed by a jewel shown at the Paris Exhibition of 1867; a diamond spray of lilac, bought by the Empress Eugénie. It was believed that the jeweller had kept a spray of real lilac next to him while he was working.

Flowers and leaves had pervaded the styles of many other less expensive jewels. Some of the prettiest of the early nineteenth century evolved from the fashion for coloured gold, in small jewelled nosegays. Gold can be mixed with different metals to alter its final colour; copper produces a red-gold and silver a greenish tint. These subtle variations were effectively used for the stalk and leaves, while the flowers were composed of coloured stones or — very often — charmingly demure clusters of turquoises. The pansy, symbolising

Fig. 9.4. Two gold hearts decorated in the floral style of the 1830s and 1840s. Top: the basket of flowers is made of two-coloured gold and set with stones whose initials spell the romantic message 'Regard', to emphasise the meaning of the flowers. Below: this bracelet padlock shows the favourite forget-me-not, its petals formed by turquoises, and the leaves beautifully engraved. There are flowers on both sides of these hearts. (Brian and Lynn Holmes)

Fig. 9.5. Ivory was carved into large and detailed flowers. Left: a realistic rose. Right: a rose seen from the side, with all its tightly gathered petals. Late 19th century. (Bellamy)

'thoughts', was very subtly portrayed in amethyst and citrines. These little flower brooches, with coloured gold foliage, date from around 1830.

Favoured Flowers and Materials

The abundance of blossoms and foliage which trailed over brooches, lockets, bangles and ear-rings during the peak of Victorian romanticism was in part the result of a fashionable interest in the language of flowers. Excessive nineteenth century sentiment found ample expression in the study of the elaborate symbolism of nature. Several books were published listing the meanings of every species imaginable, referring to ancient tales and Eastern romances to capture young imaginations. In the 1850s, Mrs A.C. Burke compiled a miniature guide to the language of flowers. This was followed by another small volume in 1866, called *Language and Sentiment of Flowers*, compiled by 'L.V.' with 'floral records', suitable poems and colour illustrations. In 1869, *The Young Ladies' Journal* published their own book on the subject.

Ivory was an ideal medium for expressing this fascinating interest. Beautiful roses, lilies of the valley, acorns, lilac, chrysanthemums and many other flowers could be intricately carved on brooches, ear-rings and pendants. Parian was a creamy-coloured porcelain used mainly for figures, but it lent itself to jewellery as a cheaper, very pretty imitation of ivory. Mary Brougham of Burslem was considered the leading manufacturer of Parian jewellery.

Coral was very often carved into clusters of flowers and leaves, while tortoise-shell was more often fashioned to resemble branches and twigs. The red chrysanthemum, meaning 'I love', was a popular subject for coral carvings. A pendant and ear-rings of about 1860 would show the flower in delicate details of its tiny petals, perhaps surrounded by leaves, twigs and tiny rosebuds. Another use for coral was found during a mid century craze for grapes and vine-leaves. Gold would be worked into leaves and tendrils, sheltering succulent bunches of faceted, polished coral grapes.

Seed pearls also very often represented the grapes in such pieces. These tiny pearls, mainly from China and Madras, were still in vogue in these early Victorian years, and their main use was in floral jewellery. The pearls were strung on white horsehair on to a background of mother-of-pearl; very few perfect examples of this delicate work have survived.

Ivy leaves seemed to cling to every smooth surface of gold or silver: they covered lockets and bangles, and entwined themselves around the frames of brooches and pendants. Many brooches can still be found, shaped as a single ivy leaf of pavé-set turquoise or malachite. According to the language of flowers, the ivy signified 'Friendship, fidelity and marriage'.

Florentine mosaics, on black marble backgrounds, more often than not depicted flowers using white agate, cornelian and lapis-lazuli, with malachite leaves. Piqué jewels used flowers and tendrils of inlaid silver, gold or mother-

Fig. 9.6. Flowers as hair-ornaments. Right: silver and silver gilt filigree hair-pin with delicate spray of flowers. The right-hand flowerhead is mounted on a spring so that it trembled. About 1868. Left: a small hair-comb mounted with a steel flower, cut and faceted to catch the light. About 1830-40. (Galérie 360)

Fig. 9.8. (Opposite page)
*Turn-of-the-century jewellers
favoured the long misshapen
'Mississippi' pearls, used here
to create a flower with two
drops of unequal lengths.
The chain is set with tiny
baroque pearls, and a similar
flower forms the clasp.
(Bellamy)*

of-pearl. Gold filigree and turquoise forget-me-nots sprawled over brooches and ear-rings of white chalcedony. Cornflowers, daisies, convolvulus, roses, fuchsias and too many more to mention were also favourite motifs and, of course, the forget-me-not was especially suitable for mourning jewels.

For a time in the second half of the nineteenth century, the flower motif, in endless variations, delivered its romantic message through every form of jewel. When, after the Silver Jubilee of 1887, the Birmingham jewellery trade planned to step up production of cheap silver items, designers concentrated on this craze for sentimental symbolism. The popular silver 'love' brooches catered for a demand from the lower and servant classes; all but the very poor could afford them. Girls' names and flowers, often overlaid with pink gold, were the main forms of decoration, combined with outlines of hearts, horseshoes and lovers' knots to express friendship, love, faith and sometimes patriotism. These brooches make a good starting-point for the modest collector of flower jewels. (See Chapter 5, Silver of the Late Nineteenth Century.)

Art Nouveau

This was just the kind of jewellery that repelled sensitive and aesthetic Art Nouveau craftsmen, who instigated the next change in flower representation

*Fig. 9.7. Gold grape and
vine leaf ear-rings, a popular
theme for jewellery around
1840; the leaves were made
from finely chased coloured
gold. Below: a pendant and
matching ear-rings in
Florentine mosaic set in gold
mounts. About 1860.
(Ewing)*

through their turn-of-the-century jewels. The emphasis was again on nature, but the idea of trying to copy specimens exactly was repulsive. Designs were based on certain romantic flowers or leaves — lilies, sycamore leaves, honesty — but they were interpreted by the individual artist, with a deep understanding for the gems and materials used.

While jewellers remained true to nature, their main aim was to create something of real artistic value. W. Fred, talking of contemporary Austrian jewellery at the turn of the century, said, 'Crude masses of naturalistic flowers are really of no account whatever, for a bouquet of diamonds can never have the exquisite charm of a fresh, sweet-smelling bunch of real blossoms.'

From these beliefs emerged a new and haunting stylisation of flowers in jewellery, with nature acting as abstract inspiration rather than a model.

Collectors of flower jewellery will find specimens in every period, and in every price range. The true collector will probably concentrate on Georgian sprays, or nineteenth century realism in diamonds but, of course, these can be very expensive. Those who prefer to collect smaller, easy-to-wear accessories, will enjoy the carved ivory bouquets, small stained bone pendants carved as single roses, shamrocks of Connemara marble, or Scottish thistles in cairngorms and agates. In this way, with careful and imaginative taste, the flower acts as a fascinating theme to link your choice of romantic, symbolic and, above all, decorative jewels.

Fig. 9.9. Gold spray brooch with rose blossoms, buds and leaves, entwined with laurels. Several of the leaves are inscribed with 'Traviata', 'Lucia', 'Romeo', 'D. Juan', 'Barbero', 'Estrella', 'Dinorah', 'Linda'. This brooch is believed to have belonged to Adelina (Adèle Juana Maria) Patti, the celebrated Spanish soprano. The inscriptions are names of operas in which she sang; the laurels signify her victories and successes. (Wartski)

10. Animals in Jewellery

From the earliest times, in ancient Egypt, Greece and Rome, the custom of wearing jewels for religious purposes, or to ward off evil spirits, was closely linked to deep magical and superstitious beliefs about certain animals.

The Egyptians in the fourth century B.C. incorporated their sacred beetle into gems to be worn as amulets or used as seals. These scarabs were carved in the shape of the beetle and the underside was engraved with a hieroglyphic motto. As the skill spread throughout the ancient worlds, the beetle was replaced elsewhere by symbols appropriate to different civilisations, and eventually the carving of scarabs led to the development of cameo-cutting.

From then, either as charms or as beautiful adornments, animals and insects have been portrayed in jewellery through the ages, successfully adapting themselves to the tools and techniques of centuries of craftsmen and to the passing whims of fashions.

In English jewellery, animal motifs were carefully nurtured by a national characteristic. Because of its personal nature, jewellery for both men and women has at times expressed sentiments of deepest love, respect and grief. It was natural then that the Englishman's affection for animals should be shown in his jewellery: while the gentleman would publicise his love of hunting through sporting motifs, the lady could emphasise her delicacy and femininity with the almost intangible beauty of a butterfly's wings.

Superstition too played its part in keeping animals in fashion. The serpent is probably one of the best known and most successful motifs drawn from the animal world. Its popularity stemmed from an ancient Greek and Roman reverence for the snake as a guardian spirit and symbol of wisdom. Curled round the frame of a Georgian mourning brooch with its tail tucked in its mouth, the serpent was a suitable reminder of eternity, or brightly jewelled on the wrist of a Victorian lady it was seen again as proof of an everlasting love.

The versatility of the snake, however, was particularly unusual, and different ages favoured different animals, enabling today's collectors to gather a complete menagerie of animal jewels. As ancient cameos and their subsequent copies were carved as miniature versions of contemporary paintings and frescoes, animals and mythical beasts were often included, but only in the late Renaissance did the whole jewel itself take an animal form.

The second half of the sixteenth century saw the development of a later and

Fig. 10.1. English blue enamel and diamond snake bangle. About 1840. (Landsberg & Son)

more elaborate Renaissance style. As the amount of jewellery worn by women increased, the new rich styles of decoration found perfect expression in the art of jewellery production. It was a time when jewellers were truly artists, and when all personal accessories and clothes were jewelled. The introduction of the irregularly shaped baroque pearl accelerated a fashion for animal jewels, for the imagination of artist-craftsmen transformed these rare pearls into the bodies of fantastic or terrifying beasts.

Erasmus Hornick of Nuremberg produced designs for such jewels in 1562. Building around the pearl, he and other designers added enamelled gold and gems to head, wings or legs, finally creating pendants shaped as dragons, eagles, sea-horses, mermaids or hybrid monsters. The taste for such pendants spread to several countries, and in Spain in particular, which was a centre for goldsmiths, the corresponding fashion bred less extraordinary species: there the more passive dove, swan, lamb or rabbit were favoured. A very fine collection of these pieces, including the famous Canning jewel (shaped as a merman) is in the Victoria & Albert Museum, and the use of the baroque pearl and superb enamelling on back and front can be seen to full advantage.

From this impressive beginning animals accompanied almost every jewellery fashion through the ages, but it is easy to see that in certain eras animals and insects as decorations are more dominant than in others.

During the seventeenth and eighteenth centuries, flower forms were generally preferred, but the serpent with its mythical associations was creeping into Neo-classical designs, and by the end of the eighteenth century many chains and necklaces carried a snake motif. On late eighteenth century watches, chased gold decoration often portrayed hunting scenes, and a stag's head, perhaps, or gundog might be carved on a gentleman's seal.

Improved paste jewels that successfully imitated diamonds and precious stones lent themselves readily to fast-changing vogues and to novelty styles which could be more easily discarded in favour of the next whim, and animals made an appearance at this stage. French butterfly brooches, silver-set, would have white wings and a body of coloured pastes. Small jewelled birds were worn in elaborate eighteenth century coiffures, and were perched quivering on top of that popular hair ornament, the aigrette. Doves (symbols of the Holy Ghost) and swallows were favoured at this time too.

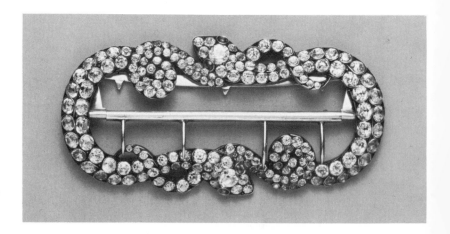

Fig. 10.2. Fine paste buckle, designed as two entwined serpents, late 18th century. (Peter Edwards)

Plate 20. (Previous page) This subtly shaded enamel-work flower jewellery was very popular around the turn of the century. Some petals have a matt surface, while others are opalescent to give a satin sheen. A great deal of this work was American. (S. Rogers and M. Ventura; Peter Edwards)

Plate 21. The kind of enamelling seen on these purple and green-tipped leaves is almost a Liberty hallmark. The gold leaves were cupped and the enamel poured in to give a gem-like effect. Here combined with amethysts on a necklace and brooch, there is a strong Arts and Crafts feeling in the pieces. (Bellamy)

Plate 22. (Above) *Realistically vicious wolf's head brooch, pavé-set in diamonds with ruby eyes, enamelled teeth and tongue. (Hancocks & Co)*

Plate 23. (Right) *Reverse crystal intaglio of a heron. Finely painted and showing the mother-of-pearl background, in a gold mount, 1860s. (Ewing)*

Plate 24. A group of 19th century animal jewels. Note the frog (symbol of wedded bliss) in diamonds and turquoises, which is typical of the 1860s; the lion on a seal of about 1830; and the elegant swan in coloured gold on a slim bar-brooch from the turn of the century. This amusing collection shows the effect of a carefully chosen group. (Ewing)

Fig. 10.3. Diamond, turquoise and enamelled parrot ear-rings; the birds are looking inquiringly out from their hoops. About 1860. (Phillips)

But it was the nineteenth century and the Victorians especially who admitted almost every species of animal and insect into their jewellery.

They seem to have introduced animal motifs along with the fashion for mosaic jewellery, which lasted from about 1820 to 1850. At this time, travel had become much easier, and the first package tours to Europe were being organised. The most fashionable sites to visit were the newly discovered ruins of Pompeii and Herculaneum. The new breed of holiday-makers inspired a whole range of mosaics. (See Chapter 13, Mosaics in Jewellery.) The picture would be bordered by black or coloured glass, and framed in gold or by stones such as lapis-lazuli or malachite.

Somehow or other the repertoire of classical sites began to include pictures of birds portrayed in minute detail, and a necklace of linked mosaic plaques might be composed of a series of different birds engaged in different occupations: a cockerel driving a bird-pulled chariot, for example — the Roman flavour was still present!

The other animal seen frequently on Roman mosaic work is the King Charles spaniel. The same rather pampered and aristocratic-looking dog was shown nestling on a velvet cushion. Again the work was fine and the mosaics were accomplished in great detail, but unfortunately the delicacy of these pieces has made perfect examples relatively rare and expensive today.

The middle of the nineteenth century marked the onset of a fever for novelty, and for gimmicky fashions. From this time until the end of the century, animals and insects enjoyed their greatest popularity as jewels. Styles changed rapidly; some survived quietly for the rest of Victoria's reign, while others had bright but brief lives, and it is difficult to disentangle from the maze of concoctions the beginnings and ends of certain fashions. Although the serpent was worn throughout the century on some of the most beautiful animal jewels, the height of its fashion came in the middle of the century. The motif received an extra boost from Queen Victoria's choice of an emerald-set serpent as a betrothal ring.

Rings could have either single or double heads, jewelled faces with cabochon ruby eyes, a single diamond, or just plain gold coils. Chains were

Fig. 10.4. Carved horn
cicada pendant. The horn is
stained a delicate pink to
lighten the wings and add to
the effect of translucency.
Turn of the century. (Private
collection)

made of links like the scales of a reptile. Supple bracelets curled around the
wrist while short necklaces or collars fastened tail-to-mouth around the neck.
Some of the prettiest and most benevolent-looking heads were completely
pavé-set with turquoises or enamelled in rich royal blue and studded with
diamonds. Necklaces were worn with a heart-shaped locket hanging from the
serpent's mouth. At this time, the mid century fashion for pavé-set turquoises
was also applied to frogs; with a similar respect for their magical qualities, the
Victorians transformed their natural ugliness to beauty.

The 1860s saw the arrival of the reverse crystal intaglio. In these jewels, a
design was cut into the back of a cabochon crystal. This was then painted and
backed with a piece of mother-of-pearl, so that an animal's head would be seen

floating inside the crystal. This fashion caught on quickly: while racehorses, sporting animals, foxes and every kind of game bird were worn on men's cuff-links and stick-pins, ladies captured colourful birds and butterflies and insects under crystal.

The insect world, traditionally so repellent to fastidious young ladies, was of great ornamental value to jewellery at this time. The bee, possibly because it was the emblem of the Bonapartes, was much worn in the 1860s. This was soon accompanied by the ordinary housefly. For an unknown reason, the fly appeared often beautifully and realistically executed in gold and jewels on lockets and brooches or, most effectively of all, it landed on faceted crystal pendants. By the 1870s beetles were crawling all over hats and veils, progressing from rose beetles to detailed stag-beetles. Even such repulsive bugs as woodlice or earwigs adorned parasols, necklaces and ear-rings. In her book *The Art of Beauty* (1878), that daunting fashion critic, Mrs Haweis, condemned the presence of slugs and snails (there was a craze for fossilised snails) in places where they would not be allowed to reside if alive. Nevertheless, flies, beetles, grasshoppers, dragonflies persisted in many forms while the Aesthetic Movement was encouraging ornaments derived from nature.

The most pleasant result of this insect vogue was the butterfly jewel. Although quietly popular for some time, the butterflies came after the plague of insects, most being made at the end of the nineteenth century. The possibilities of interpretations of the beautiful wing-markings were fully explored. Coloured stones were combined with gold and diamonds, and often pastes were used instead to enlarge the range of colours; bodies might be made of turquoise, or shimmering opals. The quality varied tremendously. Butterflies were especially popular on the tiny pins of the 1890s worn in the hair or tucked into folds of bows or lace, especially for evening wear, as they were almost always made of diamonds.

By the 1890s and *fin de siècle*, animals as novelty jewels had been well exploited. The enormous amounts of mass-produced bar-brooches and lace-pins still available now will offer endless examples to any would-be collector: hens, birds, swans, bats, kittens, monkeys, dogs, storks, bears, fish, or the honeymoon brooch of bee and crescent moon.

The lizard deserves particular mention in the list, as many fine quality brooches were made in its shape. As the Roman symbol of wedded bliss, the reptile was luxuriously and respectfully set with diamonds and rubies, and the discovery of the green demantoid garnet in the 1860s added to the beauty and realism of the lizard brooch.

A short but intense fashion for sporting jewellery in the 1880s and 1890s added yet more animals to jewels. Very fashionable for country wear, sporting brooches were worn by women anxious to break the previous strict rules of etiquette denying them such healthy pastimes. Motifs included eagles, ducks, parrots, hounds, grouse, rabbits and squirrels, to mention just a few. Gentlemen adapted stick-pins to the fashion, wearing similar animals.

Art Nouveau jewellers and artists had for some time used nature as inspiration for designs, but despised what they saw as the vulgar and petty fashions of the 1860s. Their interpretations of animals in jewels are based on an almost impressionistic view of the colours and lines and dragonflies

Fig. 10.5. A wise owl, perched in a garland of branches, in coloured gold. This same owl appears in many different forms, often perched on a crescent moon or on crossed twigs. Late 19th century. (Brian and Lynn Holmes)

Fig. 10.6. Plique à jour *bat brooch with diamond body, the wings and ears imaginatively decorated with the skilful translucent enamel, perfected by French turn-of-the-century jewellers. French, about 1890. (Hancocks & Co)*

Fig. 10.7. Three 1920s plastic frogs, used as toggles. Very stylised design. (Private collection)

and peacocks rather than the novelty appeal of certain animals portrayed in realistic detail.

Unusual materials such as horn, natural or stained, were carved into dragonfly pendants; the translucence of insect wings was captured by the *plique à jour* enamelling; while the fantastic peacock's colours were seen, true to nature, in dense blue and green enamels. The favoured opal was particularly suited to expressing the natural colourings of insects.

Collectors have an enormous variety of animals to choose from, although many no doubt start by choosing a single pet silver cat or jewelled dog. You could limit your collection to a particular period — the late nineteenth century offers the best possibilities — or choose animals on stick-pins or bar-brooches. But perhaps most rewarding of all is to come across a short and forgotten undocumented animal fashion. While sorting through the well-known butterflies and dogs, you may discover a necklace to match the brooch with perhaps that tiny but wisest owl, perfect in three-coloured gold, with minute ruby eyes, perched patiently on a smooth gold crescent moon, an aged but timeless observer of this everlasting animal kingdom.

11. Stick-pins

Tie-pins, or stick-pins, have been collected for their elegant efficiency or bizarre flamboyance, throughout their relatively short history. The disappearance of more formal clothes for men made them, for a while, some of the less popular items in antique jewellery. Now as they seem to be coming back into fashion, there is a growing interest in these jewelled pins. The greatest attraction to collectors is the endless variety of motifs and ornaments used on stick-pins, especially on late nineteenth century examples. As appreciation of Victorian jewellery grows, the decorative evidence provided by stick-pins fascinates a wider circle of antique dealers and customers.

Neckwear for gentlemen had become a separate item of clothing by the early eighteenth century, when the cravat or neckcloth replaced the large falling collar. The arrangement of the neckcloth gradually assumed enormous importance, notably amongst the Dandies and followers of Beau Brummell: and a discreet jewel, nestling in the immaculate folds of the linen or lace, was one of the few items of jewellery which was considered acceptable.

In the eighteenth century, pins were shorter than those made in the next century, and were shaped in the middle into a zigzag pattern to keep them in

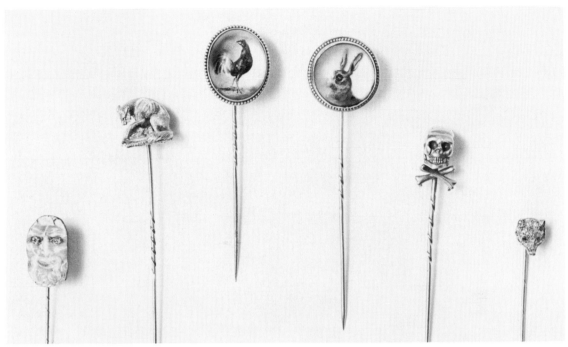

Fig. 11.2. Left to right:
carved opal head, diamond
eyes, about 1890; chased
gold model of a fox and
partridge, probably by Hunt
& Roskell; reverse crystal
intaglios of a fighting cock
and a hare (an unusual
motif), both about 1860;
19th century gold skull and
cross-bones, the motto of
the 17th Lancers; and a fox
head, set with rose diamonds
and ruby eyes, 1880-90.
(Hancocks & Co)

place. Pastes or single foil-backed stones in closed settings were popular.

The passion for mourning jewels that thrived in the last quarter of the eighteenth century affected designs of cravat-pins. (See Chapter 7, Mourning Jewellery.) These were made in the fashionable marquise shape, and a frame of gold would contain a miniature scene painted in sepia on ivory. The scenes depicted were often excessively sentimental and morbid, including all the emblems of grief and mourning: the weeping willow, urn, tombstone and a bereaved, sobbing figure.

By the early nineteenth century, more adventurous motifs were being worn by the Regency Dandies. Cravats had altered in appearance, but not in their importance to the gentleman's whole costume.

The limitation of size was the only obstacle put in the way of jewellers, who produced tie-pins to meet every new demand of the insatiable nineteenth century appetite for novelty. During this period, the jeweller's pride of production overcame any difficulty. The pins themselves were now made with a spiral ridge near the top to secure the tie.

It was not only jewellery fashions that formed the heads of these pins: sentiment, patriotism, memories of historic events and political sympathies were at times all shown by the stick-pin which a gentleman wore in his tie.

The fashion for cameos, swept in by the late eighteenth century wave of Neo-classicism, remained for most of the nineteenth century, and naturally many were made, or reset, for stick-pins. Their quality varies tremendously and, while it is possible to find a fine early cameo or intaglio set in excellent nineteenth century gold-work, the combination is rare. More common examples consist of later stones carved with Victorian interpretations of the 'classical head'.

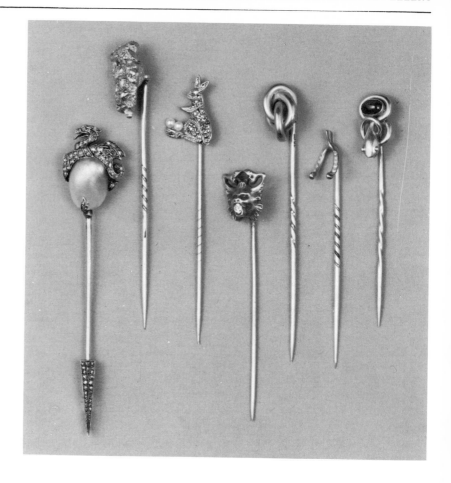

All the mid nineteenth century jewellery styles can be traced on stick-pins. The serpent appears frequently, sometimes coiled around a cone of agate, or with jewelled head and eyes. Carved coral enjoyed great popularity; pearls continued to be great favourites; pavé-set turquoises were also widely used. Diamonds were worn with evening clothes.

Queen Victoria's purchase of Balmoral in 1848, and her love of all things Scottish, bred the fashion for pebble jewellery (including tie-pins) of silver or gold set with agates, citrines and amethysts. These blended well with the muted colours of country clothes and with tartans.

One jewellery style that was applied mainly to gentlemen's jewellery was the reverse crystal intaglio. The back of a cabochon crystal was carved, painted and then backed with mother-of-pearl. Animals, game birds, insects and stags' heads were favourite subjects and each appeared in realistic detail, suspended inside the bubble of crystal.

By the second half of the nineteenth century, the pursuit of novelty was in full swing and stick-pins lent themselves perfectly to every passing whim. The insects seen everywhere on ladies' jewels, parasols and veils appeared just as frequently to land on gentlemen's ties. Houseflies and beetles were made in gold, or jewelled with pavé-set diamond wings and a pearl body.

The greatest boost was given to the range of tie-pin motifs by the sporting

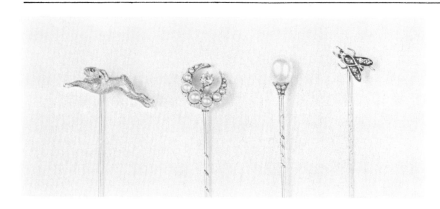

Fig. 11.4. Group of typical late Victorian pins: a running hare with ruby eyes, in chased gold; a gold crescent set with pearls and a diamond; a single pearl set with rose diamonds; rose diamond fly set with ruby eyes. (Simeon)

jewels that developed in the 1880s and 1890s. Every animal associated with hunting or riding was used as a model for stick-pins. The large number of these illustrated shows the importance of this fashion: the fox's head, along with many other animals, was often covered with rose diamonds. Hares and dogs were shown in full run. The enamelled terrier (Fig. 11.5.) is much more unusual. The attention paid to details of eyes, muscles and expressions is worth studying. Gold has been chased to represent the hairs of the animal's coat, and its eyes were set with tiny stones, sometimes minute cabochon rubies.

One particularly rare example of a political emblem is also illustrated (Fig. 11.5.). It is a three-dimensional 18 carat gold model of Austen Chamberlain (1863-1937), the father of Neville Chamberlain. The style of the pin resembles that of a nineteenth century cartoon. As Chancellor of the Exchequer,

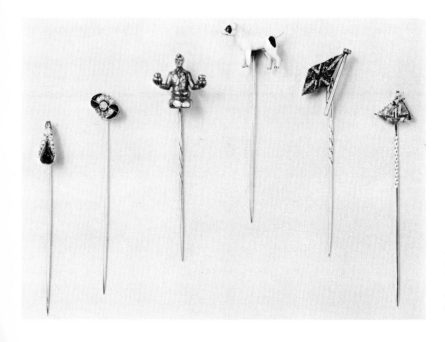

Fig. 11.5. Left to right: Cartier pin of platinum set diamonds and a cabochon Burma sapphire, about 1925; French pin with diamonds, onyx and emerald propellors, mounted in platinum; rare political stick-pin, of Austen Chamberlain. Unusual sporting motif of a terrier, 18 carat gold and hard enamel, diamond eyes; gold and platinum patriotic model of a Union Jack, set with diamonds, rubies and sapphires; model of a sailing boat, set with fancy flat cut diamonds, mounted in gold. Tiffany pin of diamonds and calibré sapphires, set in platinum and gold. About 1928-30. (Private collection)

Fig. 11.6. Fine early 20th century pins, showing ingenuity in the cutting and combination of precious stones: Right to left: elegant Edwardian ruby and diamond pin; sapphire and diamond box in perspective; diamond and sapphire question mark; gold and ruby hand; champagne glass made of specially cut diamonds; ruby and sapphire Union Jack. (Brian and Lynn Holmes, S. Rogers and M. Ventura)

he is shown emerging from a huge loaf of bread holding a small loaf in each hand. This was probably part of the anti-Chamberlain propaganda put out by the Liberals who were urging free trade, in opposition to Chamberlain's idea of protected trade within the Empire. The large loaf represented the size that would be obtainable under free trade, while the small loaf, supported by Chamberlain, showed what the same amount of money would buy under protection. The symbolic loaf of bread had been used in a similar way during the campaign for the Repeal of the Corn Laws (1845-6). Superb detail on the stick-pin includes a rose-cut diamond monocle and an enamel orchid buttonhole.

The sophisticated age of the 1920s, its attitudes and atmosphere are reflected in its jewellery. One way of wearing and collecting the style can be through the tie-pins made at the time.

Signed pieces always fetch high prices, but the importance of the signature must not be overemphasised. The superior design and quality of workmanship on many unsigned examples is often overshadowed by a signed, though inferior, piece. Geometric patterns plus the unprecedented combinations of precious stones and platinum settings, are some of the well-known features of this period. All of them were concentrated in perfect proportion on the heads of tie-pins.

Another attitude which can be detected in designs of the 1925-35 period is an obsession with speed, movement and new scientific developments. One pin illustrated incorporates emerald propellers in the tiny platinum shape which is set with diamonds and onyx (Fig. 11.5.).

An attempt at reviving the fashion was made by the Scarf Pin Society, set up in 1951 by a group of gentlemen. The Society had 25 members, with three permanent officers, known as King Pin, Linch Pin, and Safety Pin — Founder, Secretary and Treasurer respectively. Members met at an annual dinner, and lots were drawn for them to borrow certain pins which were the property of the Society and which they could wear for the dinner and throughout the following year. New acquisitions were shown at the dinner on velvet cushions.

The Scarf Pin Society commissioned pins, to be made with rubies, sapphires, emeralds and diamonds, representing the colours of the Society. It continued until the mid 1960s. The object of the Society was 'to re-unite those few gentlemen whose pleasure it is to bring a little colour into a drab world by the wearing of a scarf or tie-pin'.

12. Cameos and Engraved Gems

No collection of Victorian jewellery would be complete without a cameo, and no collection of cameos would be justly representative without some choice examples made in the Victorian era. Yet, for some time, Victorian cameos were largely ignored and despised by connoisseurs. Although, in general, later nineteenth century cameos can only rarely compete in beauty or quality with late eighteenth century specimens, nonetheless a search through the variety of Victorian adaptations can be fascinating and fruitful. The story of cameo carving is well documented and can be studied as deeply or as briefly as a collector wishes, but it is an area in which it is most important to develop an understanding of the subject by handling the pieces, closely examining the carving and materials, and taking note of the subject matter.

The art of gem-engraving was developed in ancient times and spread through Egypt and Greece to Rome, with subject matter based on pictorial presentations of classical stories and ideals. The art of cameo-cutting can be traced to the ancient Egyptian carving of the sacred beetle or scarab. Hardstones were engraved, or cut into the shape of the scarab, as amuletic symbols. As the custom spread to other lands, the beetle was replaced by other subjects.

Since that period, there have been two main revivals of the art: the first was in the late Middle Ages and Renaissance period, when there was a great renewal of interest in classical learning, encouraged by art patrons such as Lorenzo dei Medici and François I of France. The art went out of fashion during the seventeenth and early eighteenth centuries, but was revived with the wave of Neo-classicism that lasted roughly from about 1760 to 1820. The great archeological discoveries of this period led to a new interest in ancient culture; consequently very fine cameos and intaglios were produced. With the coming of the Victorian age, this Neo-classicism was replaced by the Romantic-Gothic style, which transformed the rôle and the art of the cameo. It disappeared as one of the highest forms of art, but remained as one of the most popular items of decorative jewellery until the 1880s.

New collectors searching in shops and markets will find that nineteenth century cameos are most plentiful. Probably the first variation they will face is the difference between early nineteenth century classical cameos and later nineteenth century romantic carvings.

The Renaissance which resulted in a substantial renewal of interest in classics led to a new school of gem-engraving and produced excellent cameos. This harmony was disturbed in the seventeenth and early eighteenth centuries, when the prevailing artistic styles — the florid Baroque and Rococo — and a shift of emphasis on to outward appearances and decoration were not conducive to cameo-carving. When gem-engraving was attempted in this period, the results were not totally successful.

The next period of fine cameos came with the Neo-classical revival of the late eighteenth century, when again there was a total commitment to classical art and ideals. As before, cameo artists felt the need to provide inspiration for the people, through models and engravings of gods and heroes and of meaningful stories from mythology. The figure and personality of Napoleon was also an encouraging influence on the revival of cameo-carving. Apart from his own love of cameos, he represented heroic strength as the head of a state and a new social system. About 1810, when his power and leadership were at their greatest, Napoleon was himself depicted on cameos, his portrait carved in the style of an ancient Roman Emperor. Such a cameo might be given by Napoleon and the gift would be considered a great honour and token of esteem. The art of cameo-carving became a perfect expression and diffusion of the Neo-classical spirit, and was raised in esteem to the same rank as painting, sculpture and architecture.

Fig. 12.1. Agate cameo in gold and enamel mount. The banded agate cameo is of Charles IV of Spain, and is signed by William Brown. About 1800, the mount is about 1870. (Sotheby's)

It is interesting too that cameo-carving is at its best in male-dominated societies, where masculine characteristics of heroes like Hercules and Zeus were most valued, and where cameos were regarded as pure works of art and not merely as adornments to feminine beauty. This change of attitude is one of the main distinctions between early and later nineteenth century cameos. During the 1830s, Neo-classicism gave way to a new era of Romanticism; in this case, a Romantic-Gothic style, which coincided with the accession of a female monarch, who was a very dominant and influential figure — Queen Victoria. This change of public taste seems to have stopped the flow of the finest cameos which were produced in the classical atmosphere; however the cameo, far from disappearing, remained in favour as an item of decorative jewellery for another fifty years.

For purists and cameo-connoisseurs, this debasement of the art spoilt cameos and gem-engraving. It is true that the quality of the cheaper cameos, at the lower end of the market declined steadily. But to collectors of Victorian jewellery, the cameo was one of the most popular and versatile fashions of the age. The discipline of Neo-classicism had been discarded for freedom to follow and mix any number of influences on design. These included the Neo-Renaissance style which naturally brought the cameo to the forefront of fashion. Society in general loved outward show, material signs of success, and beautiful women were regarded as showcases for their husbands' wealth. Men bought cameos to give to women as ornaments, and as indications of their own ideal view of the female as a rather helpless nymph, a projection too of their sexual desires. The rather superficial, empty-headed and frail Victorian female is reflected in carvings of stereo-typed, expressionless classical heads. These were the basic differences between a classical and a romantic age, that switched the rôle of the cameo from a high art form into a pretty ornament to beauty.

Fig. 12.2. (Below) Early 17th century Venetian agate cameo, with a double-headed blackamoor carving of extremely fine quality, mounted in chased coloured gold.

Fig. 12.3. (Bottom) A third stone cameo on the base of Fig. 12.2, taking the place of the original seal. (Nicholas Harris)

How Cameos Are Made

The difference between a cameo and an intaglio is that, on a cameo, the design is carved so that it stands up in relief from the background; while on an intaglio, the design is incised into the stone. This often gives the cameo a decorative advantage, and sometimes more immediate appeal to the collector, because the design of the figure or head can be seen and appreciated at a glance. The most prized cameos of all periods were carved from hardstones, such as agates with their different coloured layers of grey, brown or black with a white streak. The skill lay in using these bands so that the subject which was carved from the creamy white layer, stood out from the dark background, thus creating a small sculpture. The most common combination was the rust and white of the kind of agate called sardonyx. Shading and details were then achieved by variations, perhaps by working on a dark band seen through a thin white layer, or by interpreting natural shading as skin tones or facial expressions.

Many other materials have been used with varying success. Precious stones were carved in ancient times and during later revivals, but are not as effective as banded agates. Imitations of stone cameos have been created in glass, pottery and later in shell, coral, opal, jet, ivory and lava. Agates can also be artificially coloured; the dark layers are porous, and so can be soaked in various solutions to produce different colours.

The main tools used were drills with heads of iron, impregnated with diamond dust to cut the stone, and lubricated with olive oil. Apart from these necessities, cameo-carving requires patience — a large cameo could take several years to complete — and skill, particularly in judging and improvising

on the layers, which could change suddenly and unpredictably in both thickness and direction.

Cameo-carving is an art form that was conceived and developed by ancient craftsmen, centred around their strongest beliefs about the powers of the gods; about the struggles and imperfections of mortals and the strength of human character in the face of adverse conditions; about the state, rulers, social and political systems. A deep awareness of these aspects of life inspired the carving of subjects to represent them and to encourage or humiliate man. Whenever these classical ideals have been revived and upheld at different times through the centuries, the inspiration for an expressive art has also been recalled, and cameo-carving has thrived.

Cameos of the Neo-classical Period

Late eighteenth century Classicism had affected architecture, furniture, ceramics and costume: cameos were obviously the most appropriate fashion accessory. The 'Grand Tour' had become an integral part of a good education and took in the recently excavated sites in Italy, including Pompeii. The aristocrats on the Grand Tour created a good market for the shell-cameo copies of wall-friezes and Renaissance paintings made by cameo-carvers of Rome and Naples and these were brought back to England or France by their proud owners. After Napoleon's Italian campaign in 1796, many fine cameos from Rome found their way to France and captivated artists, craftsmen and collectors, including Napoleon himself. He set up a school for gem-engraving under Jeuffroy (1749-1826), a medallist, and in 1805 he added a Prix de Rome for gem-engraving to those awarded for painting, sculpture and architecture. Napoleon also had some of Louis XVI's cameos mounted as jewels, thus encouraging the fashion of wearing cameos as jewellery. This was an important feature of costume of this period, and one that is illustrated in many portraits of the Empress Josephine and other female members of Napoleon's family.

In spite of their low intrinsic value, cameos were mounted with diamonds, pearls and precious stones, although they were also suited to more modest settings. It was usual for a fashionable lady of the early nineteenth century, clothed in a Grecian-style high-waisted dress, to wear cameos on her belt, her

Fig. 12.4. Unusual stone cameo, believed to have been carved about 1750 by Calabresi, although there are conflicting reports. The scene shows Mars and Venus taken in the toils of Vulcan, with all the gods and goddesses looking on. (Landsberg & Son)

Fig. 12.5. Gold-mounted shell cameo, designed as a diadem. The cameo is about 1780, the mount a little later. (Landsberg & Son)

necklace, one on each bracelet, on her diadem, and also on a band worn around the forehead.

Genuine antique cameos were rare, so modern gem-engravers produced stone cameos in the antique taste, to provide adequate supplies. At this time, cameos were being made of shell and moulded glass, as well as from coloured stones, in particular emeralds, Jasper or malachite. The craze for cameos was so great that in Paris 'confiseurs' made cameos of chocolate, with features of Greek or Roman profiles traced in white sugar. This huge demand for fashionable cameos worn as jewels was accompanied by a desperate mania amongst connoisseurs and collectors to own genuine antique gems, and it seems there was a great deal of cheating and faking going on. In Italy, for example, it was quite common for an unscrupulous dealer to push a new stone intaglio into the neck of a turkey or fowl, where the gastric juices and rough insides produced almost the same effect as the aging of thousands of years. Such devious practices were resented by contemporary engravers, who were always anxious to prove that their own gems came closest to the antique. Many stories were told of cameo artists claiming so-called classical gems as their own.

One such is told of Giovanni Pichler, a member of a famous family of gem-cutters. Pichler carved a very fine cameo of a female head. He broke off a corner of the stone and then gave the rest to a dealer to show to some connoisseurs, who all confirmed that it was without doubt a genuine antique gem. Then Pichler produced the broken fragment and claimed the piece as his own work.

The best-known story of this kind is told of Benedetto Pistrucci, an excellent artist and lively personality, who was patronised by Napoleon's sister, Elisa Bacciochi. One of Pistrucci's cameos, 'Flora' was sold by the notorious dealer Angelo Bonelli to the famous collector Payne Knight, who bought it at a very high price, believing it to be a very fine ancient Greek cameo. Bonelli had paid Pistrucci very little for the work some time before. When Pistrucci was working in England, at the house of Sir Joseph Banks, Payne Knight proudly showed the Flora cameo he had just purchased, declaring it to be a superb Greek example. Pistrucci recognised the gem and set about proving the work as his own. Payne Knight never believed him, in spite of all the proof, including Pistrucci's secret mark.

This was just one instance of the ways in which Pistrucci had been cheated by Bonelli. These dubious dealings were the reason why he finally decided to leave Italy for England. Pistrucci had discovered, long before the Flora incident, that Bonelli habitually rubbed out his signature and replaced it with a fake Greek one. The artist then started to hide a secret mark in the hair, or folds of a costume. In England, Sir Joseph Banks became a good friend and patron of Pistrucci, and the Italian was eventually appointed chief engraver at the Royal Mint, where he designed the St George and the Dragon group for the back of the crown (five shilling (25p) piece). In some ways, Pistrucci's work spanned both Classical and Romantic ages because, although he was trained in the Classical tradition, he actually worked rather later. He was particularly good at designing commemorative medals, and did the coronation medals of both George IV and Queen Victoria.

The finest gem-engravers of this Neo-classical period tended to concentrate on intaglios rather than cameos. Jean Laurent Natter, of Nuremberg, was a famous eighteenth century cameo-cutter, highly skilled in copying antique gems. He studied in Venice and then Rouen; and many of his gems were later acquired by the fourth Duke of Marlborough for his magnificent collection.

Other important gem-engravers also worked for state mints. Marchant

Fig. 12.6. Pair of Italian gold-mounted shell cameo bracelets, each with one large and two smaller cameos. The larger ones show 'The Triumph of Alexander' and 'The Departure of Hector', both after Thorvaldsen. The smaller ones represent 'The Grief of Achilles' and 'Priam Pleading with Achilles for Hector's Ashes', both after antique carvings; and 'The Education of the Gracchi', and 'Titus', both after M. Federico, called 'Il Prusiano'. The mounts are embossed gold frames, linked by coils of interlaced snakes with chased heads. About 1840. (Sotheby's)

(1755-1812), a German who had learnt his craft in Rome, was an assistant engraver at the Royal Mint. Marchant was at one time a pupil of another famous worker, Edward Burch, librarian at the Royal Academy. Edward Burch R.A. was a sculptor and gem-engraver who exhibited at the Royal Academy from 1771 to 1808. He died in 1814. Giuseppe Girometti (1780-1851) whose work is again prized by collectors, worked at the Papal Mint in Rome.

Philippo Rega became the head of the Naples Mint, and cut a portrait head of Lord Nelson (now in the Hull-Grundy collection at the British Museum) in about 1798, at the time of Napoleon's Italian campaign.

Other important signatures and names of skilled Neo-classical engravers include Amastini, Charles and William Brown, Morelli, Antonio Berini, working in Rome in the late eighteenth century and early nineteenth century; and Benjamin Wyon (1802-1858) who was known mainly as a medallist and who designed and engraved the great seals of George IV, William IV and Queen Victoria. Their eagerness to prove their skill in imitating the antique, luckily led most artists to sign their work, and it was usual for them to use a Greek signature. This was a tribute to the ancient Greek engravers (Renaissance carvers followed the same practice) and in this way they also showed their admiration for Classical art.

Luigi Pichler was one of three brothers — one of whom is mentioned above — who were all accomplished gem-engravers. He was perhaps one of the best of the Classically-inspired artists. He too signed his name in Greek letters. Pichler worked for Prince Poniatowsky of the Polish Royal Family, copying his collection of classical gems which the Prince aimed to supplement with fakes.

Subjects of late eighteenth century and early nineteenth century cameos and intaglios are very strictly classical, which is part of their strength and success. There were extremely fine portrait heads of ancient leaders and heroes, Hercules, Homer and the Roman Emperors for example, as well as scenes and characters from mythology and copies of ancient statues and sculptures. A good knowledge of ancient history and mythology is extremely helpful in identifying subjects. The lines on these engraved gems are always strong, clear and well defined but beautifully fluid and superbly detailed. This is seen particularly in facial expressions and features, in the folds of robes and curls of hair. The subjects and the carvings all show a great nobility and a total involvement in Classical art and ideals.

Nineteenth Century Cameos

The main disadvantage of Victorian cameos is probably their very large, even unwieldy, size. Apart from this they do offer some exceptional engraving and some very different and interesting examples for collectors. The quality of engraving varies enormously, but it is important not to judge these later works by the mass of indifferent examples, nor to compare them with earlier cameos. They should be appreciated for their own merits and as products of their age.

With the Victorian era came major changes in subject matter, materials and technique in gem-engraving. Subjects were chosen for attractive appearances rather than mythological significance or an upholding of high ideals. On the whole, they became prettier and more feminine as befitted an item of female adornment; and eventually they were reduced to a standardised classical head in many cases. Contemporary features also crept into Victorian cameos, so that Victorian clothes or jewels, for example, were mixed with a classical coiffure, or a totally nineteenth century lady was depicted, often an image of Queen Victoria. Helpless nymphs and goddesses, unidentifiable as specific characters, were very popular; as were the more obvious mythological scenes such as the three Graces. Scenes became very elaborate, filled with flowing robes and swirling clouds.

Famous people of the time were very often taken as subjects, and these should be carefully examined as some can be very fine indeed. Heads of the Prince Consort, statesmen and court beauties were common. Lord Byron was favoured as a witness to the current romanticism, together with characters from contemporary literature. This group of subjects would make an interesting theme for a collection of Victorian cameos.

Of the vast range of materials used for cameos, shell was the favourite of the period and the most successful imitation of stone cameos. Collectors concentrating on nineteenth century cameos should fully explore the use of shell, because it was so typically Victorian, and then look for something unusual in this area. Shell cameos had been carved since the fifteenth or sixteenth centuries, with some produced in the late eighteenth century, but the nineteenth century craft was revived about 1805 in Sicily. Shell cameos were carved in the same way as hardstone cameos, the layers and colourings of shell providing similar opportunities, and it was also an easy material to work. There were two main varieties of shell most suitable for cameo-carving; the species of helmet shell and the queen conch shell. The large helmet shells with brown and white layers yielded a rust, cornelian-colour background and the queen conch was pale pink and white. The best carvings were achieved with the top part of the shell, where the white layer was deep enough for detailed working.

A suitable piece of shell would be fixed to the top of a stick to be worked upon. As with hardstone cameos, all the outside superfluous layers were first cut away to leave the background layer and then the design was drawn on the white section. The cameo-cutter kept changing to finer drill points until he obtained the desired degree of detailing. Polishing was an important process and on the shell cameos, the brown background is always shiny and smooth. The points used for polishing were softer than those used for cutting, but were very similar in principle. Again they were lubricated with oil mixed with polishing powder; this sometimes was sapphire dust. Polishing can rub out the finest details of carving and so the processes of finishing and polishing were often repeated several times. Onyx, again very often used for Victorian cameos, is particularly hard and takes a beautiful, high polish.

Shell carvings became the most typical and the most common of Victorian cameos, representing both the very best and the very worst of nineteenth century work. They showed the change in subject matter and provided the widest scope for Victorian romantic interpretations of the 'Classical' style. The male profile, most common in the early nineteenth century, had been replaced by the female portrait by the middle of the century. Young girls' heads are found most frequently, ranging from fine detailed examples to empty, expressionless, rigid classical profiles. More easily identifiable heads were depicted

Fig 12.7 Group of 19th century cameos, one particularly unusual showing Cupid in a cage and illustrating skilful use of the stone to create this effect. The pendant on the right is English, late 18th century, in the style of Pichler. (Serpent mount, Brian and Lynn Holmes; Victorian female head, Peter Edwards; the rest, Nicholas Harris)

Fig. 12.8. Well-executed stone cameo of an angel, mid-19th century, in gold frame. (Ronald Benjamin)

too, again of classical inspiration. They included Hercules, Socrates (with an admirably high forehead), the lively youthful Pan, and a respectable version of Bacchus. Feminine figures were of Minerva, Venus, 'Night' and 'Day' (represented by ladies' heads with either a moon or sun in the background) and the favourite profile of Medusa. There was a significant and interesting change in the appearance of this awesome character in nineteenth century cameos. Her terrifying aspect was rapidly transformed into a meek and innocent expression. The snakes in her hair were distasteful to Victorian young ladies, and were duly replaced by flowers; while the wings on her crown were moved to her back to conjure up less sinister visions of fairy tales and angels.

In the true Victorian fashion, shell cameos also became huge and elaborate, sometimes depicting biblical scenes with crowds of onlookers. Chariots ascending to heaven through fluffy clouds accompanied by cherubs and drawn by horses, groups of dancing nymphs or a herd of frolicking ponies were also popular. A further effort at glamorising the cameo was made by setting them with precious stones, so that a head or profile would appear to be dressed in jewels. These are called cameos *habillés* and they are extremely rare. Ear-rings might show a pair of characters such as the romantic mythological lovers Cupid and Psyche.

Generally, however, subjects became very tame showing little of the ferocity of the Roman Emperors or gods, or the strength and characters of heroines and goddesses. Nineteenth century shell cameos did, however, excel in one particular range of subjects, and that was copying sculptures. It seems that some of the most skilful artists were employed in creating shell cameo versions of famous sculptures by names such as Canova or Thorwaldsen. It is worthwhile considering this aspect as a basis for a collection. There are excellent examples of cameos after the work of named sculptors in the Hull-Grundy collection in the British Museum.

Unusual Materials

About 1830 some carving of shell cameos had begun in Paris, but the work was done there by Italians who remained specialists in this art. The real impact of cameos on fashion came in about 1840, and it was from this time that mechanical methods of carving were developed to cope with the demand. Many Italian workers were employed in London too, and some English artists also attempted cameo-carving, so that both Italian and English manufacturers exhibited shell cameos at the Great Exhibition. Some of the most elaborate shell cameos were made in France, possibly by Italians, during the 1860s. This was due to the fact that they had become popular again under the Second Empire. They were mostly large, heavy-looking and crowded with involved and detailed carving.

Stone cameos were also worn at the height of the cameo fashion, but perhaps a little later than the shell cameos of the 1840s and 1850s. There was some excellent work done at this time by distinguished carvers; many of whom signed their work. The best of these is Luigi Saulini (1819-1883), who worked in the 1850s and 1860s. He was the son of another famous carver, Tommaso Saulini (1793-1864). His work represents the best of nineteenth century cameos, and it is useful to look at some of Saulini's work, as a basis for comparison. There are examples in the Hull-Grundy collection.

Other fine cameo-carvers working at this time include the Italians, Paolo Neri, Bassi and Luigi Isler. The early nineteenth century artist, Pistrucci, had two daughters, Elena and Eliza Maria, who also became talented engravers in the middle of the century: they had returned to Italy with their mother. Eliza's work was shown at the International Exhibition in London in 1862, represented by a sardonyx cameo of 'The Death of Adonis'.

Fig. 12.9. Tortoise-shell cameo depicting Medusa, with entwined serpents in her hair, and wings. Mid-19th century. (Ewing)

At this time, stone cameos made of sardonyx, stained agates and particularly black and white onyx were all very much admired. Colours were used well, and the blackamoor's head motif is often seen carved as an onyx cameo. Another very effective subject was a lady's head veiled in sheer drapes, in the image of Queen Victoria. In such carvings (there is a fine example by Saulini), a thin layer of white was worked to show the background beneath, giving the impression of a fine fabric.

Throughout the nineteenth century, there was a colourful and inventive selection of materials adapted for cameos, to satisfy an ever-growing demand and to introduce an element of novelty and change to an easily bored public. Malachite had been used in the early part of the century: often several cameos would be mounted as a necklace and joined by several fine gold chains. Lapis-lazuli can be found sometimes and coral was carved in the 1840s (see Chapter 2, Coral Jewellery). Ivory and jet were used (see Chapter 7, Mourning Jewellery). Jet was particularly appropriate for mourning cameos which often showed the head of a veiled widow.

Lava was popular for a while; especially with tourists visiting Italy and Pompeii, who took home mementoes of Mount Vesuvius. These lava cameos are usually matt grey or dull greenish-brown and beige in colour. They are often very intricately carved with archeological motifs, grotesque masks or satyrs and bacchantes, and were made into large suites of jewels.

Fig. 12.10. Lava cameo bracelet, showing portraits of famous Italian writers including Petrarch, Dante, Boccacchio, Ariosto. Lava is found in many colours from grey through olive to terracotta. (Brian and Lynn Holmes)

Mounts and Settings

As the cameo found a firm place in Victorian jewellery, the settings became more important. Usually they follow the current styles of jewellery and goldwork. Early on, during the 1830s and 1840s, mounts were still quite delicate with gold filigree, rope-work, scrolls and pearl-set borders. A little later, in the High Victorian period around the middle of the century, as cameos became larger, more crowded with subjects and cut in much higher relief, settings became correspondingly heavy. Elaborate gold mounts could be enamelled, set with precious stones, or decorated with Etruscan style goldwork. The fine cameos of Saulini were set in exquisite mounts made by Castellani, Civilotti (see Chapter 15, Signed Jewellery of the Mid-nineteenth Century), or other excellent jewellers. Robert Phillips mounted shell cameos in very fine gold frames and John Brogden also surrounded cameos with his particular style of intricate gold decoration. Any cameo worth the attention of such revered jewellers and goldsmiths must have been very fine and again this proves the skill that did emerge in Victorian cameo-carving.

Earlier cameos were often remodelled in the early nineteenth century; sometimes they were repolished, or supplemented with diamonds and precious stones. Later on, many good Victorian mounts were set with much earlier cameos. It is therefore important for collectors to look carefully and separately at both the cameo and its setting.

Fakes in Cameos

Excellent imitations of cameos were diligently worked by those who spotted the opportunities offered by the fanatical craze of the Neo-classical period. There were obviously not enough examples of the genuine article to be shared amongst the avid collectors.

Jasper was a kind of fine white stoneware developed by Josiah Wedgwood in 1774-5, which could be coloured with metallic oxides. From the 1770s, Wedgwood used his new Jasper stoneware to create a kind of fake cameo in which a white bust, or classical scene was cemented on to a stained background. They were very often mounted in cut-steel on jewels, objects of vertu and especially on châtelaines. Wedgwood worked in close association with Matthew Boulton, the Birmingham manufacturer of cut-steel. Wedgwood's subjects followed traditional classical themes but also included

Fig. 12.11. Wedgwood 'imitation' cameo. The white relief against the blue Jasper background depicts a classical scene. (Brian and Lynn Holmes)

later famous figures such as Milton, Isaac Newton, plus recent or current monarchs. It is interesting to follow the change from Classicism to Romanticism in popular Wedgwood cameos too. As Dora Jane Jansen points out in her catalogue *From Slave to Siren*, women were employed in the design and manufacture of Jasper cameos, so it is not surprising to find a strong feminine influence on subjects, materials and design. Even Queen Victoria took lessons in cameo-carving. Wedgwood cameos remained popular in the early years of Queen Victoria's reign, but the quality and delicacy declined as the century progressed.

In the midst of the late eighteenth century passion for engraved gems, a Scotsman called James Tassie (1735-1799) found a way of producing accurate copies of antique cameos or intaglios. He started work in London in 1767, where he developed the technique of taking sulphur moulds from the gems, the sulphur being mixed with a white wax. Fake gems were then cast in a paste which could be coloured, transparent or opaque. A catalogue of the

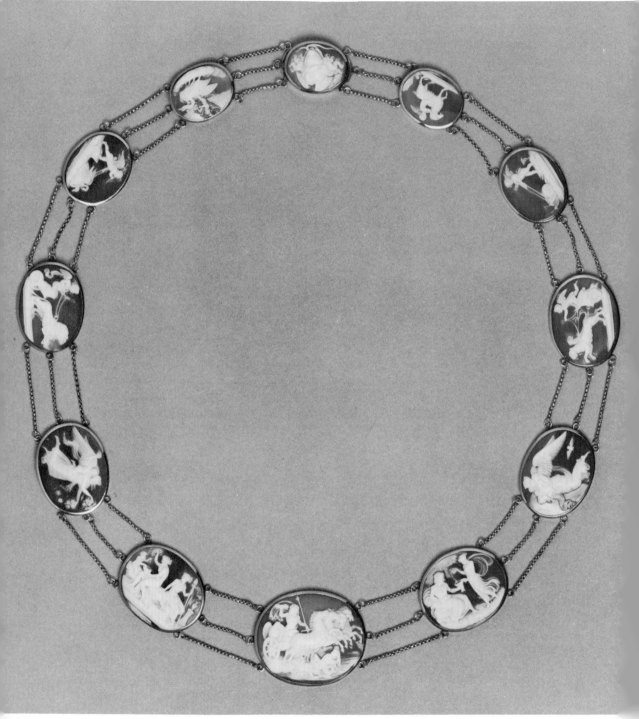

Fig. 12.12. Cameo necklace, about 1820, with some of the stone cameos carved in the manner of Thorvaldsen. (Wartski)

period by R.E. Raspe listed 15,000 of Tassie's imitation gems. They were enormously popular at the time; firstly because they were very attractive, and secondly because they were completely accurate as copies, in the original colours. They were also extremely cheap, at a time when genuine hardstone cameos were sought after and expensive. The intaglios were far less expensive and more plentiful than the cameos which were much harder to make. Tassie supplied Wedgwood with many of the moulds for his stoneware 'cameos'.

The Victorian versions of Tassies were the glass-encrusted cameos created by Apsley Pellatt from 1819 onward, used mainly for the decoration of glass. Pellatt used clear crystal which was inset with the figure or subject in a kind of white porcelain. He made paste casts from earlier and exceptionally fine intaglios, including many taken from the engravings of Pichler.

Nineteenth century fakes mostly consisted of doublets, made in the same way as Wedgwood cameos, with a cast relief cemented on to a background of coloured stone. There were other imitations of cameos throughout the century, many made in coloured and moulded glass or cast metal.

Eventually the fashion for cameos dwindled, when all avenues had been explored. In the 1870s, Neo-Renaissance jewels with enamelled mounts could be set with fine cameos, but by the 1880s, cameos were completely out of favour, replaced mostly by medallions or miniatures. Another possible reason for their decline in popularity was the disappearance from fashionable costumes of the shawl, an item of clothing which had often been pinned in place by a cameo.

Buying Cameos

Most of the cameos within reach of the average collector will be nineteenth century in date and there are many of these around, in varied forms. This survey of nineteenth century cameos has stressed the extremes of quality:

Fig. 12.13. Gold and blue enamel English bangle, made towards the end of the first quarter of the 19th century, with a 17th century double portrait cameo of the typical Neo-classical type. (Nicholas Harris)

there were some exceptionally fine cameos, like those of Saulini, which are true collectors' items; and at the other end of the scale, exceedingly poor quality cameos. Generally the mechanically-made cameos are the worst, and, if at all possible, should be avoided by a really discerning collector. From a more practical angle, cameos can look very decorative and very 'Victorian' when worn with modern clothes. Perhaps the best to choose for this purpose are the finer ladies' heads and less obvious mythological scenes, from a purely decorative point of view.

A collection of nineteenth century cameos will certainly benefit from some basic theme or direction to guide your choice; and it is more interesting to collect shell cameos engraved in the manner of a named sculptor, such as Canova or Thorvaldsen, or those depicting well-known contemporary figures. It is always best to look for something unusual in a shell cameo, and this will also help to distinguish between good and very average pieces. Cameos rather than intaglios have also been stressed in this chapter, because the immediate decorative aspect of the cameo appealed more than the 'hidden' talent of the incised intaglio to the Victorians. So far more cameos were made during that period.

Time, experience and that precious collector's eye and instinct will tell you how good or bad a cameo is, if it is hand-carved or mechanically-made. Otherwise, the best test is to run a thumb over the surface of the cameo. If the lines feel sharp, i.e. very definite and precise, it is usually a machine-made cameo. If the edges are more fluid and smooth to the touch, it is more likely to be hand-carved. Of course, no such test is infallible, and you should use your own judgment and intuition first. Mounts or settings can alter prices dramatically and, if a collector is only interested in cameos, it is wisest not to buy one set in an elaborate or expensive mount. As with all jewels, always buy the best quality you can afford.

13. Mosaics in Jewellery

Interest among the collectors of the crafts of the early nineteenth century Neo-classical period has long been centred on cameos and engraved stones. But there was another ancient art form which was skilfully revived at the same time: this was the art of mosaics transferred by its Italian nineteenth century exponents from frescoes and vast ceilings on to small boxes, objects and jewellery.

Mosaic decoration is formed when small pieces of stone, glass or other hard materials are fitted together to produce a picture or design. Many different substances can be used, but stone and glass are the most common and were both used in the earliest, ancient mosaics.

The tiny fragments of these substances in various shades and shapes are called 'tesserae'. The tesserae were held together by a cement made from a mixture of crushed stone, sand and water. Sometimes this cement was coloured, along with the 'grout' used to fill any gaps between fragments and to produce a smooth surface. The actual materials used in mosaics changed very little from ancient times through the ages, and techniques remained virtually unaltered until the late eighteenth century.

The history of mosaics runs on very similar lines to that of cameos; both have their roots in ancient civilisations. Both were studied and developed during the Renaissance. At that time, mosaics were still used to cover vast areas in churches and palaces. It was not until some time later that their purpose was extended to smaller decorative objects, this was done initially by Florentine craftsmen.

By the late sixteenth century, two important centres for the production of mosaics had been set up, one in Rome and the other in Florence. The mosaics produced at these two centres, from their inception to the end of the nineteenth century, were entirely different in style. This stems basically from the differing attitudes and functions of the two original establishments.

Early Florentine Mosaics

In Florence, the workshop called the Opificio delle Pietre Dure was set up around 1580, under the direction of Francesco I dei Medici, Grand Duke of

Tuscany (1541-87). Experiments in stone-working had already been carried out under the guidance of his father Cosimo I the Great (1519-74). Francesco concentrated even more on the arts, and brought together the Florentine crafts-men with a tradition of stone-working and the 'foreign' artists, such as the Milanese specialists in rock crystal and the Venetian masters of glass and porcelain. Franceso's architect Buontalenti followed and organised all these skills, added a German specialist. Finally in 1580 they appointed Giovanni Bianchi Bonavita from Milan as director of mosaic and inlay work in stone.

This gathering of craftsmen really marks the beginnings of the Opificio, although it was Francesco's brother, Ferdinand I (1549-1609), who actually gave the factory a more definite and official status in 1588. Very fine work was done here over the years. In the second half of the seventeenth century, outstanding achievements were largely due to the sculptor Giovanni Battista Foggini (1652-1725) and the gem and stone carver, Giuseppe Antonio Bar-tolommeo Torricelli of Fiesole (1659-1719). This period produced beautiful objects for the Grand Ducal palaces, including cabinets, tables and smaller objects inlaid with pietra-dura (hard stones such as jasper or agate).

When French troops entered Florence in 1799, Marie Louise de Bourbon became Queen. She was succeeded by another female Regent, Napoleon's sister, Elisa Bonaparte Bacciocchi who was made Grand Duchess of Tuscany in 1809. She was well known as a patron of the arts. Stone-working flourished under both these rulers. The Opificio continued into the nineteenth century, but economic crises forced it to change production and policy. However it still exists today, although its activities now mainly involve restoration.

The pietra-dura technique involved the use of semi-precious and precious stones and marbles. These included agates, chalcedony, cornelian, lapis-lazuli, onyx, malachite, mother-of-pearl, and many others. Thin slices of these stones were cut with a small saw or a copper wire and then were fitted closely together, usually into a bed of black marble, to form a pattern.

Favourite Florentine subjects were flowers, leaves, birds and fruit. The main feature of these Florentine mosaics is their purely decorative quality: abstract designs and stylised flowers with a strong sense of the natural beauty of the stones themselves. This characteristic separates Florentine work from that done in Rome.

Early Roman Mosaics

About the same time as the founding of the Opificio, the Vatican mosaic workshop was established in Rome in 1576, principally to provide decora-tions for the interior of St Peter, Rome. From the start, this workshop aimed to translate great Italian paintings and ancient frescoes into mosaics, and continued to work in this way, sometimes to replace fading paintings or reproduce them in miniature.

The Romans worked with glass tesserae, which were intrinsically worthless next to the Florentine pietra-dura. But the coloured glass fragments enabled mosaicists to obtain the subtle shadings required when copying paintings. It is possible that a plan for the painting was first engraved on to a copper or metal plate, and the mosaics filled in rather like painting-by-numbers, under a microscope. It was by a very gradual process that the use of mosaics was ex-

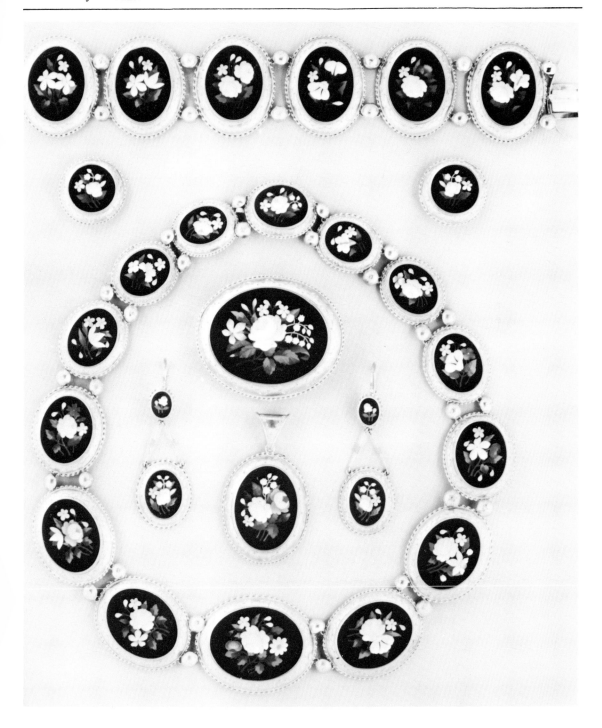

Fig. 13.1. An example of Florentine mosaic work at its finest: bracelet, studs, necklace, ear-rings, brooch and pendant in gold mounts with applied filigree decoration. the sensitivity to stones, colour, flower arrangement and proportions was never sacrificed, even on the smallest section of an ear-ring. (Landsberg & Son)

tended to less exclusive objects for a wider market and led eventually to a very popular Victorian jewellery fashion.

Visitors to Rome and Florence on the 'Grand Tour' in the late seventeenth and eighteenth centuries admired the fine mosaic work. Many English tourists brought home pietra-dura panels to decorate their furniture, or Roman mosaic plaques. The Florentine variety was far more expensive and, as European travel became cheaper and more easily available, the Roman mosaics became the more popular souvenirs.

The Influence of the Neo-classical Revival

A revival of interest in classical art, architecture and beauty gave an extra impetus to the fashion for mosaics. This Neo-classicism began in the latter part of the eighteenth century and the fashion continued until the 1830s. The new interest in Greek, Roman and Egyptian antiquities was stirred up by the archeological discoveries at Herculaneum and Pompeii during the years 1738 to 1756, as well as those in Greece and Egypt. Several volumes were published about these excavations, spreading the information and influencing current tastes.

Visitors flocked to see these very romantic ruins and the most suitable souvenirs were undoubtedly the Roman mosaic plaques depicting the buildings and best-known sights of Rome and, occasionally, Athens. Added to this, the scenes were made in an art form that was itself deeply imbued with the classical spirit.

From the middle of the eighteenth century, Roman production of mosaics thrived and this continued success was partly due to the introduction of a new

Fig. 13.2. Late 18th century Roman mosaic plaque of hunting scene full of movement, superb anatomical detail and clear, rich colours. The dogs' collars are picked out in vivid red, unusually bright for this kind of mosaic. As always, the setting is the countryside. (Landsberg & Son)

Fig. 13.3. Early 19th century Roman mosaic in the style of Antonio Aguatti, master of animal mosaics. His development of the micromosaic technique enabled him to show the texture of the animal's fur and skin, and bring naturalism and life to studies of dogs. (Landsberg & Son)

technique. Experiments at the Vatican workshop towards the end of the eighteenth century led to the development of the micromosaics, which widened the whole field of subjects to be interpreted.

By the new technique, the opaque glass substance was pulled into long strips, known as *smalti filati*. By stretching these canes of coloured glass, this process produced an enormous range of different shades of colour. This meant that, when each strip was cut into minute slices, each tessera could be coloured in one of some 20,000 tints. This enabled mosaicists to execute the most perfect, detailed copies of paintings, because they now had at their disposal as many colours as the artist had on his palette.

It is thought to be Giacomo Raffaelli who was responsible for the invention of micromosaics, and he showed examples of this work in 1775. The celebrated Antonio Aguatti also worked on the technique and improved it in the early nineteenth century.

It was this process that brought mosaics into extensive use on boxes, trinkets and jewellery. The pictures greatly appealed to emerging Regency tastes in England, as they moved away from the classic, restrained simplicity of the Adam period and towards more picturesque and colourful designs.

Identifying Neo-classical Mosaics

Early micromosaic plaques of the late eighteenth and early nineteenth centuries are characterised by rich but subtle colours, and subjects which best illustrated the versatility of the new technique. Looking now at these examples, we can see how smooth the surfaces are: the joins or grouting cannot be felt with a finger-tip, and are barely visible to the naked eye. The tesserae are minute, sometimes 1,400 particles would fill 1 sq. in. (6.5 sq. cm.) of these micromosaics.

Landscapes were very popular subjects with wide expanses of sky, sea and rolling hills. There was usually some water in the scene; rivers or waterfalls

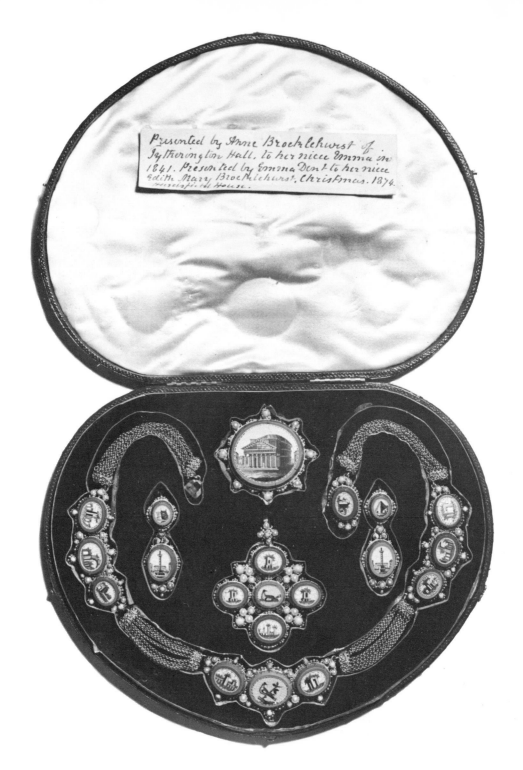

Fig. 13.4. Mosaic suite of necklace, ear-rings, brooch and pendant in its original box. The plaques showing typical views of buildings of Rome, and birds, are set in light blue glass frames and delicate gold mounts with pearls and turquoises in an earlier style. The original box, still intact, has a note about the jewel's history 'Presented by Anne Brocklehurst of Tytherington Hall, to her niece Emma in 1841. Presented by Emma Dent to her niece Edith Mary Brocklehurst, Christmas 1874. Hurdsfield House.' (Cameo Corner)

Plate 25. (Previous page) *The variety and colour of stick-pin motifs: the cockerel's head, flower and girl's head are all Art Nouveau; the iris is by Tiffany; the man in the moon is a very popular motif; and the coral leg with garter is a typical Victorian frivolity. (Brian and Lynn Holmes; Nicholas Harris; S. Rogers and M. Ventura)*

Plate 26. (Top left) *Sardonyx cameo of Napoleon, signed Dies, about 1810.*

Plate 27. (Top centre) *Renaissance cameo in a 19th century mount.*

Plate 28. (Top right) *Stone cameo of Apollo, by Girometti, early 19th century.*

Plate 29. (Left) *Stone cameo by Tommaso Saulini (the father of Luigi Saulini), about 1845.*

Plate 30. (Bottom left) *Classical stone carving by A. Vaudet in gold, pearl and diamond mount, about 1800.*

Plate 31. (Bottom right) *Classical head carved in malachite. (26-31, Hancocks & Co)*

Plate 32. (Top) *Different types of mosaic jewellery. Above: late 19th century gold and mosaic suite of brooch and ear-rings. Below: mid-19th century Italian plaque bracelet. (John Joseph)*

Plate 33. (Left) *An early 19th century example of the spaniel mosaic. Later, more commercial examples show them on cushions, rather than in this rural setting.*

Plate 34. (Above) *Gold brooch by Castellani, about 1860. He often used mosaics of Byzantine inspiration. (33-34, Hancocks & Co)*

were particularly favoured, as great skill was needed to capture the beauty and movement of these natural phenomena. These must have appealed to the English love of peaceful countryside, as did the hunting scenes, full of action and lithe animals, attacking or devouring their victims. Animals remained very prominent features of mosaics; dogs, birds and horses are the most common, and butterflies with exquisitely shaded wings.

Classic pastoral scenes were popular for a time, and in the second half of the nineteenth century especially, peasants or early Romans were shown grouped around their straw huts, calmly tending sheep or hens. These were all subjects taken from earlier paintings.

Sentiment occasionally crept into mosiac work. One example in a private collection shows a seascape with a ship in the background heading out to sea; there are craggy rocks in the foreground and two doves, one in flight and the other perched securely on the rock, each holding in its mouth one end of a white ribbon pulled into a lovers' knot. The inscription in French, traditionally the language of love, reads '*Le plus loin, le plus sure*'.

Other symbols of romance more commonly found are the altar of love, Cupid's bow and arrows, Cupid in his chariot and — most common of all — Venus's doves, shown billing and cooing over a basket of flowers.

One of the most frequently copied and well-known of ancient mosaics was the Capitoline doves, described by Pliny the Elder in his history of art. The doves are shown on the rim of a wide goblet or dish of water, one is drinking and the others are pluming their feathers. Raffaelli successfully copied the original at the beginning of the nineteenth century.

Ruins were depicted from the late eighteenth century onwards but it was not until about 1820 to 1830 that these scenes of ruins and landscapes became commercially popular for tourist souvenirs and jewellery. Favourite spots shown in these mosaics included the Temple of the Sibyl at Tivoli, the Greek Temple at Paestum, the Pantheon, the Colosseum, and the Trevi fountain. Sometimes they were just beautiful views of landscapes, interspersed with mosaics of birds or animals. Then they acted as a record of a memorable tour, like an early version of the photograph album.

In the 1820s it was customary to have a suite of gold jewellery made using several mosaic plaques, each of which showed a different place of interest. The glass mosaics were set in frames of coloured glass, blue, red or black, or occasionally aventurine quartz or lapis-lazuli. These were then mounted in gold in the current fashion. This was very often in the 'cannetille' style of gold filigree work (see Chapter 3, Nineteenth Century Gold-work) surrounding each plaque. Bracelets were made from wide bands of gold mesh, and the mosaic would form the clasp. With some pieces, it seems that the cannetille work remained in use with mosaics for some time after it had gone out of fashion for other jewels.

Another way of setting the plaques was to link them by three or more fine gold chains '*en esclavage*' as it was called. Each plaque might then be fitted into a gold mount with no glass frame.

One of the most famous and accomplished mosaicists, working in the early part of the nineteenth century in Rome was Antonio Aguatti, whose family before him had worked in the same medium. Aguatti specialised in the subtleties of the micromosaic, which he greatly improved in his own workshop. He introduced even more colours to the strips of glass, as well as different shapes of tesserae. His technique lent itself perfectly to his own speciality — the portrayal of animals, the textures of their furry coats, and their movements. His poodles and spaniels are superb.

Aguatti had been supervised by one of the greatest mosaicists, Giacomo Raffaelli, working in the late eighteenth and early nineteenth centuries. Aguatti, in his turn, was master to Michelangelo Barberi, who worked from about 1820 to about 1860. From this time, the spaniel remained a favourite subject for later mosaics.

Fig. 13.5. A close-up of the brooch from Fig. 13.4. (Cameo Corner)

Mid-nineteenth Century Mosaics

As demand grew and the new generation of tourists was less discriminating, jewellery incorporating mosaics of ancient ruins became rather stereotyped around the 1840s. This lowering of technical standards can usually be spotted by larger tesserae, bolder colours and less refined shading of sky and grass or water.

Excellent mosaics were still being produced in Rome, perhaps for a different market. Exquisite baskets of flowers, with carefully textured basket-weave, were set in black glass for brooches or bracelets, and plaques for boxes.

Following the style of earlier eighteenth century Italian artists, suites of mid-nineteenth century jewels were made with plaques each showing a different figure in peasant costume: a wandering musician, grape-pickers, an old philosopher. Very often these had a border of tesserae in white ringed with red. Religious paintings offered, of course, a whole different range of subjects, but probably these were more for home consumption in Italy. They included pictures of the Madonna and heads of the Apostles, all stunning copies of great early Italian paintings.

About the middle of the nineteenth century, mosaic crosses were made, set in the fine gold frames typical of Roman gold-work of the period. Castellani (1793-1865), and his sons who carried on the famous jewellery workshop in Rome, incorporated mosaics into many of their fine gold brooches. These

Fig. 13.6. Fine gold ear-rings set with Roman mosaics of sunflowers on a bright blue background. About 1870. (Peter Edwards)

mosaics were inspired more by Byzantine art, and are most often seen in blue or green. The brooches were small and usually round, in a plain gold mount, and had a Greek or Latin inscription inlaid into the mosaic in bold Roman capitals. (See Chapter 15, Signed Jewellery of the Mid-nineteenth Century.)

A slightly different kind of Roman mosaic can be found on some later nineteenth century jewels, with a distinct change in colour, style and technique from the earlier smooth pictorial plaques. Mounted in gold, or even gilt metal, these mosaics in bright shiny colours, are often dominated by an opaque white background. The tesserae appear to be rather large and coarse, and do not fit together so smoothly, producing an uneven, raised surface.

Wide bangles of the 1860s, with exquisite gold-work around the back, were covered at the front with complicated classical scenes or rather grotesque but intriguing Bacchic masks in brightly coloured mosaics. The large raised capital letters spelled out 'ROMA' on the gold section, showing that they were souvenirs of the city. At the time, they would cost about £30. Later, little bar-brooches and heart-shaped brooches were made in a similar way, with birds or flowers, in deep blue, red or rust, on a white or turquoise background.

This kind of mosaic was also frequently used on jewels inspired by the Egyptian craze, which started in the 1860s and reached a peak around the

Fig. 13.7. Suite of gold and mosaic jewellery in the Egyptian style, about 1870. The background of this very colourful suite is turquoise, effective in its rich gold setting. The headdress is white and gold with a dark blue and red decoration. The border key pattern is in red and white. (Cameo Corner)

1890s (see Chapter 14, Egyptian Revival Jewellery). The Suez Canal had drawn public attention to the Middle East and especially to Egypt, and it became the height of fashion to wear Egyptian-style jewels in rich colours, particularly turquoise and gold, with motifs of scarabs, sphinxes and hawks' heads. Pendants, brooches, ear-rings and necklaces were made in mosaic, with no apparent attempt at a smooth surface or the illusion of a picture. They just had the opaque glass particles arranged to form striking multicoloured Egyptian motifs.

Nineteenth Century Florentine Mosaics

The Florentine jewellery of the mid-nineteenth century has a very distinctive impressive character that is instantly discernible from Roman mosaics.

It was the same style of work for which Florence had been famous in the seventeenth century. A great deal of skill was required in choosing, cutting and fitting stones. While work of this kind was still being done in the Opificio, many other workshops in Florence were set up.

Brooches, bracelets, ear-rings and necklaces were made, often in very grand suites, and consisted of individual plaques, usually round or oval. Black Belgian marble was used to form a matt background, and into this a variety of hard 'semi-precious' stones was very carefully fitted, arranged in sprays of flowers and leaves.

Subjects were mostly flowers: white daisies with golden flower centres; delicate lilies of the valley; bright red tulips; or roses in a very pale pink marble which contrasted simply and beautifully with leaves of shaded olive green. Other suites were outstanding for their rich, multicoloured bouquets, incorporating every possible stone: malachite, lapis-lazuli, cornelian, turquoise, red, white, rust and pink marbles.

Occasionally, the grape and vine motif was interpreted in pietra-dura, the lustrous grapes made from discs of mother-of-pearl. The butterfly, favoured by seventeenth century mosaicists, made another colourful appearance. In all these subjects, each piece of stone, each petal, leaf or flower centre was immaculately cut, and the natural shading or veins of each stone helped to create the naturalism that characterised the finest of Florentine work.

The gold mounts were typical of the period, being heavy and impressive. They were often encrusted with filigree trails, rope-work or granulation, or applied with garlands of vine leaves.

Derby Marbles

Black marble, similar to that used in Florence, was quarried in Derbyshire, and had been used there for some time. Derby had been a centre for jewellery in the eighteenth century, and lapidaries had gathered in the area to work on local stones. In the nineteenth century, Derbyshire stone cutters and craftsmen turned to producing an English pietra-dura. This was encouraged by the Duke of Devonshire, who was glad to see use made of the marbles on his Derbyshire estates — and lent pieces from his own collection to be copied.

Fig. 13.8. Florentine mosaic cross pendant. (Eleanor Hutton)

Fig. 13.9. English version of
Florentine mosaics, made in
Derbyshire, with a purple
and yellow pansy in a silver
frame. (Cameo Corner)

It can be difficult to identify Derby marbles as they are often termed, but generally they were less refined. Their flower inlays of local fluorspar often lacked the naturalism and colouring of Florentine work. This small cottage industry made trinkets, boxes, brooches and crosses for visitors and tourists. Their wares were kept suitably simple and inexpensive so they were very limited in their use of exotic stones such as lapis-lazuli and turquoise. Single flowers were more common than exuberant bouquets.

Yet more imitations of mosaics were worn in the late 1860s and 1870s, made with backgrounds of jet. Similar arrangements of white, pale pink and greens were copied on small brooches and ear-rings.

Mosaic jewellery, and particularly Roman mosaic plaques, may seem a rather specialised area for collectors, requiring perhaps a little more time and study for true appreciation. Buyers are also often unsure of prices, as there is little intrinsic value to assess and justify the cost. However it is the workmanship which should be considered in the same way as a painting — that carries even less intrinsic worth in its paint and canvas.

If it were at all possible to carry out similar mosaic work today, the cost would be staggering and entirely impractical. For these reasons, and for their beauty and delicacy, mosaic jewels have become real collectors' pieces, wonderful examples of a skill and craftsmanship which cannot be repeated.

§14. Egyptian Revival Jewellery

Ever since the Pharaohs of ancient Egypt were buried with their treasures to protect and equip them for the after-life, their sumptuous tombs have been rifled and looted, and endless tales told of wondrous discoveries in eery surroundings. Of all the valuable treasures in these ancient tombs, the jewels were the most amazing, because of their beauty, their extravagance and the strange and complex symbolism which they presented. These dramatic jewels began to exert their fascination on the nineteenth century public, already feverish with a passion for newly-discovered ancient works of art. Astounding discoveries at Pompeii, Herculaneum, Nineveh and in Egypt had yielded enticing specimens of classical crafts, and had created an enormous clamour in society to own and wear such original jewels. The scarcity of originals, particularly in the case of Egyptian examples as so many had been stolen, naturally led to a demand for good reproductions, and this demand affected jewel design for the rest of the century.

The Etruscans had inspired magnificent gold- and metal-work; the Romans, who had perfected the art of gem-engraving, were imitated in the late eighteenth century and throughout the nineteenth century; from the Egyptian discoveries, it was the colourful jewellery which most fired the imagination and led to European interpretations of the Egyptian style. Although formalised and adapted to contemporary fashions, the jewels were loaded with typical symbols and imitations of decorative techniques, so that they finished by looking more Egyptian than most of the originals.

The lure of the exotic had permeated jewellery and artistic design once before, at the end of the eighteenth century. After Napoleon led his expedition to Egypt in 1798, obelisks, pyramids and papyrus columns appeared on furniture and on jewellery for a while; but this period was more absorbed with classical Greece and Rome. It was not until the mid-nineteenth century, in the light of recent excavations and publications during the 1860s, that an Egyptian style again began to make an impression on jewel design. This was first sparked off by the discovery, in 1859, of the jewellery of Queen Ah-Hotpe (of the early 18th dynasty). The coffin of the Queen, along with jewels and gold-work, was found by one of the agents of Auguste Mariette, the Frenchman who had been appointed as Conservator of Monuments by Said Pasha. Eventually, after a daring recovery of the jewellery stolen by a jealous rival, Mariette was able to present his treasure to Said, whose eyes were then opened to the importance of these discoveries. From then, appreciation of their magnificence spread through the Western world.

While historians were still contemplating these finds, and designers and jewellers were working on their implications, the Suez Canal was opened, in 1867, and Egypt was brought very much to the foreground of public attention. Thus the Egyptian revival was well and truly launched. Evidence of its popularity was shown in the contents of the Exhibitions of the 1870s, where there was a definite preference for jewels with Egyptian motifs. In 1867, Phillips showed an enamelled necklace with scarabs and in 1872 T. & J. Bragg of Birmingham exhibited their versions of Egyptian-style jewellery.

At this stage, Egyptian Revival jewels were made in gold, in the current archeological manner, and there was almost no attempt to simulate the elaborate ancient techniques and colourings. It was a matter of changing the identifying motifs on these Victorian jewels, from a ram's head or a lotus flower to a sphinx or a scarab, using granulation, filigree and rope-work. These gold Egyptian-style jewels most often appeared as large, heavy brooches in suites with long matching ear-rings. A popular type of brooch was circular with a raised scarab or sphinx's head in the centre, bordered by a simple design of leaves or lotus petals and some rope-work. Edwin Streeter, of Conduit Street,

Fig. 14.1. Enamelled gold and gem-set brooch, based on an Egyptian deity, with lotus flower motifs. Made by Carlo Giuliano, marked C.G. (Wartski)

Fig. 14.2. Gold suite, brooch and ear-rings typical of the 1870s style of Egyptian and general archaeological revival, incorporating classical motifs and scarabs. (Harris and Edwards)

London, offered this kind of die-stamped gold suite, which was partly machine-made, with a choice of classical motifs. (See also Chapter 15, Signed Jewellery of the Mid-nineteenth Century.)

A little later, during the 1880s and 1890s, the Roman mosaic was adapted to an Egyptian influence, again on brooches and suites, set in classic-style gold or gilt metal mounts. Very often a low carat gold was used. The idea of mosaics was seen as a way of capturing the colour and richness of original jewels. These mosaics had rough, uneven surfaces, usually with dense white backgrounds, while motifs were shown in strong colours of royal blue, turquoise and cornelian-red. Designs blended hieroglyphics, zigzag designs, sphinx heads, winged scarabs and other well-known symbols. (See also Chapter 13, Mosaics in Jewellery.)

Ancient Motifs and Materials

As colours and symbols become more varied and important in Egyptian revival jewellery towards the turn of the century, it is useful to know something about the jewels they imitated. A little knowledge of the key motifs and materials of the Egyptians helps a great deal in enjoying and collecting the revivalist jewels.

Much of the original jewellery and adornments was funerary, and therefore made specifically for the burial chamber; although tomb paintings show that very similar jewels were also worn during life, by both men and women. Beliefs about death, judgment, the after-life, and the gods and goddesses played a very important part in ancient Egypt, leading to elaborate burial rituals, and the luxurious and extravagant tombs of the Pharaohs. Preparations for a Pharaoh's burial jewels would begin almost as soon as he became king. Even the poor people were dressed in their finest garments and buried with their most treasured possessions, often a simple string of beads.

Jewels, in life and death, were primarily worn as amulets to protect the wearer from hostile physical powers or from the Evil Eye. Hostility could come from the climate, striking as flood, drought or disease, or in the form of dangerous animals such as crocodiles and scorpions; but the unseen powers of the Evil Eye were considered just as harmful. This need for protection from these evil forces led to the use of a series of symbols which occur throughout the jewels: they were copied and adapted throughout the various revivals. The outlines of the original symbols were developed from everyday objects or from aspects of Nature which were considered to have protective qualities. The study of these amulets is a wide and fascinating subject, but we will only cover a few of the main symbols which are easily recognised.

The scarab is one of the most common motifs and this represented a species of beetle worshipped by the Egyptians as a symbol of the sun-god. This was the kind of beetle which rolled its food in the shape of a ball of dung along the ground to its burrow. In this action, the Egyptians saw a parallel to the sun, pushed across the sky in a similar way. Another belief was that young beetles came from this ball, and this led to more involved associations with the idea of rebirth after death. Egyptian scarabs were carved images of this beetle and they were at first purely amuletic, although later their flat backs were engraved and used as seals, replacing cylindrical forms.

Scarabs were moulded from faîence or carved from glazed steatite or, occasionally, from stones such as amethyst, lapis-lazuli or cornelian. The intricacy of the carving varied from minutely detailed representations to a few impressionistic lines. The size of the scarab varied too, according to its purpose; the large winged scarabs, usually carved from green stone, were those placed over the hearts of the dead. These 'heart-scarabs' were inscribed with a text from the Book of the Dead, to ensure that the heart did not give evidence against its owner during the Last Judgment. With all these responsibilities, the scarab played an important part in Egyptian culture. It was widely copied through the revivals and occasionally original scarabs were set in Egyptian-style jewels, greatly increasing their value and attraction at the time.

Perhaps just as common as the scarab amongst ancient Egyptian amulets is the 'wedjet' eye, or the eye of the sky god Horus, who was believed to be ever-watchful for the presence of the Evil Eye and able to counteract its effects.

The Eye of Horus was one of many symbols that came into being with the development of hieroglyphic signs, which were used both in writing and as protective amulets themselves. The repertoire of symbols and their later imitations is based on standard motifs. The 'sa'-sign, which looked like a rolled-up papyrus shelter, came to mean protection. The 'ankh' in the shape of a 'T' with a loop (a sandal strap), the 'tyet' (a girdle tie) and the 'djed' (a column of trimmed papyrus stalks) signified life and well-being. The sacred cobra was the sign of power and also a protector of the king. The falcon was another symbol of the god Horus, and of the king; the vulture was the emblem of the goddess Nekhebet; and the lotus flower was the symbol of resurrection. A fresh lotus flower was often worn as a natural adornment; it was often translated into a more lasting aid to beauty as a jewel motif. Certain jewels also denoted rank. The fly, seen on necklaces with fringes of golden flies, was introduced to jewels through the Order of the Golden Fly; it was awarded principally for valour. These are some of the most common symbols that occur on revival jewellery, together with more obvious associations of the sphinx, pyramids and mummies.

Fig. 14.3. Gold hinged bangle, set with green stone scarab flanked by vultures, decorated in the archaeological style of gold-work. About 1870. (Anne Bloom)

Materials were chosen by the ancient Egyptians for their bright glowing colours and not for any value or rarity. Gold was the main component of jewels, as it was obtainable in Egypt, easy to work, and always remained bright and gleaming. Gold also had magical qualities, as it was the colour of the sun, and reputedly the flesh of the gods. Silver was used, but far less frequently as it was rarer than gold. The colouring of the jewels is based on the use of three main stones: cornelian, the colour of life blood; turquoise, representing vegetation; and lapis-lazuli, which had to be imported from Afghanistan and was the colour of the sky and sea. Green felspar sometimes took the place of turquoise and amethyst was quite often worked. Sophisticated glass, pottery or faîence extended the range of materials, and the Egyptians developed techniques for adding coloured inlays, especially in cloisonné work.

Favoured Forms

Collars were the most important items of adornment; they were often worn as marks of rank, and took different forms. They were usually composed of deep rows of beads, and sometimes covered the chest and shoulders. The pectoral was a particularly colourful and distinctive breast ornament, usually a large rectangular open-work plaque depicting a story or a symbolic scene. The fine craftmanship devoted to pectorals cleverly incorporated many of the favourite motifs, by means of elaborate inlays and chased gold-work. Diadems, circlets, wig ornaments, bracelets, armlets, anklets, simple pendants and, to a lesser extent, ear-rings were all part of the fashionable person's jewellery. So the

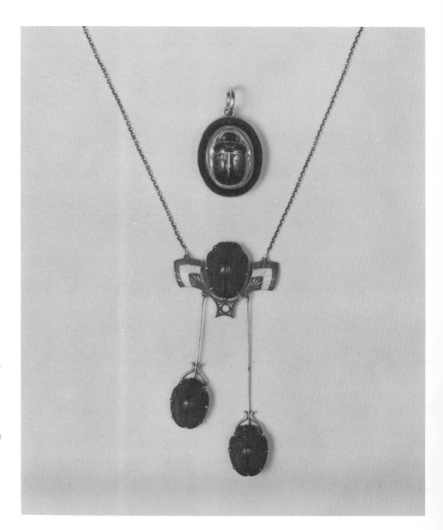

Fig. 14.4. Two early 20th century versions of Egyptian revival. Below: pendant following the form of negligée pendants fashionable in Edwardian jewels, set with real scarabs (the actual beetle preserved) with a green-blue sheen, yellow and green enamel mount. Above: gold locket, enamelled in deep green with scarab motif. (S. Rogers, M. Ventura)

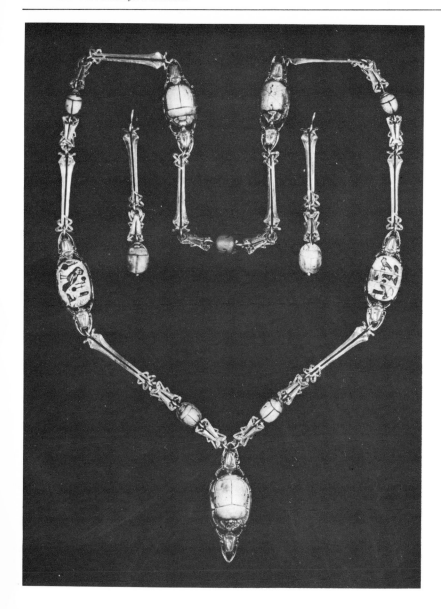

Fig. 14.5. Enamelled gold necklace set with large and small scarabs, stamped 'Lalique'. Later adapted to make a pair of matching earrings. (Sotheby's Belgravia)

rich, bright colours and magical symbols form the major characteristics which lent themselves admirably to dramatic copies in the nineteenth and twentieth centuries.

To return to the late nineteenth century, it was appropriate then that the Egyptian-style jewels which emerged in the 1860s and 1870s should be made entirely of gold and that later Roman mosaics should be influenced by the originals' brightly coloured appearance. The Egyptian fad lingered into the 1880s and 1890s when Sarah Bernhardt's portrayal of Cleopatra sent everyone wild for jewels of turquoise and oxidised silver. Her performance added to the drama of the jewels; slithering silver and turquoise-studded serpents coiled around the upper arm, and theatrical pendants like ancient pectorals enamelled with vultures and falcons became the rage. From 1891 to

1894, René Lalique made Bernhardt's stage jewellery for her parts as Iseyl and Gismonda. Many of his jewels around this time are composed of dramatic, vigorously writhing entwined cobras, with enamelled scales and gaping mouths. Some necklaces in the form of enamelled and jewelled plaques are also reminiscent of Egyptian pectorals; while a tiara made by Lalique in 1899 — again for the stage — is directly Egyptian-inspired. This large aluminium and glass tiara was made for Madame Bartet in her role of Bérénice. It is made of figures of Isis, joined by their wings and interspersed with lotus flowers and carved ivory petal-shaped plaques.

The Egyptian Revival of the 1920s

The Egyptian style with its glamour and colours obviously had a great appeal and the life of the fashion was extended into the early part of the twentieth century by intriguing explorations. These culminated in the glorious discovery of Tutankhamun's tomb in 1923 and the most complete and beautiful collection of ancient Egyptian jewels. The theatrical aspect had also helped to keep the fashion alive. Even those who did not follow archeological discoveries were introduced to Egyptian ornaments by the mesmerizing movie-screen. In 1917, the well-publicised silent film-star, Theda Bara, triumphed in *Cleopatra*. Publicity posters showed her in a stylised setting, costume and jewels. In the 1920s, Valentino played the devastating sheik, and in 1934 came Cecil B. de Mille's lavish production of *Cleopatra,* billed as a 'Love Affair that Shook the World'.

Tutankhamun's ornaments had also shaken the world of design; a new kind of Egyptian Revival jewellery was born at this time, mostly on the continent. The geometrical shapes of the rectangular pectorals and the stylised figures suited and further influenced the artistic ideas of the 1920s. The jewellers did not attempt to copy ancient Egyptian techniques or their complicated inlays of compounds, but translated the original colour scheme into rich enamels, adding modern hardstone scarabs where necessary. Silver-gilt replaced the original rich gold; but lapis, turquoise and cornelian were still used, although less extravagantly than in the originals. Authenticity took second place to appearance; the style, drama, and atmosphere which created the overall impression of each jewel, were the criteria of success.

The enamel work is of a surprisingly high standard, irrespective of the humble materials. Even on small brass brooches, a scarab shape may be attractively enamelled in a deep, metallic blue-green in imitation of the glaze on ancient faïence scarabs. Small slim rectangular pendants represented similar scenes to those on pectorals, and were enamelled in minute detail. A typical bracelet consisted of small oval plaques enamelled and linked by carved stone scarabs. Necklaces were delicate but elaborate with many appendages set with turquoises. They were draped with fine chains from which hung stylised lotus flowers, mummies, ankh or sa signs and perhaps a central falcon with spreading, colourful wings. In this case, the actual form of the jewel bears little or no resemblance to an original but the effect is obtained through accurate and evocative motifs. Brooches were made on similar lines, from silver gilt with bright turquoise, rust, royal blue and white enamels. They were shaped as lotus flowers or, very often, as the vulture or 'Ba' bird. This represented

Fig. 14.6. French powder compact on silk chain with a tassel; a typical Art Deco accessory incorporating the Egyptian influence in its brightly coloured enamel decoration. (Bellamy)

the 'ba' or soul of the deceased, with the head of a falcon and outstretched wings.

It is interesting to find that the skilful translucent *plique à jour* enamel was applied to these cheaper jewels as well. It can be found on a metal brooch or pendant, perhaps a copy of the ancient vulture collar, where the body is set with marcasite and the wings enamelled in green *plique à jour*. These are often German made. The silver gilt and enamelled pieces seem to be mostly continental (French or German) and are found stamped 800 or 900 indicating the quality of the silver, varying with the country of origin. Apart from these fashionable jewels, there was a demand for souvenirs, as more tourists made trips to Egypt and journeys down the Nile. These souvenir trinkets can be recognised as they depict scenes of famous sites, the pyramids, the sphinx, rather than copying ancient jewellery motifs.

Belt-buckles, ear-rings, and tiny charms were all adapted to the Egyptian taste. Rings were copies of scarab rings, with the stones set in a swivel mount and authentic gold wire wound around the shoulders. A favourite charm was the 'Moses basket', a tiny gilt or metal casket, its lid ususally roughly enamelled with an Egyptian scene, opening to reveal a moulded metal baby Moses inside. Little mummy charms could be made simply of silver, or enamelled in detail, again opening to show a mummy inside its case. One novelty in this style was the propelling pencil, which was hidden inside a gilt and enamelled mummy. This was pulled out for use with the pencil lead appearing from the top or bottom of the charm.

Collecting Egyptian Revival jewellery is a very specialised area: its dramatic appearance and bright colours, as well as the cheaper materials of the 1920s interpretations, may be an acquired taste. But once collectors succumb to their charm, they will find a rich source of style and originality to explore. Compared to the amount of Etruscan-style late nineteenth century jewellery, there are relatively few pieces of the 1860s and 1870s to be found with an Egyptian influence. Quite large numbers of twentieth century gilt and enamel pieces were made and there should be a good choice, ranging from small brooches and mummy charms to the more sought after and elaborate necklaces.

Plate 35. (Facing previous page) *Group of 1920s Egyptian Revival jewellery, showing ancient motifs adapted to current fashions. Plique à jour enamel is used for the brooches' wings, surprisingly as the technique was difficult and time-consuming. (Ankh brooch, Cosliff, Antiquarius; rest, Bellamy)*

Plate 36. (Previous page) *Gold and enamel 'bulla' set with cabochon emeralds by Civilotti. (Nicholas Harris)*

Plate 37. (Above) *French Gothic-style enamel bracelet, set with pearls, by Morel. (Nicholas Harris)*

Plate 38. (Left) *Late 19th century pendant cross and chain, enamelled and gem-set in the distinctive manner of C. & A. Giulano. (Hancocks & Co)*

Plate 39. (Previous page) *Turn-of-the-century animal novelty jewels: one lizard is set with demantoid garnets; the other is enamelled with diamonds inset, as is the fish. One butterfly is set with rubies, diamonds and a cabochon emerald; the other is more stylised and dates from the early 20th century. (Anne Bloom)*

Plate 40. *Open-work Renaissance-style pendant in enamelled gold, set with diamonds, cabochon rubies and pearls. Signed with the mark attributed to Robert Phillips and 'C.G.' for Carlo Giuliano. (Private collection)*

15. Signed Jewellery of the Mid-nineteenth Century

An awareness of the importance of jewels as documents of social history has grown considerably during recent years. Marks and signatures have been more fully researched and explored by jewellery historians, and inquisitive dealers and collectors in their efforts to learn about craftsmen, their techniques, inspirations and intentions. As respect for nineteenth century jewellers grew with this new knowledge, the signed jewel has assumed a greater value as a collector's piece. Its mark or signature labelled it definitely as the work of one of the best craftsmen of the period and provided clues to dates, origins of styles and influences.

One of the most distinctive features of the jewellery industry in the second half of the nineteenth century is the reappearance of the individual jeweller. This trend also marked an important change from the eighteenth century jewellery trade. It was around the 1830s and 1840s that fashions, customs, novels and artistic design were all tinged with the romance of the Renaissance and Middle Ages, and jewellers too were inspired by the complete individual Renaissance craftsmen, exemplified by Leonardo da Vinci or Cellini. It was partly this inspiration and revival that produced many fine jewellers who combined the talents of designer, academic, historian, craftsman and businessman, and influenced the course of nineteenth century jewel design. The two names and signatures dominating mid nineteenth century jewels are undoubtedly those of Fortunato Castellani and Carlo Giuliano, both of whom worked in very different and very distinctive styles.

F.P. Castellani

Castellani's achievements centred around the firm's brilliant copies of ancient Etruscan gold jewels. In this case again, the signature is important as it places the piece very firmly in the nineteenth century. It may seem impossible today to confuse a nineteenth century copy with the ancient original, but mistakes have been made, especially in the last century.

Fortunato Pio Castellani (1793-1865) had established himself as a jeweller and an antique dealer by about 1814-15, when he went to work in his father's workshop in Rome. At the start of his career he was involved in making very

Fig. 15.1. Fibula brooch made by Castellani, set with an ancient cameo of clasped hands. (Hancocks & Co)

traditional jewellery in French and English styles; and it was not until the 1820s that he became interested in classical jewellery, and especially in the Etruscan metal-work that was being excavated at the time. Castellani quickly recognised the passion that was growing in society for these ancient ornaments. He realised, too, that there would be a great demand for good modern copies of the originals. Apparently he was right in his assessment of Roman society, and its eagerness to follow the fashion leaders.

When the Princess of Canino appeared in public in the 1830s wearing genuine Etruscan jewels, she sent everyone nearly mad with jealousy, according to an article by Shirley Bury ('Alessandro Castellani and the Revival of Granulation', *The Burlington Magazine*, October 1975). The

Fig. 15.2. Bracelet made by Castellani in gold, set with carved stone scarabs. (Hancocks & Co)

Princess was the wife of Lucien Bonaparte, and the suite of jewels had been found on her estate near Rome. Castellani probably began by making fakes to satisfy this demand and from this he progressed to honest reproductions. These would also have been eagerly greeted by foreigners who were making the Grand Tour and visiting Rome; they helped to spread the style outside Italy as they returned home.

Around 1828, Fortunato Pio acquired a new friend and business colleague in Michelangelo Caetani, Duke of Sermoneta (1804-83) who was to remain a life-long friend and adviser to the Castellani family. In 1836, through Caetani's influence, Castellani and his son Alessandro were invited to give their opinions and advice on the wealth of gold Etruscan ornaments excavated at the Regulini Galassi tomb at Cervetri. This was a turning point in his career, because the metal-work which Castellani saw and examined there, gave him first-hand experience of the fascinating but mysterious Etruscan technique of granulation. The thousands of minute beads of gold scattered as delicately as a frost over smooth gold surfaces, along with their wonderful visual effect and sophisticated technique both captivated and puzzled him. From then on, he was determined to discover the secret of granulation and to reproduce this beautiful Etruscan decoration on his own jewels.

Meanwhile, he continued to make jewellery in a classical style using gold and filigree. He searched relentlessly through documents and archaeological evidence for the secret of the process. Eventually, in a tiny village in the Umbrian Marches, Castellani came across a group of peasants working with practically the same processes as those used in Classical times, and he immediately brought these peasants to work for him in Rome. It is not absolutely certain that it was from these peasant jewellers that Castellani learned his method of granulation, but it must have brought him a great deal closer to classical metal-working techniques and designs.

Fig. 15.3. Small bulla in gold and mosaic by Castellani. (Phillips)

Fortunato Pio's eldest son, Alessandro (1824-83), carried on the research into granulation, but the family's workshop was closed in 1848 due to political problems, and remained unproductive for 10 years. Alessandro emerged again around 1858, according to Mrs Bury, after imprisonment in the Castel St Angelo for his patriotic activities, but he was now an exile from Rome and decided to live and work in Naples. Fortunato Pio had retired in 1851, and Alessandro and his brother Augusto (1829-1914) carried on the business. The best jewels seem to have been made after the reopening, in the late 1860s and 1870s.

Alessandro still enthusiastically continued his research into granulation and antique jewellery. He travelled extensively, often to Paris, and to London where in 1861 he gave a lecture on 'The Revival of Classical Jewellery' to the Archaeological Institute. He went to Philadelphia in 1876, also to lecture. Alessandro was a very learned man, an academic as well as a shrewd businessman, but he also had the most thorough understanding of technique, design and every aspect of jewellery-making. While studying and writing treatises, he never neglected experiments at the workbench.

In spite of all his work, Castellani never solved the mystery of granulation; although he came very near to it. In the 1930s, Littledale discovered that the granules had been fixed by a technique which made use of the different melting points of fine gold and gold mixed with small amounts of copper.

Castellani's method had been to use an 'arsenite flux and an impalpably fine solder' to secure the grains and wires to the gold surface.

The Castellanis exhibited jewels at the 1862 International Exhibition in London. It seems that their granulation technique was still being perfected at this time, but it was not long before their finest Etruscan-style jewels attracted enormous attention at the Paris Exposition Universal of 1867 and at later European exhibitions. Their gold jewellery was widely copied in Britain, Europe and America, for the rest of the century. Simple bar-brooches and bangles with a version of Etruscan decoration were still appearing in jewellers' catalogues in the 1890s. In fact Etruscan styles were being made right up until the 1930s by Alfredo Castellani, but these were most probably of lower quality.

The family business, well-run by the two brothers, thrived during the 1860s and 1870s, even after their father's death in 1865. Castellani opened a branch in Paris in the Champs Elysées, about 1860, and from here they exerted a very strong influence on Parisian jewellers. They also set up a branch in London, in Soho, which was later carried on by Giuliano. Through this outlet they again influenced London jewellers. All the Castellani workshops in Rome, Naples, Paris and London were very large and efficient, and Castellani even employed ladies for finer goldsmithing techniques. The bulk of the stock sold at their various branches consisted of more standard pieces, in archaeological styles, all of very fine quality.

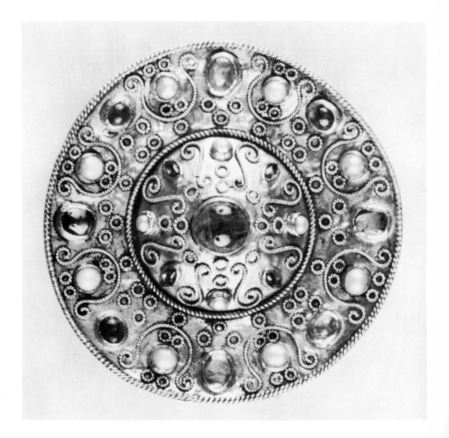

Fig. 15.4. Circular gold brooch made by Wièse, a pupil of Froment-Meurice, showing Castellani's influence on Parisian jewellers. It is set with cabochon emeralds, rubies and pearls, and bears the engraved signature of Wièse as well as an impressed mark. (Wartski)

Fig. 15.5. Gold, enamel and diamond necklace and ear-rings, made by Fontenay, a French jeweller working in the Etruscan style. The gold-work incorporates amphorae, lotus flower motifs, granulation and filigree work. About 1870. (Nicholas Harris)

Popular lines were gold brooches shaped as fibulae; lockets in the form of the ancient *bulla* — a round ornament worn by Etruscan and Roman youths as an amulet — necklaces with fringes of shells, amphorae or masks; and brooches set with deep blue and green mosaics in a Byzantine style with an inscription in bold Roman capitals. Some other brooches and bracelets were set with cameos or carved stone imitation scarabs, and occasionally with antique intaglios or scarabs, coins and medals.

In the 1860s, Castellani made gold mounts for a group of cameos by Saulini. (See also an article on Saulini's cameos by Malcolm Carr, *The Connoisseur,* June 1976.) These settings for other gems would also be signed. More spectacular pieces, some of which are probably never seen today in the trade, were most likely commissions, or experimental or sample pieces. There are some very fine examples in the Victoria & Albert Museum, London, including one gold necklace with a pendant head of Achelous, bearing the marks of both Castellani and Giuliano, and a pair of bracelets, one with the rare mark of Alessandro Castellani. The marks he used were two capital crossed Cs, back to back, either alone or in a diamond-shaped frame. The signature of Alessandro Castellani is rare; see Fig. 15.6. A jewel must bear the Castellani mark before it can be definitely attributed to the firm.

Fig. 15.6. Mark of Castellani, a monogram of two 'C's which Robert Phillips (see below) may have emulated.

C. Giuliano

Carlo Giuliano is the other major name and influence in later nineteenth century jewellery. He, too, lived and worked in London and was the head of a family of craftsmen who were certainly amongst the most creative and skilful jewellers of their age. The family drive and ambition helped turn this talent into commercial success.

When the exiled Alessandro Castellani reopened a workshop in Naples in 1858, Carlo Giuliano was one of the young Neapolitans employed there. He became one of their leading craftsmen, and it was possibly the expansion of the Castellani firm which brought Giuliano to London in the first place. It is also thought that the English jeweller, Robert Phillips, sponsored Giuliano when he first came to England. Perhaps it was Robert Phillips himself who spotted Giuliano's talents while visiting Naples and advised him to move to England. This advice was obviously remembered when Giuliano was offered the opportunity of moving to London to manage Castellani's new Soho workshop. Once installed in Soho, he followed up Phillips' offer, and soon after his arrival he severed connections with Castellani. In 1860, he took over the workshop at 13 Frith Street. It was only another three years before he was able to enter a mark at Goldsmiths Hall, as designer and manufacturer of his own pieces.

He still recognised the need for help and patronage from the right quarters, and his jewellery was sold through Harry Emmanuel, the successful English goldsmith and jeweller, at his shop in New Bond Street. It seems that Emmanuel also exhibited Giuliano's work at his stand at the Paris Exposition Universal of 1867, for an account of the Exhibition in the *Art Journal* illustrates a pendant, shown at Emmanuel's stand, which is identical to the Giuliano pendant now in the Victoria & Albert Museum. In a similar way, Giuliano also made jewellery for Hunt and Roskell.

Fig. 15.7. Gold fringe necklet made by Giuliano, with mask motifs, hung with lapis-lazuli beads from blue and white enamel links. (Wartski)

The result of these successful business relationships was that Giuliano was soon able to open and finance his own retail shop in 1874 at 115 Piccadilly. He obviously had a great flair for business and confidence in his future success, for his shop was set up in grand style, providing a suitable setting for the work of an 'Art Jeweller' as he now called himself. But apart from this glamorous image, it was the style and quality of his jewels that promoted his reputation and ensured success.

Giuliano, too, looked to the past for designs, and although he was undoubtedly influenced by Castellani's Classical revival gold-work, it was the Renaissance that captured his own imagination. The richly enamelled jewels of the sixteenth and seventeenth centuries provided inspiration and scope for his own abilities. The intentions and attitudes of medieval craftsmen seemed particularly in tune with his own. He was primarily concerned with beauty, creating jewels which were works of art, whose value lay in craftsmanship and design and not in the precious stones themselves. He cared little for the intrinsic values of the materials with which he worked. This attitude showed a complete break with jewellery fashions of the first half of the century.

One of the most important aspects of Giuliano's work is the originality and imagination he brought to his designs. Renaissance jewels were his

Fig. 15.8. Brooch enamelled with a cherub by Giuliano. (Phillips)

inspiration: they stimulated his own ideas and were only rarely models for exact replicas. Working on Renaissance principles of design, and improving their techniques, he translated a past style into his own highly individual (and wearable) jewels, concentrating on neck ornaments, pendants and necklaces. He used delicate, open gold scroll-work, enamels, and stones chosen for their colour, such as peridots, pink sapphires, brown zircons, baroque pearls and occasional sprinklings of rose diamonds. He was a complete master of the art of enamelling, using various techniques of ronde bosse, champlevé, and cloisonné, in exquisite colour combinations or the startling contrast of black and white, suppressing colour completely. His designs appeared to be traditional but he cleverly chose to express his own adventurous ideas within a refined, tasteful and acceptable framework. This attitude contrasted with that of Art Nouveau jewellers, such as Lalique, whose ideas had to be expressed by complete innovations, breaking entirely with the past, irrespective of wearability or customers' tastes.

Giuliano appears today less dramatic, perhaps, but he was highly creative as a jeweller. The fact that his thoughts were successfully interpreted in jewels also shows the measure of his technical skill and knowledge. Apart from these Renaissance-style pendants, Giuliano produced a varied repertoire of jewels and objects, absorbing several different influences. He used the Egyptian style of the late 1860s for example, and the Etruscan granulation developed by Castellani; both very effectively. Giuliano was surely amongst the many admirers of this technique and he practised it himself very skilfully. (See also Chapter 14, Egyptian Revival Jewellery.)

Giuliano also had a brother Federico, who had come to London hoping to join the successful jewellery firm, but this did not work out and Federico

Fig. 15.9. Enamelled and gem-set pendant by Giuliano. (Phillips)

Fig. 15.10. Butterfly brooch in gold and enamel, made by Giuliano. (Landsberg & Son)

opened his own shop in 1883 together with his son Ferdinando. The quality of their jewels did not match that of Carlo's work.

Giuliano's two sons Carlo and Arthur, continued to run the Piccadilly branch, with Novissimo, after 1895. The jewellery changed gradually, corresponding to new tastes, but continued to be traditional and feminine throughout the sensations and madness of Art Nouveau. Unfortunately, the business became less successful in the opening years of the twentieth century; standards of design and manufacture declined. In 1912 the firm moved to 48 Knightsbridge and finally closed in 1914 after the death of Arthur Giuliano.

Carlo Giuliano's mark was 'CG'; that of his sons, 'C & AG'; on a small oval plaque which was soldered to the piece, often on the loop of the pendant. For this reason Giuliano's signatures are easier to fake. His marks are sometimes added to the 'Holbeinesque' enamelled pendants of the 1870s, but a deception should be easily spotted by an eye familiar with the genuine articles. (For further information see 'The Giuliano Family' by Geoffrey Munn, *The Connoisseur*, November 1975.)

One necklace, mentioned above, and now in the Victoria & Albert Museum, bears the marks of both Castellani and Giuliano, suggesting that ties between the two jewellers were not completely broken. It seems possible that while Augusto Castellani was exiled from Rome on political grounds, between 1848 and 1858, he travelled to London and may have made an arrangement for Giuliano to act as an agent for Castellani's jewels in London.

Another link with the Castellanis and their technique, as suggested by Geoffrey Munn of Wartski, can be traced through Giuliano's designer, Pasquale Novissimo. Novissimo was also a native Neapolitan, and it is likely that he had worked for Castellani at the Naples workshop before he left Italy for England. He was Giuliano's chief designer, from the opening of the Piccadilly shop in 1874 almost until he died in 1914.

Novissimo painted watercolour designs from which the customer was able to choose. A highly skilled craftsman himself, he was also a designer of exceptional taste and talent, with a superb sense of colour, proportion and an awareness of the natural beauty of the materials he worked. From this information, it seems probable that Novissimo may have introduced Castellani's granulation technique to Giuliano's workshops. Lack of financial backing prevented Novissimo from setting up his own business, and he continued as chief designer for the sons Carlo and Arthur Giuliano after their father's death in 1895.

Other Important Designers

There were very many skilful jewellers who worked in a similar style to that of Castellani from the 1860s to the 1880s, some of whom also signed their work. Giacinto Melillo (1846-1915) was an employee of the Castellanis, and produced some exceptionally fine jewels in the classical manner, which were very closely linked to the work of his master. Melillo joined the Naples workshop as a very young apprentice. He was greatly influenced by excavations at Pompeii and Herculaneum. Later in his career, he sometimes directly interpreted bronze sculptures into jewels. For instance, an antique door or cupboard handle showing a head of Medusa was skilfully copied by Melillo as a silver brooch.

There is a bracelet, signed 'GM', by Melillo in a private collection. It is very similar to those made by Castellani, which are now in the Victoria and Albert Museum. Unfortunately Melillo's work is rarely signed, but with experience and study it can be recognised. Its excellent craftsmanship equals that of Castellani. An unsigned piece by Melillo may well fetch far less than a signed Castellani, even when it is of equal or superior quality.

Apart from jewellery, Melillo also made larger pieces of silver, again inspired by ancient originals, and the signature would then usually be in full — G. Melillo — on a tab of silver hard-soldered to the object. (For

Fig. 15.11. Gold brooch by Melillo, with amorino and cornucopia. (Private collection)

Fig. 15.12. Gold brooch in the Italian archaeological manner, with filigree and granulation. This bears the mark once believed to have been that of Doria; a diamond-shaped cartouche enclosing a fleur de lys and CD. This is now generally thought to be that of Robert Phillips, the retailer. (Wartski)

information on Melillo, see 'Giancinto Melillo — A Pupil of Castellani' by Geoffrey Munn, *The Connoisseur*, September 1977.)

Robert Phillips of Cockspur Street, London was one of the earliest firms to specialise in Italian archaeological style jewels of very fine quality. For some time, a mark in high relief, thought to read as the initials C.D. with a fleur de lys, was generally accredited to a jeweller called Carlo Doria. Almost nothing was known about him except that he worked for Robert Phillips, because jewels bearing this mark were invariably found in a Phillips' box. Now Geoffrey Munn has suggested that the monogram is in fact back to back P's in emulation of the mark of the Castellani atelier — the back to back C's. This theory is supported by the fact that the Prince of Wales' feathers appear on Phillips' notepaper, as part of a Royal Warrant. Robert Phillips also had a mark 'R.P.' and later 'R.P.' within a shield, which seems to have been in use before the adaptation of the Italianate signature in the early 1860s. In 1885, the control of the firm passed to Alfred Phillips whose mark was 'A.P.'; and by 1927 the business had closed.

Fig. 15.13. Mark previously thought to be that of Carlo Doria, now attributed to Robert Phillips.

The name Carlo Doria was found in a periodical by an enquiring dealer some time ago but now there are no traces of that periodical or of the origins of the name. However it seems probable that an Italian jeweller called Carlo Doria was working for Robert Phillips in the 1860s. The jewels themselves are comparable in quality to those of Castellani, with rich granulation and wire-work in gold, sometimes with the addition of light enamelling and semi-precious stones. See also *The Connoisseur*, September 1979, in an article by Geoffrey Munn.

John Brogden, an English jeweller working between 1842 and 1885, was again inspired by archaeological finds. Particularly impressed by discoveries at Nineveh, he tended more towards Assyrian styles. He was a goldsmith of great skill and was adept at both granulation and filigree work. Brogden produced some Etruscan-style jewels, which were shown at the Paris Exposition of 1878 and praised by Alessandro Castellani in a report on British jewellery shown there. He used the marks 'JB' or 'BROGDEN'; both in a rectangular shield.

Fig. 15.14. Gold bangle with lion's head motifs, made by Erik Kollin for Fabergé, about 1880. It is a replica of a jewel from the Scythian Treasure. (Wartski)

Erik Kollin had worked as a goldsmith for Fabergé since the 1860s and was the only Fabergé workmaster to be interested in the archaeological style. He was influenced and inspired by the Scythian treasures of the Hermitage in St Petersburg and made copies of ancient gold ornaments in the 1880s.

These and many other signatures and marks are important to collectors and historians, who have amassed the kind of information gathered here. Marks add interest and historical background to a piece of jewellery, providing guidelines to dates and styles, and leading often to details of the jeweller's life. At the same time, it is important not to overemphasise the signature or use it as a crutch for personal taste and judgment. Sometimes a signature can influence opinion and a decision to such an extent that the merits of the piece itself are ignored. This leads to high prices being paid for signed but often inferior pieces. The confident and experienced collector should be able to recognise fine craftsmanship and design without an identifying mark.

16. The Famous Jewel Houses

Names such as Giuliano and Castellani dominated the jewellery scene in the second half of the nineteenth century and were very much a part of the cult of the individual craftsman. This phenomenon found its place in an increasingly industrialised era that turned to the Renaissance and Middle Ages for direction, and found there the perfect model of the complete Renaissance artist-craftsman.

Following this wave of individual revivalist jewels, or more accurately coinciding with it, came the rise of the great firms of jewellers, who probably enjoyed their finest hours during the sumptuous Belle Epoque.

Throughout the nineteenth century and the early part of the twentieth, traditional diamond jewellery for formal tastes and occasions continued to be made alongside the more adventurous jewels with their changing and controversial designs. Even the most famous and artistic of jewellers had begun their careers making this kind of jewellery, learning basic techniques before putting their own ideas into practice. Both the jewels themselves and the firms that specialised in them were modelled on the grand French eighteenth century style, centred on the court and the fashionable aristocracy.

During the Second Empire, the French Crown Jewels were remounted to suit the Empress Eugénie. These diamond jewels formed an important part of the jewellery displays at the international exhibitions held in the mid century and set the tone for formal jewellery for the rest of the century. The popularity of this kind of jewellery contributed to the successful growth of many of the great firms of jewellers. Several of these were established in the middle of the nineteenth century and still exist today.

It must be stressed that, as with all signed pieces, these jewels should be judged on their own individual merits, and the marks should act purely as a guide or insight into their origins. The firms were often family concerns, handed down through the years, and their work spanned very long periods and vast changes. They all produced a large proportion of very standard and commercial pieces, as well as the more distinctive jewels. The second half of the nineteenth century also saw the establishment of American firms, who now became trendsetters in their own right, after years of following European, and particularly Parisian fashions.

Fig. 16.1. HM Queen Victoria-Eugénia of Spain wearing a Cartier diadem of pearls and diamonds set in gold, 1929. (Cartie

Cartier

The name of Cartier conjures up visions of exceptionally fine diamond and coloured stone jewellery, of the 1920s, in very strong and stylish designs. In fact, the firm began as early as 1847, founded by Louis François Cartier, who made jewellery in a small workshop in Paris, which he took over from his master, Picard. His father, Pierre Cartier, had specialised in making powder flasks and rifle butts, and with this skill he had introduced his son to the art of the goldsmith.

The talent of Louis François, his originality and good taste could not remain long undiscovered, and soon attracted the attention of the Princess Mathilde Bonaparte. Her influence led him to the fashionable circles surrounding her cousin Napoleon III and Empress Eugénie, and their patronage enabled him to open a small shop in the Boulevard des Italiens, in 1859. More prestigious names were added to the Cartier clientèle when the Paris Exposition Universal of 1867 drew rich and famous personalities from all over the world.

But the French Empire fell in 1870 and the Cartiers had to work hard again to maintain their success and reputation. Cartier's son Alfred came to work with his father in 1872; then in 1898 the three grandsons, Louis, Pierre and Jacques joined the business. It was at this time that they moved to 13 Rue de la Paix, amongst the most fashionable jewellers in Paris. Here, too, they were close to the salon of the couturier Worth, a great friend of the Cartiers.

Among Cartier's many influential customers was the Prince of Wales (later Edward VII) who commissioned 27 diadems for his Coronation in 1902. He managed to persuade the jewellers to open a branch in London. In 1902,

Fig. 16.2. 1920s diamond collar, made by Cartier, in the traditional elegant Edwardian style. (Landsberg & Son)

Cartier, London was established in New Burlington Street, at the same address as the Worths, and in 1904, it transferred to its present position at 175 New Bond Street. Several Royal Appointments followed, the first in 1903, by the House of Portugal, and then in 1904, the King and Queen of England.

The Cartiers were very interested to see that many wealthy American customers were visiting their Paris shop, and in 1907, Alfred sent his son Pierre to America to look into the situation with a view to opening another branch. Pierre was very favourably impressed by the growing affluence and quickly set up a New York Cartier on Fifth Avenue in 1908. The magnificent building was swapped by Cartier for a two-strand necklace of black pearls.

After Alfred's death, Louis remained in Paris, Jacques managed the London House, and Pierre the New York branch. Louis was the leading light behind the Cartier genius for innovations in jewel fashions. He revived the traditions of watchmaking, creating wristwatches that were elegant fashion accessories, and timepieces soon became a speciality of the House.

In London, Jacques soon decided to open a London workshop rather than import jewels from Paris and this proved to be another successful step in the firm's history, for Jacques continued to acquire an impressive list of clients, which included the Maharajas and Eastern Princes. Cartier has managed to grow with the times, to foresee and create jewel trends and changing markets and still maintain its high standard of production and its distinguished customers.

Fig. 16.3. Gold enamel and diamond compact, decorated with black enamel palmette and lotus bud motifs. The centre, front and back, has rose diamond monograms, with a cabochon sapphire and rose diamond thumbpiece. It hangs from a finger ring by enamelled chains, with enamel and rose diamond beads at intervals. About 1925, Cartier. (Sotheby's)

Fig. 16.4. Cartier as master of the Art Deco style: a diamond, emerald, black enamel and aquamarine brooch, mounted in platinum. (Landsberg & Son)

Boucheron

Another name that still stands for beauty and quality was first heard in Paris in 1858, when the firm of Boucheron was founded by Frédéric Boucheron (1830-1902).

Boucheron had begun to learn his craft by training under Jules Chaise (1807-70), the famous French engraver and chaser. This aspect of gold-smithing was considered extremely important in France at this time, and many famous later nineteenth century jewellers had been apprenticed at an early age to one of the leading engravers or *ciseleurs*. French jewellers insisted on the utmost perfection in every aspect of their work.

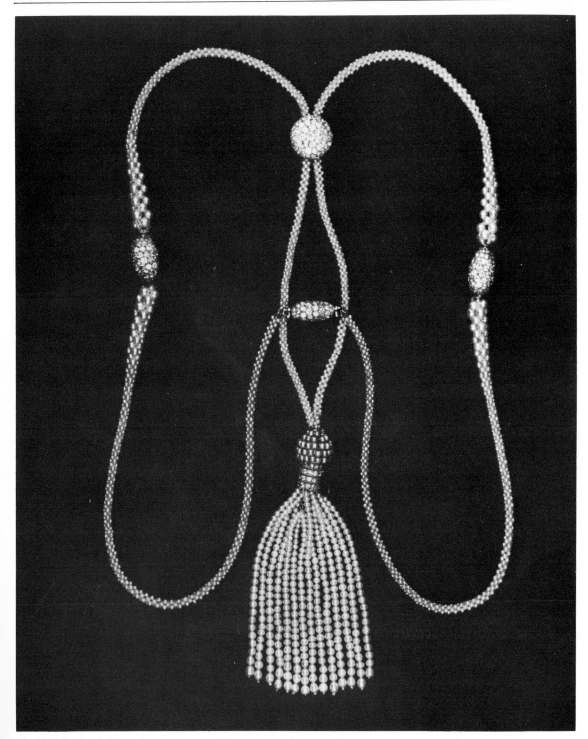

Fig. 16.5. Pearl and diamond sautoir made by Cartier. About 1920. (Phillips)

*Fig. 16.6. Pair of cufflinks
with invisible-set sapphires
and diamonds in platinum by
Boucheron of Paris.
(Landsberg & Son)*

By the 1860s, a promising start to his career had enabled Boucheron to move from the Rue Royale to fashionable premises in the Place Vendôme. Here he was able to show to best advantage his fine versions of grand, traditional diamond jewellery, which was so popular at the time. He was a regular exhibitor at the Paris Exhibitions and specialised in beautiful flower-sprays.

Boucheron employed several craftsmen and designers, all highly skilled in different areas and perhaps the best known is Jules Debût who designed a great deal of the jewellery shown by Boucheron at the 1878 Exposition. This combination of different specialist craftsmen ensured the firm's success in the latter part of the nineteenth century. They adapted well to the change in designs at the turn of the century, making some excellent Art Nouveau jewels, exhibited in 1900, and later Art Deco pieces. Boucheron London was founded in 1907 and moved to Bond Street in 1913.

Chaumet

Chaumet is also still very much in existence, in London and Paris. This company is known for exquisite suites of large and valuable stones, but again the firm has kept pace with changing fashions and successfully altered its outlook to suit the modern market.

The business was founded in Paris in about 1780 when Etienne Nitot opened a small jeweller's shop in the Rue St Honoré. An interesting stroke of good luck set Nitot on the road to fame. One day he went to help the victim of a carriage accident outside his shop. This casualty turned out to be the First Consul, Napoleon Bonaparte, who promised to repay Nitot's help and hospitality. This promise was obviously not forgotten, for in 1803, Nitot was commissioned to make the Consular sword, to be set with the famous Regent diamond from the ancient crown of France, and Napoleon granted an advance of 2,500,000 francs for the work.

The small jeweller's business had acquired a serious customer, and the following year, Nitot received an order for Napoleon's Coronation, when he was crowned Emperor by His Holiness Pope Pius VII. Nitot made the magnificent crown, known as the Crown of Charlemagne, which can be seen in the Louvre in Paris. He was also given the commission for the jewelled tiara which was to be a gift from the Emperor to the Pope.

After his death in 1809, Etienne Nitot was succeeded by his son François-Regnault Nitot, and it was his workshop that produced the parures ordered by Napoleon for the Empress Marie-Louise, including the particularly fine ruby and diamond set worn by the Empress at her wedding to Napoleon.

In 1811, the Emperor commissioned another sword and the Regent diamond and other stones removed from the first sword, together with stones from the coronation sword of Louis XVI, were set in it.

In 1815, when Napoleon fell from power, the Nitot business was taken over by Jean-Baptiste Fossin, a former employee, who took premises at 75 Rue de Richelieu. He later moved to number 62, the home of the business until 1905. Fossin was successful during the Restoration years and received an appointment from the King in 1830, when his son Jules joined the business.

Jules Fossin (1808-69) ran the firm until 1862, when Prosper Morel succeeded as head of the business. Prosper Morel was the son of the famous silversmith who had worked at one stage for the Fossin family. Morel's son-in-law was Joseph Chaumet (1854-1928) and he joined the firm in 1874, eventually taking over from Morel as director in 1889. His son Marcel succeeded him and his sons Jacques and Pierre manage the business today.

Fig. 16.7. Gold, enamel and diamond compact of envelope design, decorated with black enamel and edged with rose diamonds. About 1925, made by Van Cleef and Arpels, Paris. (Sotheby's)

The Paris branch is at 12 Place Vendôme; this house, completed in 1720, originally belonged to the Prince de Léon, and was later decorated with extremely fine paintings which still remain. Frederick Chopin lived in this house at one time, and died there in 1849. It also witnessed the famous romance of Napoleon III and Eugénie, whose family lived there.

Another interesting association of this firm is with one of the oldest and most celebrated French watchmakers Breguet, who still make watches for Chaumet.

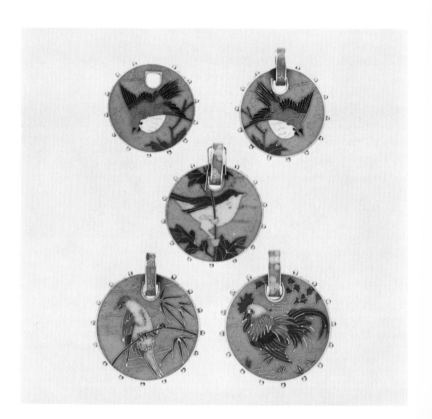

Fig. 16.8. Set of cloisonné enamel pendants by Falize. (Sotheby's)

Falize

A name that draws a second look today is that of Falize, both Alexis (1811-98) and his son Lucien (1838-97). They made an important contribution to the jewellery repertoire of the later nineteenth century, and their name has now come to be associated principally with the colourful cloisonné enamel jewellery that they perfected in the mid 1860s.

Alexis Falize had begun by working for the Maison Mellerio in the 1830s and worked his way through other Parisian jewellers, to establish his own business about 1850. It was about this time that Oriental influence on Western design began to make itself felt. In the late 1850s, Japan reopened trade with the West; so introducing its highly distinctive decoration and techniques to Victorian artists, designers and jewellers.

Alexis Falize studied Eastern enamelling and produced the most successful cloisonné enamel jewels, which he exhibited in 1867 at the Paris Exposition. In 1876, his son Lucien took over the business and enlarged and developed the firm, spreading the name by exhibiting at the 1878 Exposition. In 1880, he formed a business partnership with Bapst, which lasted until 1892.

Lucien's son André succeeded as head of the firm in 1897 on his father's death, and he continued to specialise in enamels set in very fine gold-work. Beads, necklaces, pendants and ear-rings were produced in cloisonné enamels, depicting the simple shapes of Oriental birds and flowers in clear, strong colours of flawless enamels. Necklaces often consisted of a collar from which hung several circular pendants, each showing a different motif, and enamelled in different colours both back and front. The firm's work is marked 'A.F' in a lozenge, but it is so distinctive and individual that it is immediately recognisable.

Fouquet

Falize had also been well known for jewels made in the current Neo-Renaissance taste of the 1870s and 1880s in France, and it was this style too that first attracted public attention to the famous French jeweller Alphonse Fouquet (1828-1911). Since the age of 11, Fouquet had worked with various

Fig. 16.9. Gold, enamel, pearl and plique à jour *enamel pendant designed by Georges Fouquet. (Sotheby's)*

jewellers in Paris, at one time in 1854, as a designer for Jules Chaise.

When he established his own firm, about 1860, at 176 Rue de Temple, he was still producing very conventional commercial jewels. During the 1870s, his Renaissance style of jewellery, with very elaborate gold-work and enamel, showed great promise and he began to make a name for himself. But it is really with the very intense French Art Nouveau style that the name Fouquet is linked, and this reputation was earned by the work of Alphonse Fouquet's eldest son, Georges (1862-1957).

Georges joined his father in 1891, and by 1895 he was in total control of the business. He completely changed the style, production and administration of the firm, and his main innovation was commissioning modern and *avant-garde* designers of the day, including Desrosiers, and Alphonse Mucha. Perhaps the most famous of Fouquet's jewels are those designed by Mucha for Sarah Bernhardt. In 1901, Mucha was also employed to decorate the outside and inside of Fouquet's shop at 6 Rue Royale.

Fouquet's jewels were highly original, dramatic and very modern, and he was a leading figure amongst French Art Nouveau jewellers. His mark was an inscribed signature 'G. Fouquet' or 'Gges Fouquet', but these jewels rarely come on to the market and have become true collector's items or museum pieces.

Many famous names contributed to the *fin de siècle* French jewel design; it was a period rich in imaginative and idealistic concepts of jewels as works of art. The strength of the Art Nouveau movement is reflected in the tortuous shapes taken by the free-flowing line, the startling organic motifs, and the development of brilliant techniques, especially in enamel-work.

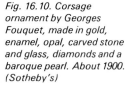

Fig. 16.10. Corsage ornament by Georges Fouquet, made in gold, enamel, opal, carved stone and glass, diamonds and a baroque pearl. About 1900. (Sotheby's)

Much inspiration had come from the East, but probably the greatest stimulation came from the reaction against the previous stale designs of conventional French jewellery. From this restive period of change, exciting influences and outrageous ideas, emerged a group of talented, creative French jewellers. Their work is described in the next chapter.

17. Signed Art Nouveau Jewellery

LALIQUE

René Jules Lalique (1860-1945) was perhaps the most talented jeweller of this period, and his name is inextricably linked with the Art Nouveau movement. The most creative and imaginative designer, and a highly skilled craftsman, he certainly exerted the greatest influence on turn-of-the-century jewel design.

So many Art Nouveau jewels were imitations of his work that it is useful to look at any signed Lalique pieces that come up for sale, to trace the original elements of design. It is important, too, to appreciate the full extent of Lalique's powerful originality, as it emerged at the close of a century that had been totally obsessed with history and past styles, the revival of classicism and the Renaissance, and of Gothic and Celtic jewels.

Lalique was born in a small town on the River Marne, the son of a merchant who died in 1876. The 16-year-old boy showed a strong love of drawing, and this talent persuaded his mother to send him as an apprentice to the jeweller Louis Aucoc. He studied at the Ecole des Arts Décoratifs, and spent some time in England, probably at art school, around 1880. When he returned to Paris, he designed and made pieces for various jewellers,

Fig. 17.1. Gold Art Nouveau ring by Aucoc, master to Lalique, bearing his poinçon (hallmark). Made about 1898-1900, as many such pieces were, in preparation for the 1900 Paris Exposition. (Editions Graphiques)

Fig. 17.2. Opal, enamel and gold brooch by René Lalique. About 1900. (Christie's)

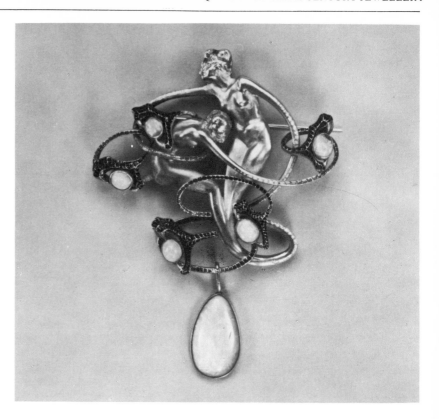

including Cartier, Boucheron and Aucoc. He continued this work in his small workshop that he bought from Jules Destape in 1884.

Soon he moved to larger premises, and it was after 1890, when he was installed at 20 Rue Thérèse, that he began to experiment and follow the direction of his own adventurous ideas. He now had a hard-earned but perfect technical jeweller's skill at his fingertips and he used this to express his own feelings about nature, art and creation.

In the early 1890s, he made the extraordinary stage jewellery for Sarah Bernhardt in her rôles as Iseyl and Gismonda. In 1894, he exhibited at the Salon du Champs de Mars, and shortly after this, in 1897, he was made a Chevalier de la Légion d'Honneur. These events, and his dedicated work on the development of a consciously new approach to jewellery, all led up to the enormous success of his most sensational jewels, prepared for and exhibited at the Paris Exposition of 1900.

A study of Lalique's jewels helps one to appreciate the work of his followers, and to recognise the certain basic characteristics that mark his work as clearly as any signature. His understanding of nature was very realistic and unsentimental; he saw beauty in the decay of flowers and plants, because this was for him an integral part of the natural process that led back to the earth and therefore to creation and rebirth. From watching dragonflies, insects and bats at close range, he was able to interpret them as the dazzling, dreamlike creatures he knew.

In Lalique's hands traditional materials seemed to be transformed, he was never intimidated by their value or by their intrinsic worthlessness. Instead, he measured value by the natural beauty of materials, their texture, colouring and their possibilities of creating a particular effect.

He introduced horn, for example, which was light and easy to work, and used it mainly for hair-ornaments, carved into clusters of leaves and flowers, sometimes stained to autumnal colours.

Lalique also experimented with new shapes. Apart from his sensuous and over-ripe plant forms, he began to use the female, nude figure as a jewel motif, mainly after 1895. Another favourite was the fantasy of a young girl's face, framed by windswept, flowing hair: again a beautiful symbol of decadence, or the same innocent face flanked by bat's wings. The violent movement of the windblown hair, or swirling robes, or symbolically struggling female limbs, is always balanced and calmed by pure, passive facial features.

He needed new techniques to express all these ideas, and one of the most effective that he explored was *plique à jour* enamelling. It involved a process that had been known to craftsmen of earlier centuries and was reintroduced to France in the second half of the nineteenth century. It was a translucent enamel, on the principles of cloisonné work, that lent itself to portraying the subtleties of nature's colouring.

From 1895 to 1912, Lalique was involved in making the series of spectacular jewels for Calouste Gulbenkian. They are now in Lisbon. As he finished this lengthy and demanding commission, Lalique felt slightly disillusioned with the many poor imitations his work had inspired, and he turned his attention more and more to glass production.

Many of his later jewels are simply engraved glass pendants. His mark is 'LALIQUE' in various forms, sometimes engraved, sometimes stamped, but original pieces are quite rare and valuable.

Fig. 17.3. Gold bangle in the archaeological style with two lion's heads, made by Tiffany. (Harris and Edwards)

The House of Vever

Second only to Lalique is the House of Vever, a family of French jewellers working in the Art Nouveau style. The name has also become well known among students of period jewellery, because Henri Vever wrote an important history of nineteenth century French jewellery.

It was his grandfather, Paul Vever, who founded the firm in the town of Metz in 1821. His son Ernest came to work with him in 1848. In 1871, when France lost Alsace-Lorraine to the Prussians, Ernest Vever fled to Paris, and managed to buy the jewellery business of Baugrand, who had died in 1870 during the Siege of Paris.

Ernest's two sons Paul (1851-1915) and Henri (1854-1942) eventually joined their father and produced the exquisite jewels in the new style that was emerging as they took over the business. Their jewels are even more scarce than those of Lalique. They were again very new and modern in contrast to previous styles — brilliantly conceived designs and magnificently produced.

Vever's work is not as wild or as uninhibited as Lalique's, although the themes are similar. The jewels have a slightly more controlled or geometric feel, that fits somewhere between the lingering formality of Fouquet and the untempered imagination of Lalique. Their mark is 'Vever, Paris'.

Fig. 17.4. Gold brooch by Vever in gold, set with diamonds, emeralds and amethysts. The maiden holding the flower is of carved pâte de verre, *against a background of* plique à jour *enamel. (Editions Graphiques)*

The Maison Vever employed several of the best-known craftsmen of the time, each a specialist in a different field, like Tourette who was an expert enamellist, and Gautrait, a celebrated engraver.

Eugène Grasset (1841-1917) was a Swiss painter and illustrator who designed several distinctive and unusual pieces for Vever. The best known of Vever's jewels is probably the 'Sylvia' pendant, made in Paris in 1900, now in the Musée des Arts Décoratifs in Paris. It uses the female shape with a daring addition of dreamlike enamelled wings, and a sinuous line of diamonds running through the design.

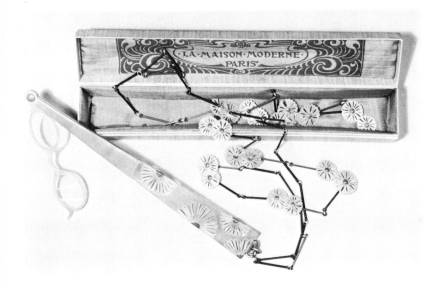

Fig. 17.5. Gaillard at his best, showing his imaginative use of unusual materials. A lorgnette made of horn, carved with openwork daisies, with orange enamel flowercentres, textured with dots. The very long chain made of blackened steel; the long links are joined by gold rings, with flowerheads at intervals. La Maison Moderne was a Paris avant-garde firm (a rival to Samuel Bing's L'Art Nouveau) directed by M. Meier-Graefe, which produced a large number of jewels by good designers. (Lewis M. Kaplan Associates)

L. Gaillard

The engraved signature of 'L. Gaillard' is the mark of Lucien Gaillard, a French jeweller who had inherited his working knowledge from his father and grandfather. He had been trained principally as a silversmith. By the time Lucien took over the business in 1892, he had been exposed to Japanese influences and was captivated by their metal-working techniques.

The Gaillard family had been jewellers for some generations, at one point specialising in gilt-copper jewels. When Ernest Gaillard, Lucien's father, took control, he abandoned this line to concentrate on new and original silver-work, making interesting brooches decorated with enamelled flowers. Around 1869 he extended his range with niello-silver jewels, buttons, bracelets, brooches (see Chapter 6, Collecting in Unusual Materials). Until then niello work had been carried out almost exclusively in Russia, Germany and Austria, but now it became a speciality of the house of Gaillard.

After the war in 1870, Gaillard began to make little gold trinkets, such as bottles, boxes, cane handles. It was at this stage too that the firm began to produce gold pieces in the Japanese style. These were beautifully encrusted with metals and various alloys. They were of very high quality and won a silver medal at the 1878 Exposition. Following the Gaillard display at the 1889 Exposition Ernest Gaillard was awarded the cross of the *Légion d'Honneur*, and he retired from business shortly afterwards in 1892.

Lucien went to work in his father's atelier in 1878 as an apprentice. Here he studied with various specialists, as he was anxious to become proficient in all branches of his trade. From this time onwards he loved his work passionately; he was an untiring researcher and diligent student of different techniques that he sought to perfect, with excellent results.

About 1878 Lucien Gaillard had been completely captivated by the arts of Japan and had made up his mind to discover the secrets of their work, their techniques of mixed metals and alloys patinating silver. In 1881, he began serious research. Gaillard was not completely satisfied with the objects made by French craftsmen who, of course, were little prepared for this kind of work, and had not had long to train and experiment. After 1900, he brought several Japanese craftsmen over from Tokyo — engravers, lacquerists and jewellers — and installed them in his workshop. Under his direction they made not only jewels, but also metal and lacquer-work, which until then had not been known in the West.

At the 1900 Paris Exposition, the Gaillard stand showed little jewellery, although there were many objects decorated in the Japanese style. After this, inspired and encouraged by the work of his friend Lalique, Gaillard turned his hand to more jewellery. He moved to larger, improved premises in the Rue de la Boëtie; and by 1902 he was exhibiting wonderful jewels, imaginative but elegant and refined, and still very much under the influence of the Japanese style. He specialised in horn jewels, pendants, combs and hair-ornaments, which were carved into simple organic shapes, and sometimes adorned with enamels or semi-precious stones. He also produced delicate jewels in enamel work, especially *plique à jour* enamel, again obviously influenced by Lalique.

Fig. 17.6. Hair-ornament in carved horn, by Lucien Gaillard. (Sotheby's Belgravia)

Fig. 17.7. Gold pendant by Count Epinay da Briort, who worked for Boucheron, set with diamonds. The girl is surrounded by mistletoe and the locket opens to reveal a mirror. Bears an engraved 'B'. (Editions Graphiques)

Other European Makers

After these leaders of the Art Nouveau jewellery scene, it is hard to select just one or two names, for there were many who worked skilfully in the same style.

Enthusiasts will perhaps come across the signature for example of Luis Masriera (1872-1958), a jeweller from Barcelona, Spain. Again his work had a firm basis of technical skills, learnt in the family business, and a thorough knowledge of enamelling taught by a famous craftsman in the Geneva School of Art.

The Paris Exposition had a devastating effect on Masriera, who then used his skills to create his own versions of the new style, achieving a winning combination of fine production and original design.

In Belgium, a major exponent of the style was the jeweller Philippe Wolfers (1858-1929). He had a background knowledge of sculpture, having been trained by Isidore de Rudder, when he joined his father's jewellery business at the age of 17. He constantly experimented, moving from work on silver to the ivory that came from the Congo at that time.

For about 10 years, bridging the two centuries, Wolfers designed jewels in his own workshop in Brussels, using precious stones, with gold and enamel. His work was delicate, but very definite in line and colour. By 1908, he had changed direction again, leaving jewel design for sculpture, so that his jewels, marked 'PW', are few and consequently rare.

Important and influential European makers are almost too numerous to mention. Perhaps less well known, but worth looking out for as examples of style and workmanship are the jewels of the Parisian firm of Mauboussin. For stunning 1920s jewels that epitomise the Art Deco movement, the firm of Lacloche is outstanding. This Parisian jeweller was established in 1897 by the four brothers Lacloche. They produced fine precious jewels identified later as much by their elegance and modern design as by their mark. (See Chapter 21, Edwardian and Art Deco Jewellery.)

C.L. Tiffany

The Centennial Exposition held in Philadelphia, U.S.A., was a turning-point for American jewellery design. Until then, the most fashionable jewels had always come from Europe: in particular from Paris, or from Italy when

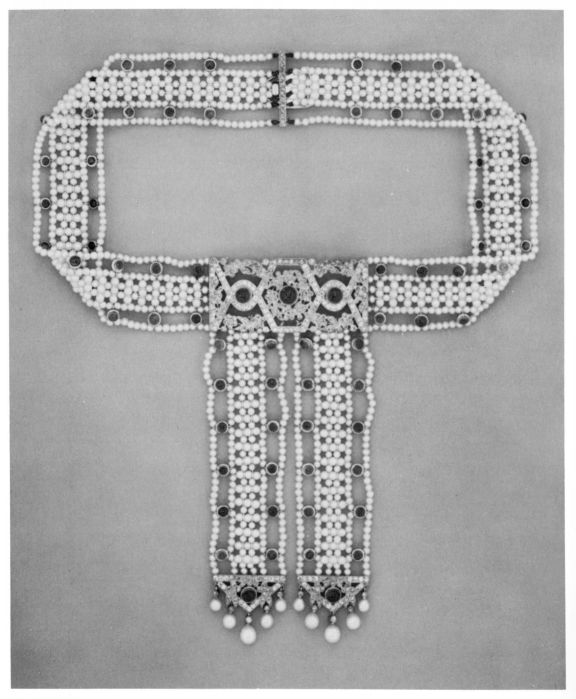

Fig. 17.8. Pearl and
cabochon emerald collar,
with the plaques set with
diamonds and cabochon
emeralds. Made by Tiffany
& Co., New York, 1915.
(Phillips)

Roman and Florentine mosaics were popular. American ability in jewel design had never been seriously considered. The 1876 Exposition saw the first signs of a successful attempt to establish an American style in its own right. Charles Lewis Tiffany (1812-1902) was among the first to encourage this move, after years of importing goods from Europe for his New York store.

In 1837, Tiffany had opened a shop in Broadway, New York City, together with an old friend, John B. Young. They sold stationery and a wide variety of pretty gifts. When this proved a success, they expanded the shop and also sold decorative objects from Europe, including some jewellery from Paris. The shop's name and popularity grew, and their stock of jewellery improved. The partners, joined in 1841 by Ellis, kept abreast of the best European fashions by making regular buying trips.

The next step was for the firm to start making their own jewellery, which they accomplished successfully, and by 1850, they had set up a branch in Paris.

The growth of this enterprising firm around the middle of the century was dynamic and they lost no opportunity of extending their horizons, taking advantage of bad times in Paris and the consequent drop in diamond prices to embark on a career of buying valuable stones and diamond jewellery. Tiffany & Company was a major buyer at the sale of French Crown Jewels in 1887.

In 1853, Tiffany had taken control of the whole business, and it became known as Tiffany & Co. Charles Lewis Tiffany was undoubtedly the force behind the huge success story of the company, and he had a talent for spotting potential fashions and exploiting them fully. He knew exactly what his

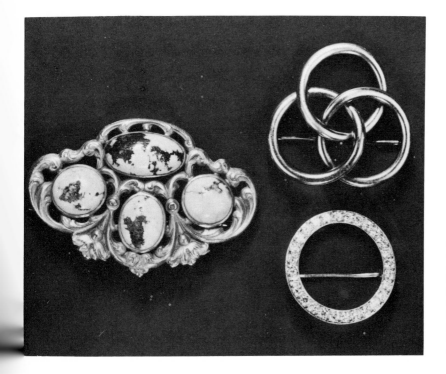

Fig. 17.9. Three brooches made by Tiffany & Co., New York, showing widely differing styles: fine gold work on a turn-of-the-century brooch set with turquoises; three linked rings of different coloured golds; and a circular diamond brooch. (Nicholas Harris)

customers wanted and determined to be the first to bring them the latest and best in jewel design.

For instance, Tiffany was very quick to sense the growing passion for Japanese styles, and his craftsmen interpreted techniques of mixed metals and delicate inlays to appeal to his clientèle. The silversmith Edward C. Moore who worked with Tiffany was instrumental in establishing this style, as he had long been an avid collector of the arts and crafts of Japan.

In 1868, Tiffany opened a London branch. On his death in 1902, Charles's son Louis Tiffany took over the firm, and he was a leading figure in encouraging the growth of a distinctive American style.

Louis Comfort Tiffany (1848-1933) was extremely talented and versatile, and lent his hand to interior design, glassmaking, jewel design, painting, and practically every aspect of the decorative arts. He was largely responsible for bringing Art Nouveau to the United States, and he himself made an important contribution to the movement, with his formula for 'Favrile' glass.

After the 1876 Philadelphia Exposition, with fresh interest in American artistic talent aroused, he established a company for interior decorating. In the 1880s, he became involved and very interested in the Art Nouveau, meeting Samuel Bing, who first displayed the new style in his shop in Paris. This influence led to the famous Tiffany glassware, and then metal-work and jewels in Art Nouveau designs followed, with Tiffany Studios producing their own distinctive versions.

The firm's mark is 'Tiffany & Co', 'Louis C. Tiffany', or 'L.C.T.' The firm remained successful through the changing styles of the 1920s and 1930s and continues to thrive today as one of the famous institutions of Fifth Avenue.

Fig. 17.10. Gold and blue enamel brooch by René Lalique, about 1900, with his usual disturbing mixture of motifs: the bats' wings surprisingly frame a young girl's head. (Sotheby's Belgravia)

Other American Makers

Tiffany is the best known name of nineteenth and twentieth century American jewellers, but other American firms were appearing at the same time, making fine quality jewellery and gradually developing their own styles. The mark 'J.E.C. & Co.' is that of J.E. Caldwell & Co., jewellers, silversmiths and antiquarians of Philadelphia since 1839. This firm is still in existence.

The late nineteenth century Craft Revival was very strong in America as

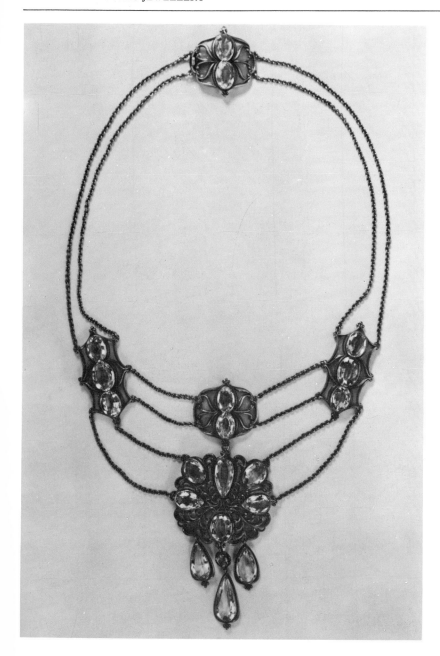

Fig. 17.11. Necklace made by Marcus, using aquamarines and blue plique á jour enamel. (Nicholas Harris)

well as in Britain. At that time, several American jewellers managed to break away, to some extent, from previous European influences and to use their own resources. The Gorham Corporation was one of these. This company had begun in the early nineteenth century in Providence, Rhode Island, and was built up to a prosperous business; especially in the late nineteenth century when their mass-production methods were the most suitable for catering to the new popular demand for Art Nouveau jewels.

This company was associated with another well known firm, Black, Starr &

Frost Ltd, of New York. Their early history is traced to the partnership of Marquand & Paulding, which began in Savannah, Georgia around 1801. The firm grew and changed directors through the nineteenth century, and was first known as Black, Starr & Frost in 1876. In 1929, it merged with the Gorham Corporation.

Marcus & Company produced stunning jewels that were distinctly American versions of the new Craft Revival and Art Nouveau styles. They made good use of enamels in strong colours, even on *plique à jour* work, which had been previously reserved for pale, subtle shading. They often combined deeply coloured enamels with diamonds and rubies, set in gold. Their workmanship is inferior to the French, but the finished product is very stylish and individual.

Other American makers include Charlton; Theodore Dreicer, a name

Fig. 17.12. Brooch by Lalique, again combining enamel and glass with gold and diamonds, and the motif of full flowers past their first freshness, their petals about to fall. (Sotheby's)

associated with good workmanship and the use of excellent stones in his jewels; and Raymond C. Yard, who had previously worked at Marcus & Co. and later became jeweller to the Rockefellers.

Some items in private collections give interesting insights into the American jewel market in the early twentieth century. Black, Starr & Frost must have catered for some very fashion-conscious customers: they sold very attractive handbags with strong Egyptian Revival jewelled designs on the frames. The bags were, in fact, made in France, and bear French gold marks, but were sold in the United States by Black, Starr & Frost. The firm's initials are very clearly printed on a silk purse attached to the inside of the bag.

Buying trips to Europe, particularly to Paris, were obviously still essential for top American jewellers, who bought either a design or the finished product. In these cases, the marks are extremely useful for identification, and for tracing the development of the American styles, and the various European influences. They also help in attributing other jewels to American origins.

There are some clear characteristics of American jewels in the early twentieth century. Platinum scroll-work settings of about 1910 are very typical. They show that Americans liked a great deal of engraving. They preferred the surfaces of metal to be filled with busy patterns, and the appearance or façade of the jewel was all-important. This attitude is especially noticeable in Art Nouveau jewels, where designs were very stylised and very good copies of original French conceptions. However they do look rather mechanised. American mass-production methods were more highly developed and refined, and innumerable Art Nouveau gold and silver jewels were turned out at low cost, using casting and stamping methods.

The firm of Unger Brothers of Newark, New Jersey, were specialists in this kind of commercial silver jewels, especially buckles, pendants and brooches. The most common motifs were flowers and leaves and the female head with flowing hair. They were in business from 1881 to 1910. Their silver was marked with the 'UB' monogram. Similar work was done by Kerr & Co.

P.C. Fabergé

Finally, no consideration of famous jewellers of this period would be complete without a mention of Fabergé. This is definitely one name that always raises the market value of a piece.

Peter Carl Fabergé (1846-1920) has become a legend amongst jewellers and his story and accomplishments are best studied through the book entitled *The Art of Carl Fabergé* written by the world expert on Fabergé, Kenneth Snowman, chairman of Wartski.

Through an enormous range of exquisite trinkets, miniature hardstone carvings, flower studies in jewels and stones, Fabergé showed amazing energy, versatility and imagination. He could change from the freedom of flowing Art Nouveau lines to the restrained elegance of the Edwardian style or a flourishing eighteenth century rococo, showing perfect mastery of decorative motifs, immaculate technical skills, and a perfectionist's attention to the smallest details, colours and proportions.

The most remarkable items, and those that mark the height of Fabergé's achievements are the jewelled 'objects of fantasy'. Very often the jewellery is not as striking or original in design, although always of superb workmanship. It was mostly made in traditional styles, in the eighteenth century French manner. Tiny miniature versions of the famous jewelled Easter eggs were made as jewels to be worn on a long chain around the neck.

Some of the most outstanding features of his work were the varied enamelling techniques, used in a spectrum of subtle or vibrant colours, particularly remarkable on large areas of guilloché enamel; the delicate three-coloured gold decoration, the use of the rose-cut for diamonds, and his awareness of the natural beauty of semi-precious stones, expressed in clever combinations with more valuable materials.

Fabergé was 24 when he took control of the family jewellery business, a successful firm that produced fashionable, traditional jewellery. The young Fabergé steered the business into a different direction, putting new emphasis on decorative objects and on individual, excellent design, rather than on clusters of precious stones.

His ingenuity was rewarded when, in 1884, the first Imperial Easter Egg

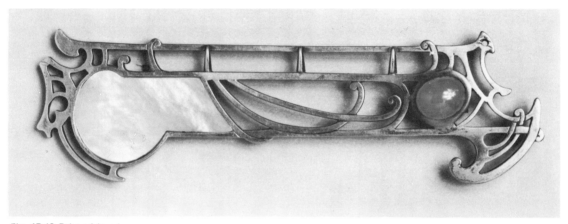

Fig. 17.13 Fabergé jewels are not as plentiful or as spectacular as his objects. This is a stylish Art Nouveau buckle, made of bowenite, mother-of-pearl and silver-gilt. (Wartski)

was presented to the Empress Marie Feodorovna. It was so well received that it led to a series of eggs which were given by the Czar Alexander III, and later his son Nicholas II as Easter gifts to their wives every year. Shortly after this Fabergé received the Royal Warrant from the Czar.

The House of Fabergé thrived, moving to ever larger premises and workshops, and the fame of the goldsmith spread to the West. The exquisite objects of such luxury and fantasy caused a great stir at the Paris Exposition of 1900, and Carl Fabergé was decorated with the *Légion d'Honneur*.

King Edward VII and Queen Alexandra (the sister of the Dowager Empress Marie Feodorovna) were amongst his most enthusiastic patrons, and they commissioned Fabergé to make hardstone carvings of the animals at Sandringham. In 1903, a branch was opened in London, moving in 1906 to Dover Street and then in 1911 to New Bond Street. After the Russian Revolution in 1917, the Bolsheviks finally closed the workshops in 1918. Fabergé managed to escape and died in Switzerland in 1920.

Carl Fabergé presided over the business and was the main source of ideas and inspiration, but the actual production was carried out in the different workshops under the supervision of workmasters. He employed specialist craftsmen, skilled at such aspects as enamel-work or stone-carving. Fabergé's work has its critics; but each piece that came from the celebrated workshops was of superb quality, impeccably finished, down to the last details of fastenings or hinges.

The work must also be seen in its setting of a restless political climate, that encouraged a leisured society to throw itself into a last fling of feverish pleasure-seeking. Fabergé gave his customers the ultimate in luxury in his objects of fantasy, with their undertones of a similarly indulgent pre-revolutionary eighteenth century France. It was in this unique atmosphere that the results of a great pride in production coupled with rich imagination won Fabergé the reputation of the last of the great goldsmiths.

Fig. 17.14. Gold and enamel pendant in its original fitted box, by Lalique.
  He uses his favourite theme of decayed autumn leaves, as part of a set based on the Four Seasons. (Sotheby's)

18. Pendants at the Turn of the Century

Embarking on a collection of antique jewellery is perhaps the hardest part for the beginner. The varied assortment offered by an antique jeweller can look like a colourful but confusing parade through the centuries, and many pieces at first seem grotesque and vulgar or overwhelmingly sentimental or morbid. But eyes unaccustomed to these sights are often first attracted to the delicate, gold and gem-set pendants of the late nineteenth and early twentieth centuries.

It was in the 1890s when these necklaces appeared in great numbers characterised by their soft outlines and a combination most often of pale stones and pearls. The last decade of the nineteenth century was a period of unrest, great change and experiment, and while those who had placed themselves at the centre of these changes were struggling with new concepts, the rest of society eventually felt the waves of their progressive ideas on fashions, architecture, literature and on jewellery.

This undercurrent of social unrest had begun as an inevitable reaction to the unpleasant side-effects of the Industrial Revolution. Along with the progress and prosperity brought by the machine had come a dehumanisation of the masses; and the increased wealth of the new middle classes had been accompanied by a lowering of standards in art and craftsmanship. As far as contemporary taste was concerned, a craze for borrowing fashions from the past had reached its peak by the 1860s. Homes were crammed with furniture, silver, ceramics and glass, all in a mixture of styles imitating the Gothic, Renaissance, Classical and others.

The vogue had spread to jewellery too, where the effects of Neo-classicism kept cameos in favour for most of the century. Gothic styles were closely imitated around the 1850s, before the Renaissance took over as a guiding influence on the rest of nineteenth century jewellery.

It was Carlo Giuliano (see Chapter 15, Signed Jewellery of the Mid-nineteenth Century), an Italian working in London, who perfected this Renaissance style. He very occasionally produced exact copies, but mostly incorporating a strong sixteenth century flavour into his own distinctive work. Another Italian, Castellani, concentrated on ancient Etruscan, Greek and Roman jewels, especially the magnificent Etruscan technique of

Fig. 18.1. Gold, diamonds and plique à jour enamel pendant and necklace in the manner of Gautrait, a French jewellery designer. About 1900. (Wartski)

granulation, which he managed to imitate with more success than anyone else, but without reaching the core of the secret. He closely copied their designs as well as techniques — with superb results. Many other jewellers of the time followed his lead.

Celtic-style jewels, too, had enjoyed an enormous popularity, with endless copies of the Irish Tara brooch and every kind of Scottish pebble being worn in the 1860s.

It was true also that mechanisation had adversely affected jewellery production. At the centre in Birmingham, which had been growing throughout the century, the quality of workmanship was steadily declining. Designs were poor and lacked originality and enthusiasm. Even the sentiments expressed in the jewels had become cheap and mechanical.

It was against this background of low-quality mass-production and stale tastes that the instigators of the Arts and Crafts Movement played out their

Fig. 18.2. Right to left: The wisteria with its flowers made of baroque Mississippi pearls was a favourite design with turn-of-the-century jewellers: Vever and Fouquet both made beautiful versions. This is a French pendant, gold with pinkish pearls, signed Arnauld, about 1900.

Classic design: the opal, diamond and sapphire cluster with two drops of unequal lengths, one a sapphire, one an opal.

Pendant of opals, green garnets (both favourite turn-of-the-century stones), diamonds and rubies.

Small gold pendant with shaded enamel leaf design, set with a ruby and pearls.

A stork, decorated in the kind of opalescent shaded enamelling, which was popular in America at the turn of the century. The outspread wings of the bird form an Art Nouveau outline. (Anne Bloom)

disgust at society with open determination to stand by their ideals. Apart from having ideas on social reform and a new moral code, they wanted to see art everywhere — not just enclosed within the frame of an oil painting — and given back to the people and their everyday lives. With a somewhat glamorised Middle Ages in mind as a model period, they encouraged the artist in every man, longing for free expression with nature as inspiration for designs. They undid the previous rigid rules of fashion, disregarded long and rigorous training for craftsmen and, above all, despising the regurgitation of past fashions, they sought a freshness in artistic ideas and the birth of 'new' designs. (See Chapter 19, Arts and Crafts Jewellery.)

The movement gathered many gifted supporters, one of whom was C.R. Ashbee (1863-1942), founder of the Guild of Handicrafts, who made valuable contributions to jewellery designs. But on the whole, the mainstream of conservative jewellery remained untouched by the movement, and those idealistic craftsmen who applied themselves to jewellery-making encountered many technical obstacles. They worked mostly in silver and with 'semi-precious' uncut stones and enamel decoration. At the close of the century, the Arts and Crafts style melted into Art Nouveau, which had a far-reaching if short-lived effect on the arts.

By the 1890s, a diluted version of the sinuous naturalistic motif had reached popular jewellery and seems to have found its way on to necklets more than any other item of jewellery. Perhaps this was because these appeared to best advantage in the deep square or V shaped décolletages of the period. These charming necklaces were, then, some of the eventual interpretations of a style which was evolved originally by the Arts and Crafts Movement and further developed in Art Nouveau. Ironically perhaps, and defeating the original purpose of the stylistic changes, the most successful of these designs were carried out on mass-produced jewels.

Necklets and pendants of the 1890s consisted of a light and feminine arrangement of stones and pearls, in a fine gold setting, sometimes resembling an Art Nouveau spider's web. The pendant would lie just on the collar-bone and hung from a delicate chain, also in a current design.

For some time, there had been a passion for pearls in jewels, used in different ways throughout the decades of the century, sometimes as a symbol of tears in mourning jewellery, or combined with turquoises in flower-like clusters. Often during the latter part of the nineteenth century, pearls were considered the only suitable adornment for young ladies. In the 1890s, half-pearls begin to appear on cheaper jewellery, used in the same way as the diamonds on high-class pieces.

In one type of necklet, pearls appear alone, set in gold with small clusters of flowers and the familiar three-drop foliage, all arranged in designs that heralded the huge and imminent impact of the Art Nouveau style. Most often, these will be found fixed to a chain to form a complete necklace. The

Fig. 18.3. Four typical delicate turn-of-the-century pendants set with pearls and a range of coloured stones popular at the time, amethysts and peridots in particular. Some have Art Nouveau outlines; others display the conventional straight lines and garlands of the Edwardian style. (John Joseph)

Fig. 18.4. The pearl and gold necklets of the late 19th and early 20th centuries. Note the flower or star and crescent motifs, the Prince of Wales chain (top) and the Edwardian double drop design (bottom). (S. Rogers and M. Ventura; John Joseph)

chain itself is usually of the Prince of Wales 'twist' pattern, which was popular at the time especially for long chains.

Another kind of turn-of-the-century pendant was not fixed to its chain and may today still be found by itself. This had a loop through which any fine gold chain could be slipped. Probably the most plentiful examples of jewellery of this period, these pendants were especially suitable for young ladies, as indeed they are now, and formed part of the jewellery production aimed at the new fashion-conscious middle classes, who were ever anxious to imitate the most costly and up-to-date jewels worn in fashionable circles. Designs of these pendants may all look similar, but enormous numbers of variations were produced, many by the Birmingham industry, which had not been slow in picking up new trends.

One of the most interesting features of their make up — and of other jewellery of the time — is the wide use of 'semi-precious' stones, in all the colours of the artist's palette. Many coloured stones were introduced to jewellery at the end of the century, when supplies of diamonds from South Africa were cut off by the Boer War. Together with the well-established half-pearl appeared stones such as amethysts, tourmalines (usually green or red), peridots (pale olive-green), opals, garnets, turquoises, pale rubies, sapphires and rose-cut diamonds.

This rose-cut for diamonds had been invented in the seventeenth century, and although improved upon by the brilliant-cut, continued in use in the eighteenth century. In the late nineteenth century, rose-cut diamonds were again widely used, mainly for cheaper items, as there was little wastage involed in cutting them. Never since this time have coloured 'semi-precious' stones regained such popularity and the vogue is well illustrated by these pendants.

Once again, the gems were enmeshed in Art Nouveau inspired shapes of flowers, leaves and the free-flowing line, which were sensually curved and folded to flatter and enhance the beauty of a young neck. After heavy and regularly-shaped suites of brooches, necklaces and ear-rings, these pendants brought light relief. They also satisfied, in a less intense manner than intended, the romantic and escapist dreams of the late Victorians. Even in their commercialised way, they helped people who understood little of the ideals and morals of the intellectuals of the time to identify with the image of the New Art. We can judge their popularity by the huge numbers of these pendants that have survived.

About this time, other makers of mass-produced popular jewellery were beginning to reap success, particularly with the pendant. Perhaps it was natural that the Art Nouveau jeweller who looked so fondly on the female form as a work of art should concentrate on the neck as one of the most sensually beautiful areas, and one worthy of his creations. Nonetheless, some manufacturers were reaching the general public with their versions of the new style of jewellery: notably Liberty, William Comyns, Charles Horner, and Murrle, Bennett & Co. These firms all made jewels in the 'modern' style of the day, on Art Nouveau lines. The results were more stylised than the pretty pendants of the 1890s and less startling than the ambitious and individual jewels made on the Continent by dedicated artists.

Liberty's chief success was with the 'Cymric' range, launched in 1899, and

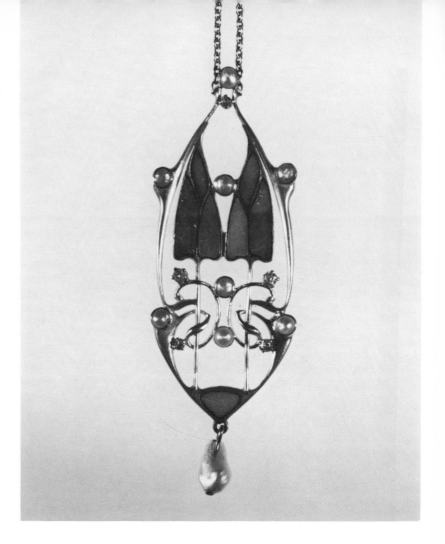

Fig. 18.5. Delicate pendant by Liberty & Co with enamel decoration and set with pearls. (Sotheby's)

made in Birmingham. Another important manufacturer was the firm of Murrle, Bennett & Co. Both silver and gold were used for pendants; rough turquoises, mother-of-pearl and moonstones were among the favourite embellishments. Enamelling, one of the main features, was frequently found in pools of mingled peacock-blue and green. Meanwhile, the more classic delicate pendant was worn throughout these passing fashions and marked the beginning of an Edwardian style. It survived in the early years of the twentieth century, until designs were gradually transformed by Art Deco devotees.

The would-be collector of late Victorian and Edwardian pendants has a vast array from which to choose and — surprisingly for such a short space of time — a large contrast in styles. It may take a little time for an unpractised eye to recognise the different types, to pick out the stronger Art Nouveau lines of a hammered silver pendant from those gently incorporated into an earlier pearl necklet, but all can be worn effectively with modern clothes and collected for their ornamental value.

One of the fascinating aspects of collecting the mass-produced pendants is that, in spite of the huge numbers produced, it is rarely, if ever, that one finds two exactly alike, however similar they may at first appear. As always, it is

Fig. 18.6. Pear-shaped pendant in gold with elaborate enamelling and a painted ivory central panel. Designed by Alphonse Mucha, it was made by Fouquet. (Sotheby's)

wise to look at as many different examples as possible, become acquainted with the different coloured stones, always asking the names when you are not certain. Study different shapes, and try them on, remembering that jewellery was made to be worn. A piece which looks dull in a crowded display cabinet, can come to life when put next to the skin.

Prices depend very much on quality, workmanship and stones and it is not difficult to distinguish between a mass-produced pendant and a fine quality hand-made example. However, unlike some popular jewellery of today, the jewels which were produced in great quantity in the late nineteenth century were made to last, a fact verified by the ever-growing displays in antique jewellers' windows. There is still much in this aspect of late nineteenth century production to attract a collector's attention. Do beware of reproductions — there are many modern copies of these pendants, intended as reproductions, so look out for a modern hallmark and wherever possible buy from a reputable dealer until you feel confident in distinguishing the genuine article.

It is important to look in museums and shops for the extraordinary creations of the period — those by Lalique, for example — which forcefully embody the spirit of the age, so as to trace and recognise their influence on more commercial, and wearable, pieces. Even in the cheaper jewellery of the time, a great deal of originality and variation in design can be studied. A single purchase can provide an enticing glimpse of a *fin de siècle* society, whose struggles, changes and questions are well represented by the endless and tortuous lines of turn-of-the-century art.

&19. Arts and Crafts Jewellery

The Arts and Crafts Movement is the name given to an artistic revolution that took place towards the end of the nineteenth century and had a very strong influence on design right through the turn of the century and in some cases up to the end of the 1920s. As a movement which offered an unusual blend of artistic, social and moral reform, it was only partially successful. Certainly it effected no ideological social change, but it did bring a new approach to design. As collectors have been finding, the fields of jewellery and metal-work were the areas most appropriate to the whole craft revival, and they had the greatest chance of achieving its ideals.

The Origins of the Movement

The movement originated in Britain and stemmed from an early nineteenth century reaction against industrialisation and the debasement of the quality of life by mechanical progress. Those who deplored these unacceptable effects of mechanisation were also pricked by a painful social conscience when they saw appalling working and living conditions, soul-destroying factory jobs, suppression of individuality and lack of artistic merit in machine-made objects. Gradually, they began to formulate ideas about a revival of 'honest' crafts and true art, freed from commercial consideration, which would bring about a cure for the social sickness implanted in society by the machine.

Early stirrings of dissatisfaction can be traced from the 1836 Government reports on design and industry, and then as the laments grew louder with the Great Exhibition of 1851, to the studies and thoughts of John Ruskin and William Morris.

John Ruskin (1819-1900) was undoubtedly the guiding force behind the movement, and a major influence on late nineteenth century design and thinking. It was his writings which laid the foundation of Arts and Crafts principles. The Great Exhibition of 1851 had paraded proof that no real work of art could be turned out under the current system of industrialism. Its massive and showy displays of rather shoddy, machine-made goods highlighted the absence of art and artists in their manufacture, and had disgusted some onlookers, including the young William Morris.

Morris (1834-96) was an undergraduate at Oxford when he read Ruskin's writings, and it was at Oxford too that he met and befriended the painter and designer Edward Burne-Jones. Morris abandoned his plans of entering the Church and decided to concentrate on art, starting his new career as an apprentice to an architect. Eventually, after painting and other experiments, he found satisfaction and the right channels for his talent in pattern designing, especially for wallpapers and textiles. He exerted his influence mainly through his own firm, Morris, Marshall, Faulkner & Company, established in 1861.

The movement gathered support in a number of ways. Ruskin's writings and ideology were distributed by F.D. Maurice in his Working Men's College, set up in London in 1854. Owen Jones' book, *Grammar of Ornament*, which was published in 1856, had a profound effect on design, with its suggestions of geometrical stylisation of nature and plant forms.

Fig. 19.1. Two pieces made by the Guild of Handicraft: a brooch with gold frame and tiny pearls and fiery orange enamel; necklace of silver with blue enamel flower motifs and mother-of-pearl centres. (The Fine Art Society)

There had also been a great deal of delving into medievalism, by A.W.N. Pugin, the architect who revived Gothic architecture and also condemned the machine and its effects; Ruskin and his colleagues had also done some research. They were searching for a model of perfection, and for evidence of a 'just' society where the artist shared his gift with the people by extending his

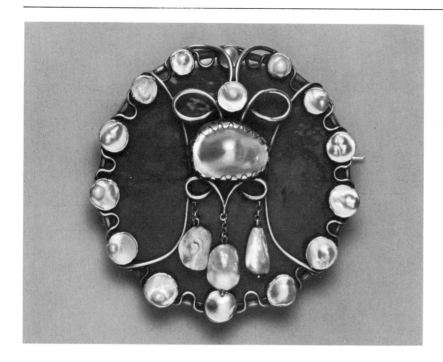

Fig. 19.2. Large brooch of silver, blue enamel and mother-of-pearl, possibly made by the Guild of Handicraft. (John Jesse and Irina Laski)

talents to all areas of crafts. They held a rather shaky belief that Renaissance artists could turn their talents in any direction and with equal success. Botticelli, for instance, trained as a goldsmith and was thought to have produced jewellery as fine as his painting. In 1853, Ruskin wrote his essay 'On the Nature of Gothic' in which he upheld the Gothic or early Christian style as a perfect example of the kind of 'life and liberty' he was striving to give to the working man. As a result of these events, the movement developed a set of guiding principles with which to work and translate words into action.

The Guilds and Art Schools

The right kind of working atmosphere had to be found to propagate the ideas, and this was done through co-operative Guilds or workshops. They echoed the two-tiered personality of the movement, because they were organised on socialist principles with the hopes of producing the resulting theoretical contentment. However they were also workshops which aimed to create handmade goods and to encourage amateur craftsmen to experiment and learn.

The first co-operative was the Guild of St George, set up by John Ruskin in 1871. It seems that his personality was too dominant for such a democratic plan, but this experiment set the pattern for the formation of further Guilds that were central to the movement. The Century Guild was founded in 1882 by A. H. Mackmurdo, a British architect and designer; the Art Workers' Guild was established in 1884 by members of the St George's Art Society, and from this developed the Arts and Crafts Exhibition Society, which was set up in 1888. Exhibitions were held in 1888, 1889 and 1890. For jewellery, the most important was the Guild of Handicraft, founded by C. R. Ashbee in 1888. Ashbee had also started a School of Handicraft in his settlement in the

East End of London. Later, in 1902, he moved his workshops to Chipping Camden in Gloucestershire, in keeping with Arts and Crafts ideals.

The Birmingham Guild of Handicraft was founded in 1890, and is also noted for its jewellery, involving many of the leading metal-workers. The Artificer's Guild was founded in 1901 by Nelson Dawson, again an important jeweller. The Bromsgrove Guild of Applied Art, founded in 1890, also specialised in metal-work and jewellery; so it can be seen that jewellery played a large part in the output of the movement.

It is also significant that so many art schools were started at the height of the movement, with leading artists as teachers. The vast amount of work by students is a particular feature of Arts and Crafts jewellery and one that should be carefully considered by collectors, when trying to attribute pieces or trace origins. Students taught by leading jewellers worked very closely to the style of their masters; and as craftsmen rarely signed their jewels, it can be difficult to identify some jewellery positively.

Principles of the Movement and their Application to Jewellery

Apart from fighting their socialist and moral battle, the leaders of the movement basically hoped to give art back to the people. They saw that there was no room left for the individual trying to create a work of art or an honest piece of handiwork, and that the poor working classes were being starved — metaphorically as well as literally — of the basic enjoyment of art in everyday life. They wanted to reintroduce the medieval-style workshop where the craftsman could develop his ideas, design and manufacture the object himself from start to finish.

Arts and Crafts principles were adamantly opposed to any specialisation in separate skills in the jewellery trade, which was one of the reasons so many Arts and Crafts pieces appear to be badly made and were unsuccessful. It was thought that the whole area of artistic design would benefit by giving an individual craftsman the central role in the workshop. In fact, it was probably ultimately more therapeutic only for the craftsman himself, as in reality these theories could not work.

The jeweller could rarely achieve sufficient skill in each area of design and production to make a satisfactory piece. Also the hand-made jewel manufactured under these conditions was far more expensive than its machine-made equivalent; finally the real tastes of the public had not been truly considered. The general buying public saw Arts and Crafts jewels as dull, amateurish and old-fashioned; ironically, only a small group of educated and aesthetically-inclined followers could appreciate or afford Arts and Crafts objects, which defeated the whole object of the movement. It was the absolute rejection of all machines which limited the appeal and the hoped-for spread of artistic hand-made wares and accompanying ideals.

The first step in applying these principles to jewellery was to dispose of the manufacturers who, as middle men, relied on machines. They put business and financial profit first, so destroying any last trace of art in jewel design. The artist was to have complete freedom of expression, and should not be bound by conventional training of the jewel trade. The idea was that there

Fig. 19.3. Well-made necklace with turquoises and pink hardstones, set in silver with rope design and pyramids of silver grains. (Bellamy)

should be no jewellers as such, just craftsmen introducing art to decorative or functional objects. All jewels were to be hand-made and their beauty was in no way dependent upon the value of the materials.

Arts and Crafts metal-workers shunned precious stones and intrinsically valuable materials; they made an effort to concentrate on inexpensive less glamorous materials and semi-precious stones. This abhorrence of value could often border on the pretentious; for example, Gaskin made a necklace of cornelians that he picked up on a beach and this product met with great approbation. According to Ruskin's ideals, it was essential not to pervert the material, but to use and translate its natural beauty, altering it as little as possible. Silver was preferred to gold; the latter was used only because of its decorative qualities. J.P. Cooper liked to use 15 carat gold because of its colour, and gold was often added to silver jewels as decoration. Beaten copper and aluminium were also worked.

Diamonds were never used and faceted stones rarely — smooth cabochons or uncut stones were the most admired, especially the deep Renaissance colours of garnets and amethysts. Turquoise as another favourite stone, particularly when it was streaked with brown matrix. Mother-of-pearl with its satin sheen and naturally undulating surface was popular along with small misshapen baroque or river pearls; these are seen most frequently as drops on

Fig. 19.4. (Top) Unusual chain with silver spirals and straight 'baton' links of gold, set with mother-of-pearl and amethyst beads.

(Below) Necklace of silver, mother-of-pearl and peridots, and two 'tooth' drops, possibly by Gaskin. Typical silver-work, with festoon chains, and clusters of granules. (Bellamy)

pendants. Long houndstooth pearls were also used in this way. Green peridots, misty moonstones and the changing glints of opals all appealed to Arts and Crafts designers. Again these preferences arose as a reaction against the many years of bright and shiny jewels, perfectly finished and matched. The natural irregularities of stones, such as turquoise matrix or the knobbly baroque pearl, and the dull hammered metal of their jewels were as different as was possible from the former regularity of form.

Claw settings were rare, because the plain collet was considered far more pleasing. Silver was often hammered out and the sections joined with bindings of wire or by decorative additions fixed to the main body of the jewel by means of flaps of metal tucked through slots and folded back. This was often rather crudely managed.

Necklaces were the favourite forms of jewels, often medieval in feeling, with loops or festoons of chains. Pendants had enamel centres or wirework designs and suspended from them was a little baroque pearl. A great many cloak clasps and buckles were made, probably because their functional nature lent itself to transformation into a work of art. Rings, brooches and bracelets can be found, but are far less common.

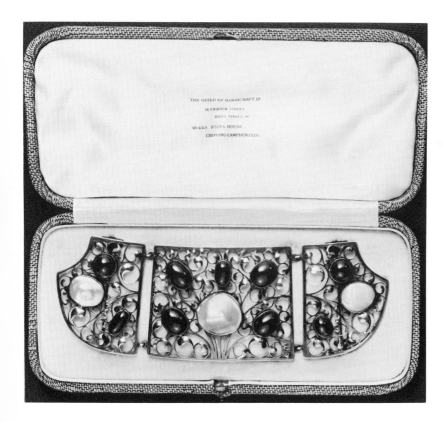

Fig. 19.5. Belt buckle designed by Ashbee for the Guild of Handicraft, in oxidised silver set with garnets and mother-of-pearl. (John Jesse)

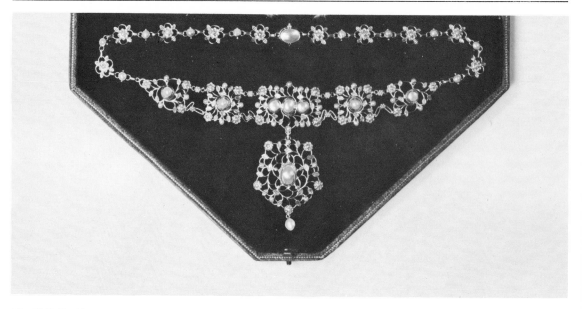

Fig. 19.6. Necklace, designed by Arthur Gaskin, in silver with mother-of-pearl and some gold decoration, made by Liberty & Co. This example shows Liberty adhering far more closely to the original design than was usual. (The Fine Art Society)

Leading Figures in Arts and Crafts Jewellery Design

C. R. Ashbee (1863-1942) was a leading advocate of Arts and Crafts theories and was associated with the design and manufacture of jewels. It is interesting to note here that so many leading craftsmen had trained originally as architects and also that there was a close connection and interchange of ideas between them. After Cambridge, Ashbee entered the offices of G. F. Bodley: at this time he was living in a pioneer settlement in Toynbee Hall in the East End. Inspired by a small evening class formed to read Ruskin, Ashbee set up his School in 1887 and The Guild of Handicraft in 1888. The latter is now best known for its production of fine jewels and metal-work.

The Guild began with three members and a capital of £50. Ashbee provided the designs and his workmen carried them out, apparently through a trial-and-error system. In 1902, Ashbee moved the Guild to Chipping Camden in Gloucestershire, but he kept his retail shop at 16a Brook Street. This move and its accompanying ambitions strained the Guild's finances until it went into liquidation in 1907.

Ashbee was particularly important in the development of Arts and Crafts jewellery and in later modern movements on the Continent. His influence can be seen in the work of many of his contemporaries. Ashbee used a great deal of turquoise enamel and a characteristic four leaf design of four softly billowing petals, among his jewel motifs. After 1900 and a meeting with Frank Lloyd Wright, Ashbee began to alter his views and finally conceded that the machine, used correctly, did have a place in society and a vital part to play in the spread of Arts and Crafts ideals and art.

Fred T. Partridge was an English metal-worker and jeweller who worked with Ashbee and the Guild of Handicraft in Chipping Camden and followed Ashbee's style very closely. His work is excellent and unusual in that it was influenced by French Art Nouveau. He made very beautiful hair-combs in

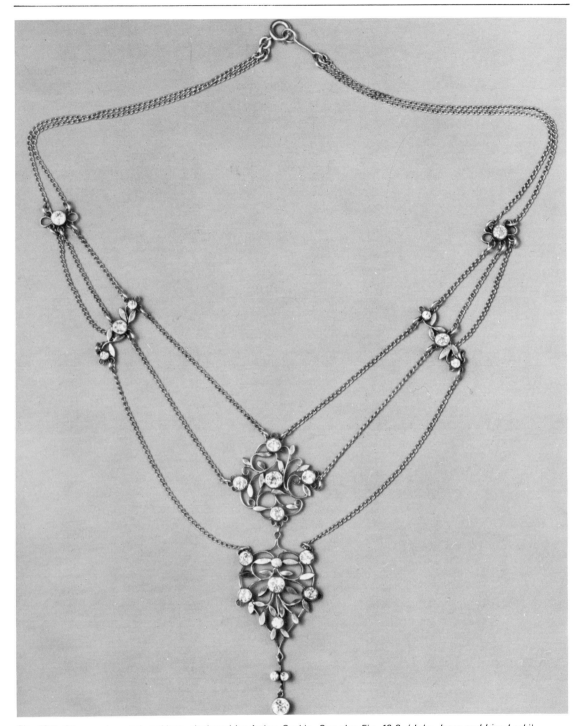

Fig. 19.7. Silver and crystal necklace, designed by Arthur Gaskin. See also Fig. 19.8. (John Jesse and Irina Laski)

Fig. 19.8. Close-up of Fig. 19.7. showing the distinctive leaves.

horn, very much in the French style, but these can be distinguished from continental combs as they were signed with his name.

Another jeweller, very evidently influenced by Ashbee, was Edgar Simpson. His designs and those of Ashbee are illustrated in *Modern Design in Jewellery and Fans* and can be compared.

The jewels of Arthur Gaskin (1862-1928) represent some of the best of Arts and Crafts work; he was an active and central figure in the Birmingham group, both making jewellery and teaching. He had many student followers. He worked together with his wife, Georgina (1868-1934) after 1899. It is a useful guide for collectors to look at some pieces of Gaskin jewellery and to recognise his very distinctive style: coils and tendrils of gold or silver wire, fine borders of rope design, clusters or pyramids of silver grains, leaves and flowers, set with small richly coloured stones and occasionally incorporating birds. Gaskin produced some designs for Liberty, but they were not usually very closely adhered to, and it was not a particularly successful venture.

Bernard Cuzner (1877-1956) was an extremely talented jeweller. He was involved with the Birmingham group, both learning and later teaching in Birmingham Art Schools, and he was greatly influenced by Gaskin. Around 1900 he was also designing for Liberty. He wrote a book entitled *A Silversmith's Manual*, recently reprinted by N.A.G. Press.

Henry Wilson (1864-1934) was another important figure, again an architect who turned to metal-working around 1890. He had worked with the architect J. D. Sedding, as his chief assistant before setting up his own workshop in about 1895. He is also known for a major practical book on jewellery-making called *Silverwork and Jewellery* published in 1903. Henry Wilson used professional jewellers to make up his designs, which probably accounts for their

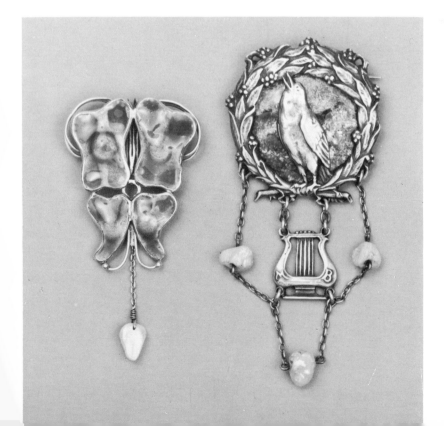

Fig. 19.9. (Right) Interesting brooch in silver, enamelled in mingled red, blue and green. This apparently comes from a design for a pendant shown in Henry Wilson's book, Silverwork and Jewellery, *but the design has been reversed and adorned with pearls and the lyre motif. (Editions Graphiques) (Left) Silver brooch with turquoise enamel, design attributed to Ashbee. (Hancocks & Co)*

success, although this practice did not comply with the Movement's requirements.

From the same architect's office and workshop emerged perhaps the most successful of Arts and Crafts jewellers, John Paul Cooper (1869-1933) whose work is very similar to that of Wilson's. Cooper in fact learnt his technical skills from Wilson's trade jewellers, but he also had a great talent and flair for designing which also worked extremely well in production. He probably came the closest to achieving the aims and ideals of the Arts and Crafts Movement. His success as a jeweller perhaps comes from the fact that he was not quite so devoted to social or moral issues. Cooper concentrated entirely on his work.

Fig. 19.10. Silver buckle, set with enamelled plaque by Nelson and Edith Dawson. About 1900. This clearly shows their highly distinctive style of enamel-work. (John Jesse)

Fig. 19.11. Fine necklace and ear-rings attributed to Sarah Madeleine Martineau, set with valuable stones and cloisonné enamels. Dated about 1914, the height of the Suffragette Movement, it seems possible that this was a commission, featuring the colours of the movement: mauve, white and green (suggestion of Mrs Shirley Bury). (The Fine Art Society)

Fig. 19.12. Buckles were a
speciality of the Arts and
Crafts workshops with Oliver
Baker leading the way with
excellent buckles designed
for Liberty & Co.
   Top left: Plain beaten
silver buckle (The Purple
shop). Top right: Liberty
buckle, silver with green
hardstone or pottery
(possibly Ruskin pottery),
beads, and a raised butterfly
motif. The design taken
directly from an Ashbee
design for the Guild of
Handicraft. (Hancocks & Co).
Below: Round buckle with
deep green and blue enamel
behind silver design of
interlaced seed-pods. This is
also counter enamelled.
(Hancocks & Co)

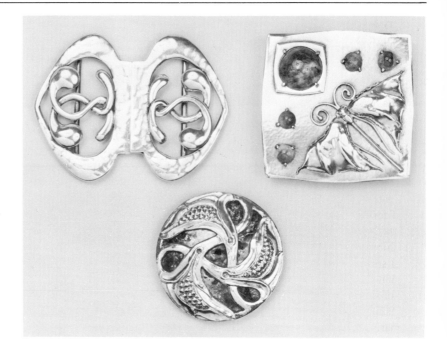

The enamelling revival was vital to Arts and Crafts jewellery, and it is probably one of its best and most progressive aspects. The hand-painted enamels
were far better, and more artistic, than any that could be commercially produced. Alexander Fisher (1864-1936) was the leading enamellist and an influential teacher of the craft. He travelled, learnt, and experimented widely
with colours and techniques using 'paillons' or flecks of metal or foil.

One of the jewellers who most benefited from Fisher's experiments and lec-
tures was Nelson Dawson (1859-1942), who worked with his wife Edith.
Their jewels can often be recognised by deep-coloured enamels of flowers and
birds; again they used very typical Arts and Crafts metal-work settings. Sarah
Madeleine Martineau is also known as a silversmith and jeweller working in
the Arts and Crafts style, but she made relatively little jewellery. The jewels
which are definitely known to have been made by these leading exponents
should serve as standards for judging and collecting other pieces, unmarked
but made by the many other jewellers working towards similar aims.

One interesting point about these jewellers and trying to recognise their
styles is their use of different kinds of leaves. Jewellers used real punches and
engraved the punches themselves, so there should be a distinct individuality
about their metal-work. The leaf motif was the connecting theme throughout
Arts and Crafts jewellery. Really the only way of learning about different
leaves is to look at as many pieces as possible — with experience and time it
may be possible to use the leaves as a kind of maker's mark. For instance,
Gaskin's leaves were always very precise and crips; but when Liberty & Co.
used Gaskin's designs, the leaves looked quite different. The Liberty machine-
made versions had far more rounded leaves, giving a less precise and more
solid appearance.

Liberty & Co. and its Designers

Modern collectors are of course very much aware of the different art movements of the nineteenth and twentieth centuries but, at the time, there were no such clear categories. In England, Art Nouveau and the Arts and Crafts Movement developed at the same time. Several large commercial firms were making jewellery in the 'modern style', based to a greater or lesser extent on Arts and Crafts designs, and with a touch of English Art Nouveau.

Classification of such jewels can often be a matter for conjecture as, strictly speaking, they should be entirely hand-made if they are to be labelled Arts and Crafts. However there is justification for including some of the mass-produced Liberty jewels in a collection of Arts and Crafts, because the firm appreciated and employed some of the very best Arts and Crafts designers, and, if for no other reason, because Arthur Liberty recognised the genius of Archibald Knox (see Chapter 20, Liberty and his Rivals).

Archibald Knox (1864-1933) was born in the Isle of Man, and made a special study of Celtic ornament at art school. He came to London in 1897, and soon after began to design for Liberty when they started their 'Cymric' range of silver, pewter and jewellery. He became their chief designer and was responsible for their Celtic revival. He had a very distinctive style with simple, soaring outlines; his use of Celtic interlacing and whiplash motifs was widely imitated. He combined the currently popular revival of ancient design with a very modern, disciplined approach to shape and an understanding of the importance of suitability of ornament to object and material.

Fig. 19.13. Group of rings showing the use of cabochon, semi-precious stones, and leaf and flower clusters. In the centre: Ring made by Sybil Dunlop, about 1920. Below: Gold and opal ring by Archibald Knox. (Bellamy; Editions Graphiques; Gooday; The Purple Shop)

Fig. 19.14. Four pendants,
three by Omar Ramsden, a
leading silversmith in the
Arts and Crafts tradition.
About 1905. Second left: An
unidentified turquoise, silver
and moonstone pendant.
(John Jesse and Irina Laski)

Liberty also bought designs by Cuzner, Gaskin and Oliver Baker. The last is best known for superb buckles of hammered silver, with curls and interlacing motifs. It also appears that Liberty 'stole' or copied designs from the Guild of Handicraft, while Ashbee disapproved of their totally commercial attitude, and condemned their alteration of original designs. Nevertheless, Liberty succeeded where the movement failed, in spreading Arts and Crafts design and in bringing art to the people in an acceptable form at realistic prices.

The enamelling revival was appreciated and encouraged by Liberty, if only from a commercial point of view. It did however give the public an opportunity to enjoy the new varieties of enamel decoration and at the same time gave the enamellists a chance to use their experiments.

Charles Fleetwood Varley produced very beautiful, hand-painted enamel landscapes, usually mounted by Liberty as lids to silver or pewter boxes, or more rarely as jewels. He was a member of the Varley family of Victorian painters, and he worked in the family tradition creating land and seascapes of deep, strong colours, very subtly shaded and bathed in sunlight or moonlight. His skill in enamels is shown in the soft haze characteristic of these pictures.

Eventually the quality of enamels in general was reduced to a kind of stereotype 'peacock' enamel of mingled blue and green. This was very easy to fire, but very effective and popular. Because the enamelling revival is so central to the Arts and Crafts Movement, it is important for collectors to differentiate between the artistic achievements of craftsmen and the commercial short-cut versions.

Fig. 19.15. Necklace and pendant of fire opals and silver, made by Edward Spencer, for the Artificers' Guild. (The Fine Art Society)

Under Fisher's influence, there developed a method of using many layers of different coloured translucent enamels to create a dreamlike effect of swirling depth and movement. Very often the main subject was a floating nymph with flowing hair and robes. Phoebe Traquair was a follower of Fisher's work and her enamels usually have a religious or spiritual character. Her enamel plaques often decorated silver or copper boxes or caskets.

Enamel decoration in the form of flowers and leaves very often appeared as settings. On a particular kind of Liberty jewel you may find a special formula for enamelled leaves — these leaves were almost a hallmark of Liberty work and produced a jewelled or gem-like effect. The leaves were 'cupped'; then translucent enamel was dropped into the recesses. This kind of jewel was made around 1910; on some these leaves frame a Varley enamel plaque.

On other occasions enamel formed a more central part of the jewel, as with Dawson's bird or flower designs, or perhaps a pendant showing a Viking ship or galleon, as designed by Edward Spencer for the Artificers' Guild.

Crafts revival jewellery continued to be made, in its purest form and in adaptations, alongside English mass-produced Art Nouveau, such as Charles Horner's and Murrle, Bennett & Co's jewellery (see Chapter 20, Liberty and his Rivals) through the turn of the century. Even after Ashbee's Guild of Handicraft closed in 1907, Ashbee continued to travel, lecture and write to spread his theories; the movement was perpetuated by new artists and craftsmen who had been taught and/or influenced by original leading figures. In 1914 there was an important exhibition of British decorative art, including that of the leading Arts and Crafts artists, which was held at the Louvre in Paris. In 1915 the Design and Industries Association was set up by many leading exponents of the Crafts revival to co-ordinate and promote British design through exhibitions. This strengthened and revitalised the continuing Crafts tradition as a decorative style, but ended the early, basic principle when it recognised the validity of the machine in modern designs.

This continuation of the style can be confusing for collectors: there were silversmiths and jewellers working from about 1915 to 1930 in the Arts and Crafts style, such as Sybil Dunlop and George Hunt. Their work is distinctive however; and experience and comparison will eventually help the collector to recognise early and late Crafts revival pieces.

The Glasgow School

Another school of design was emerging around the same time in Scotland. The leading figures were known as the Glasgow Four: they were C. R. Mackintosh, the most important of the group; J. Herbert MacNair; and two sisters, Margaret and Frances Macdonald. Margaret later married Mackintosh and Frances married MacNair. They are often associated with Arts and Crafts but their work was disliked and disapproved of in England. The Glasgow Four believed in a craft aesthetic but not in the Arts and Crafts ideology. Although jewels by Mackintosh and his followers are exceedingly rare, the Glasgow School had an enormous impact on turn-of-the-century design, especially on the Continent, and marked the beginnings of Modernism (see Chapter 20, Liberty and his Rivals).

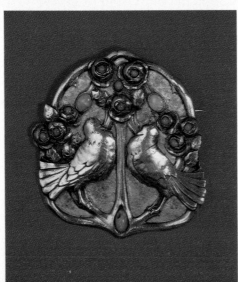

Plate 41. (Previous page) The very best of French Art Nouveau jewellery. Top: gold brooch by Vever, set with diamonds, emeralds and amethysts. The girl is of pâte de verre, *the background* plique à jour *enamel. Left: Plisson et Hartz gold and* plique à jour *enamel brooch with diamonds and a pearl drop. Right: gold and enamel brooch, set with diamonds, by Beaudoin. Below: gold locket pendant by Count Epinay de Briort, who worked for Boucheron. Set with diamonds, it opens to reveal a mirror. (Editions Graphiques)*

Plate 42. (Above) Group of jewels by C. R. Ashbee. Note the famous peacock design in silver set with opals and mother-of-pearl, and the softly moulded petals and wings.

Plate 43. (Left) Excellent, but unmarked, Arts and Crafts brooch/ buckle, set with gems in silver with enamel. (42-43, John Jesse and Irina Laski)

Fig. 19.16. Arts and Crafts jewellery at its best. Above: A well-made draped silver and turquoise necklet; characteristic of the Birmingham school, when Gaskin was teaching there. (Bellamy) Below: An early piece of Murrle, Bennet & Co, which may be included as Arts and Crafts because of its hand-finishing, hammered silver, wound wires and opals. (Private collection)

Fig. 19.17. Necklace by Mr and Mrs Arthur Gaskin, marked 'G', about 1910. It is of silver set with mother-of-pearl, turquoises and chrysoprases. (The Fine Art Society)

Some of MacNair's jewellery, possibly made by his wife, was displayed at the 1896 Arts and Crafts Exhibition, and again at the Turin Exhibition in 1902; his designs incorporated human figures and entangled wire cages. Jessie M. King was a member of the Glasgow School and she designed for the Liberty 'Cymric' range. Talwyn Morris was another follower who designed many pieces of jewellery.

Very little true craft-jewellery resulted from the American branch of the Arts and Crafts Movement. Some firms, such as Marcus & Company (see Chapter 17, Signed Art Nouveau Jewellery), followed a kind of craft aesthetic, absorbing some characteristics of English Crafts jewellery, and using a great deal of enamelling, while Tiffany followed French Art Nouveau style. There was however no design studio which could compare with the Liberty venture. Florence Koehler was the foremost individual jeweller of the American Crafts revival: she worked in Chicago.

Arts and Crafts jewellery is a very specialised area of jewel collecting, which is sometimes ignored or little understood. The jewellery can be very attractive, unusual and individual, or it can be poorly made and uninspiring in design. Collectors can also fall into the trap of thinking that the most amateurish, and obviously hand-made are the most characteristic of the movement and therefore the best. This hand-made aspect was a weakness of the movement as well as a strength; collectors should use the same discriminating judgment as with professional work when buying a piece of Arts and Crafts jewellery. They should look for the same standards of workmanship, of suitability of materials to form, of design and of proportions, as apply to other professionally-made jewels. The most successful and desirable pieces will then illustrate the merits of this artistic movement and its benefit to jewellery design.

20. Liberty and his Rivals

The growth and influence of Art Nouveau and associated artistic movements can be traced through a complex international network, involving an interchange of ideas and styles amongst separate European groups, all of whom contributed to modern twentieth century design. Art Nouveau was shortlived but intense; a creative and courageous art movement which swept through Europe and the United States during the period roughly from 1890 to 1910. Its origins and applications are diverse, drawing on many different inspirations, cultures and personalities (see Chapter 17, Signed Art Nouveau Jewellery). But as a style it is easily recognisable to collectors of jewellery, very decorative and dramatic.

Basically, the movement expressed a revolt against the long series of borrowed styles of the Victorian era, against mass-production, and against restrictions and conventions which suffocated individuality and imagination. The style was based on free-flowing sinuous lines, natural and organic motifs, such as stylised flowers, leaves, insects, and feminine, romantic dreamlike figures and faces with flowing gowns and hair. It was alive with a new movement and sensuality which were called decadent at the time. Art Nouveau affected the pure arts of painting, sculpture and architecture, but the real revolution lay in its interpretations in the applied arts: glass, ceramics, furniture, silver, graphics, jewellery and everyday objects. Each country had its own version of Art Nouveau with varying distinctive characteristics that can be clearly followed through jewellery of the period. Collectors need to go one step further in studying, observing and comparing, to distinguish between these national variations.

In France, the style was at its most pure; highly decorative, elaborate, very mobile and sensuous. Small gold pendants decorated with girls' heads and flowing hair are almost always French.

In Scotland, the Glasgow style centred around C. R. Mackintosh (see Chapter 19, Arts and Crafts Jewellery) and his work had a great influence on the Viennese Sezessionists and artists like Otto Wagner, Joseph Hoffmann and J. M. Olbrich. His style was modernistic, austere and angular and far removed from romanticised and picturesque French Art Nouveau.

German Art Nouveau again was much more geometric and restrained: it

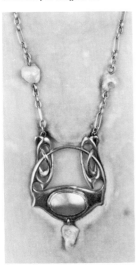

Fig. 20.1. Gold and pearl pendant by Liberty. (Sotheby's Belgravia)

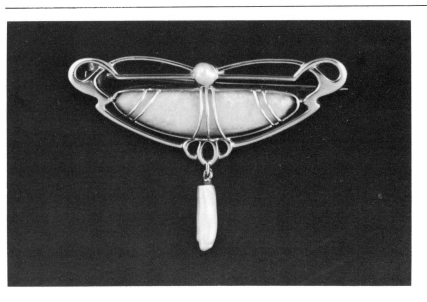

Fig. 20.2. Unmarked but very stylish gold and opal brooch with baroque pearls. About 1900. (Sotheby's Belgravia)

showed important links with the current trends in England, where the artistic revolution centred around the Arts and Crafts Movement.

The intensity of Art Nouveau was superbly expressed on jewels by great French craftsmen like Lalique and Vever (see Chapter 17, Signed Art Nouveau Jewellery) but at the other end of the scale, the commercial possibilities of a decorative new style were fully exploited in Europe, Britain and the U.S.A. Themes and motifs were adapted for mass-production to suit popular tastes, and the force of the style was inevitably diluted, to varying degrees, to make it less disturbing and more acceptable.

In England, however, the firm of Liberty & Company successfully combined powerful innovations with huge commercial considerations. In fact, one of the basic principles of the Arts and Crafts Movement was achieved by Liberty; that of bringing art to the masses. In the process, Liberty ignored another basic ideal, the rejection of the machine. Other smaller firms produced popular jewels and objects with French-style ornament, but it was the Liberty output which controlled and shaped English tastes at the turn of the century, so much so that they came to represent a national style, and English Art Nouveau.

Liberty's fame rapidly spread abroad: the name became synonymous with Art Nouveau, which was, in fact, called 'Stile Liberty' in Italy. For all these reasons, and because they are very attractive, the metal-work and jewellery made by Liberty at the turn of the century has been widely collected and sought after.

The Rise of Liberty & Co.

Liberty & Company was set up in 1875 by Arthur Lazenby Liberty (1843-1917). Liberty had embarked on his career, as a young man of twenty, when he joined the company of Farmers & Rogers as a manager in 1863. This was the time when the great interest in Oriental art and crafts encouraged

Fig. 20.3. The style to look for in the English or German Art Nouveau taste. Top right: Silver and green enamel Liberty 'Cymric' brooch. Top left: Hammered silver and blue hardstone brooch, marked 'Cymric', possibly designed by Oliver Baker.

2nd row; right: Silver and peacock enamel brooch, marked Murrle, Bennett & Co., but the same brooch appeared in an advertisement for Liberty 'Cymric' jewels. Left: Silver and enamel brooch, a Knox design.

3rd row, right: Gold, turquoise and pearl brooch, in German style, made by the firm with initials B H J. Left: Brooch of silver and Swiss lapis (a blue-stained jasper imitation of lapis) of excellent design, possibly by Patriz Huber. Bottom: German silver and enamelled stylish brooch. (Private collection, Author)

the growth of the Japonaiserie fashion and the Aesthetic Movement which affected all forms of decoration (see Chapter 5, Silver of the Late Nineteenth Century). Liberty was plunged into this atmosphere at Farmers & Rogers' Great Cloak and Shawl Emporium in Regent Street, where he dealt with goods from the Far East, cultivating his innate business sense, and watching the moods of fashions. He followed the progress of the Japanese influence, meanwhile making the acquaintance of such customers as Dante Gabriel Rossetti, Burges and J.A.M. Whistler.

When Farmer & Rogers' Oriental warehouse closed down in 1875, Liberty decided to trust his knowledge and experience and opened his own shop, an Oriental emporium, in Regent Street. The shop was called East India House and he started with a staff consisting of one shop assistant and one porter. The timing and circumstances were obviously perfect; Liberty's imported Oriental porcelain, silks, and objets d'art were enormously popular; the shop grew and new departments and ventures were added. The store developed its own personality and, instead of selling only imported goods, they commissioned exclusive designs from various craftsmen.

The 'Silver Studio' was set up by a fabric designer, Arthur Silver; this design studio supplied Liberty with their most famous textiles, and later on some silver and pewter designs. After the death of Arthur Silver in 1896, his son Reginald (Rex) Silver continued to run the studio.

The new illustrated arts magazine, *Studio International*, which was first issued in 1893, did a great deal to publicise Liberty & Company and to establish their control over public taste. The magazine had another more direct benefit to the firm, as Liberty often organised competitions for designs in conjunction with the magazine, with the intention of buying and producing the winning designs. Eventually Mr Liberty no longer had to use this method because he had found several excellent freelance designers to work for him. In 1894, the success and expansion of the Regent Street shop was such that Liberty became a public company. Arthur Liberty was then in a position to commission the best contemporary designers; through them he was to assume an important role (however resented by the Guildsmen) in the story of the Arts and Crafts Movement.

Arthur Lazenby Liberty was a particularly shrewd businessman, who knew

Fig. 20.4. Collection of silver belt buckles designed by Oliver Baker for Liberty's 'Cymric' range. These were Baker's speciality, and particular characteristics are the hammered silver surfaces and the curls or coils of silver. They were often set with semi-precious stones. (Sotheby's Belgravia)

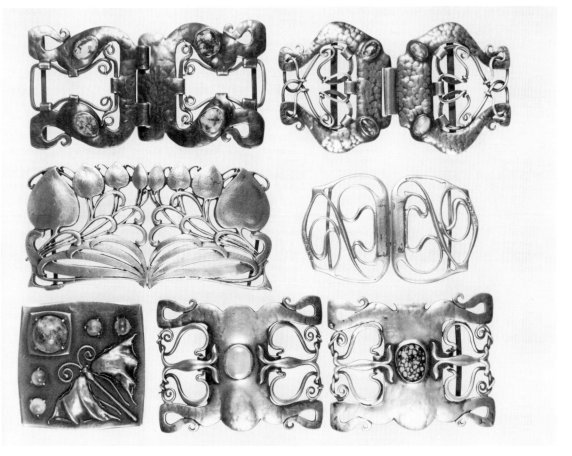

what his customers wanted before they knew themselves, and he took an interest — if a commercial one — in contemporary art and design, so that he quickly recognised the most talented artists. He saw the commercial possibilities of Arts and Crafts, and his commanding market position enabled him to disregard the idealistic attitudes concerning hand-craftsmanship and adapt the best designs for mass-production. He managed to introduce the Arts and Crafts style, in a somewhat diluted version, to the general buying public at prices they could afford.

The jewellery which is widely collected today was produced by a metal-working venture that began in the late 1890s, using the name 'Cymric'. This trade-name can be found together with the Liberty mark. The name 'Tudric' was used for a corresponding venture which launched a new range of pewter-ware. The Liberty mark for silver and gold was registered in 1894, but the first 'Cymric' pieces did not appear until 1899. It was an adventurous step to take, because gold and silver were very expensive at the time. Never before had such stylish, unconventional and *avant-garde* designs been employed for a range of cheaper, mass-produced jewels. In an advertisement in *Studio International*, Liberty claims that their 'Cymric' range marks an 'original and important departure in Gold and Silver Work' and 'a complete breaking away

Fig. 20.5. Hammered silver 'Cymric' brooch in an unusually delicate design of Celtic interlacing. (John Jesse and Irina Laski)

from convention in the matter of design and treatment, which is calculated to commend itself to all who appreciate the note distinguishing artistic productions in which individuality of idea and execution is the essence of the work'.

Of course, all Liberty customers flattered themselves that they were discerning enough to appreciate this artistic note, and rushed to buy a piece of 'Cymric' jewellery to prove it. At first, the standard of production was extremely high; pieces were sometimes hand-made, or at least hand-finished, and probably many early pieces were commissions. The finishing touches of enamels or semi-precious stones could be varied according to the customer's wishes.

A. Knox and the other Liberty Designers

The association between Archibald Knox and Liberty is important to the history of turn-of-the-century jewellery and, despite Liberty's single-minded commercial outlook, some credit must be given to him for his recognition and appreciation of one of the finest designers of the period. The Liberty mass-

production of Knox designs means that today's collectors can gather examples of his distinctive style. The artist himself did not search out fame or publicity, and his designs might not have been widely marketed, for our subsequent enjoyment, had it not been for Liberty. Even so, the policy of the company at the time was to keep the identities of their designers a close secret. It was many years before these excellent designs were widely attributed to Archibald Knox.

Knox came from the Isle of Man and was fascinated by the Celtic ornament he found there; later at art school he made a special study of the subject. It is probable that Knox began his association with Liberty's by designing fabrics and wallpapers, the firm's early specialities, and it seems most likely that he was introduced to the firm through the architect M. H. Baillie Scott with whom he worked when he moved to London in about 1897. Knox designed all the first pieces of 'Cymric' silverware which appeared in 1899. Following this initial success, Knox became their chief designer, and also inspired Liberty's Celtic Revival. Knox's early designs, of about 1899, appear to be quite close copies of Celtic art; his later work, after about 1901, shows

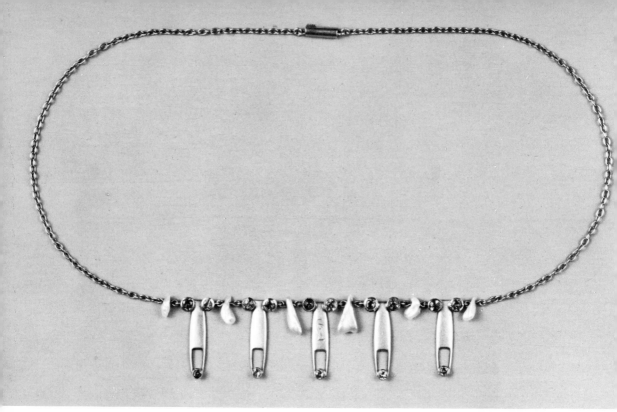

Fig. 20.7. Knox design for a
Liberty gold, pearl and
almandine garnet necklet.
(John Jesse and Irina Laski)

more stylised interpretations of Celtic ornament, more originality and an emphasis on simple elegant shapes.

Many readers may not be familiar with elements of Celtic ornament, so important to Liberty designs and therefore discussed here, but it is quite easy to get to know the basic recurring motifs and, with experience, to recognise Knox's use of them in jewellery. Certainly the best way to learn is to look at as many examples as possible; but do make sure that the dealer who assures you that the piece is attributed to Knox, is himself well-informed. You will notice clear, simple outlines; Celtic interlacing or a complex knot motif (which is more fluid and free than the Victorian lovers' knot); the famous whiplash motif, a soaring line that folds back on itself at its tip, curling around the edge of the piece; highly stylised leaves in a flattened heart-shape, a series of curved triangles or squares, all leaning to one side; and the combinations of curled, entwined wires and angular lines. All these designs are marked by a consistent control and discipline.

'Cymric' jewels were made in both silver and gold and were most often set with turquoises or mother-of-pearl; while another distinctive Knox feature was the 'floating' mingled blue and green enamels. This was often used as a pool of enamel which 'floated' underneath or within the familiar interlaced webs of silver or gold. There were small stylised leaves of gem-like translucent enamel (see Chapter 19, Arts and Crafts Jewellery) or small squares or oblongs of green or blue. Turquoises and blister pearls were very popular and Knox introduced opals into his gold jewellery, sometimes in a kind of opal mosaic. One Liberty line mixed turquoises with gold and enamels; the gold is pierced in an open-work pattern of interlacing. This cut-out Celtic design is yet another Knox characteristic.

The widespread use of 'semi-precious' stones and enamels was a by-product of the Crafts revival, and within the vast Liberty repertoire of jewels, some pieces are far more closely linked to the Arts and Crafts Movement than others. Again it is a matter of experience to distinguish between the various kinds of Liberty jewels. Several other aspects of Arts and Crafts were adopted by Liberty & Company. The extensive use of silver was in keeping with Arts and Crafts ideals, but of course it was also used because it was far cheaper than gold. Small 'Cymric' silver brooches were selling for around 7s 6d (37p) at the time. The silver was given a hand-hammered appearance, and the jewels were always hand-finished to provide evidence of the artist's touch.

As Liberty converted Arts and Crafts traits to suit popular tastes, so their workshops adapted and modified many of the designs they commissioned. This was perhaps from commercial considerations or to make the designs more their own, so that in their advertisements they could justifiably label themselves as 'inventors and designers' of 'Cymric' gold- and silver-work. For instance, one Knox design could be used for several items, and the circular motif on the cloak clasp illustrated might have started out as a button. The design was then transferred on to hat-pins, boxes, knife-rests, and many other small silver objects by the Liberty workshops. Very often, as in this case, only the decoration and not the whole shape or object was the designer's work. The alteration of original designs became a bone of contention with some of the leaders of the Arts and Crafts Movement, particularly C. R. Ashbee who blamed the failure of his Guild of Handicraft on the 'Cymric' range with its cheap and commercial variations on idealistic Arts and Crafts themes.

Liberty used the experience of professional firms who had specialised in mass-production; most of the 'Cymric' silver and jewellery was made by

Fig. 20.8. Detail of the label on a Liberty & Co. jewel case.

Fig. 20.9. (Right) Silver and enamelled belt buckle designed by Jessie King for Liberty & Co. The stylised flowers are enamelled in blue and green. (Irina Laski)

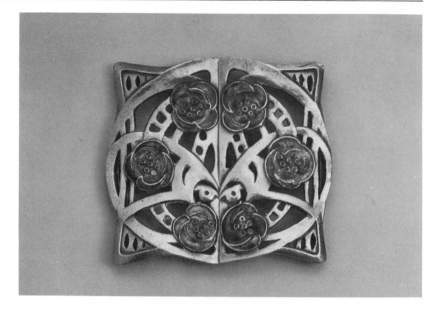

Fig. 20.10. (Below) Group of Liberty jewels. Far right: Silver and enamelled necklace, set with moonstones. The rest are very typical gold designs, some very modernistic and adventurous, using the favourite mother-of-pearl and turquoise. Note the characteristic, creamy sheen of the gold surfaces. (John Jesse and Irina Laski)

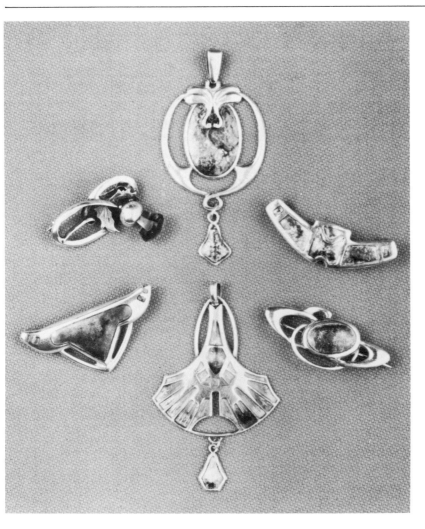

Fig. 20.11. Selection of Charles Horner jewels including the small and simple silver knot brooch set with citrine thistle, the mingled blue and green enamels and the firm's version of the Art Nouveau shape. (Private collection)

W.H. Haseler & Son, of Birmingham. In 1901, Haseler merged with Liberty, officially registering their joint company with the trade-name 'Cymric'. There were three Haselers — the father W. H. Haseler and two sons — and they had a large shareholding in the new company. It seems that W. H. Haseler also continued to produce some pieces on their own, copying Liberty designs, and it is doubtful whether this was really allowed in the agreement between the two firms.

Jewellery can bear various marks, sometimes 'W.H.H.' for Haseler; 'L & Co'; 'Ly & Co', apparently not used after 1900; and another variation 'LC&C Ld', used only in 1903.

The dominance of Liberty & Company and the huge scale of their production is proved by the names of contemporary designers who worked at one time or another for Liberty. Rex Silver, who ran the Silver Studio, also designed for the 'Cymric' range; Bernard Cuzner, Arthur Gaskin and Jessie King all contributed to the venture. Liberty's adapted their work to a greater or lesser extent with varying success. Oliver Baker's association with Liberty is best known for the very fine belt-buckles it produced. They are identifiable by lots of curls and interlacing, hammered silver surfaces, set with semi-precious cabochons.

Apart from this very stylised, Arts and Crafts inspired jewellery, Liberty catered for more delicate and traditional tastes by making the pretty, open-work gold, pearl and gem-set pendants or festoon necklaces in the Edwardian style. Knox carried out designs for this type of jewel, mostly for pendants, from about 1906 to 1909, and these were not in his typical Celtic style, although they still retained strong gold whiplash motifs. Sometimes enamel was combined with the fine gold patterns of flowing lines, which were trailed with small stones. Usually the gold jewels were unmarked, and can only be attributed by matching them to an existing design or by experience and knowledge of the Liberty style.

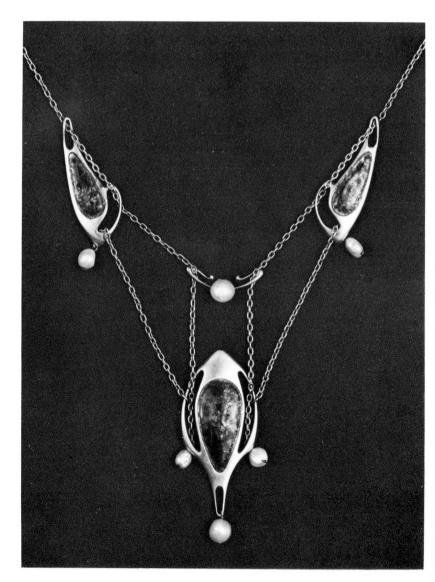

Fig. 20.12. Another example from the Liberty range of jewellery: the more substantial 'Edwardian' pendant, made in the early years of the 20th century. Here the decoration is deep green and red enamel pools mixed with smooth gold. (Bellamy)

Murrle, Bennett & Co.

The enormous success achieved by Arthur Lazenby Liberty, particularly in the field of jewellery, was bound to cause rivalry. Naturally several firms tried to produce a similar kind of so-called 'modern' jewellery. At this stage in the story, there seems to be a very complicated sharing or imitating of designs from one firm to another. A great deal of 'borrowing', copying or alteration of Liberty designs was going on; and it is not clear if this implies a business agreement or just stolen ideas.

The most successful and prolific firm of jewellers working in this style was Murrle, Bennett & Company, a name that has become increasingly familiar and sought-after among collectors. There are always some collectors who will buy signed pieces indiscriminately, but of course, standards vary. It is important to choose wisely, buying good design, workmanship and not just a maker's mark.

Very little was known until recently about the company or about the origins of their designs; but the jewels themselves are plentiful and provide great stylistic interest for any study of the cheaper jewellery of this period. Their range of designs also points to some fascinating connections with the very important Austrian and German designers of the early twentieth century. Again, the illustrations will show that their style was very distinctive, strong and in many cases immediately recognisable, while others are exactly the same as some Liberty jewels and have been taken for copies. In the light of fresh information, it seems very possible that Murrle, Bennett may have been producing these 'modern' style jewels before Liberty and, rather than copying them, sold a great deal to Liberty. The workmanship is very good and, although standards of design vary, some designs are excellent and modernistic. On the whole, Murrle, Bennett jewellery is bold and attractive.

In contemporary advertisements Murrle, Bennett & Company claimed that the jewels illustrated there 'by artists of the Modern School' are their designs and property, and give the address, 13 Charterhouse Street, London, E.C. In one advertisement, in *Studio International* around 1900, they show exactly the same Celtic-style brooch as one that appears in a Liberty advertisement. One kind of silver and enamel pendant bearing the Murrle, Bennett mark definitely comes from a design by Knox, suggesting some arrangement with

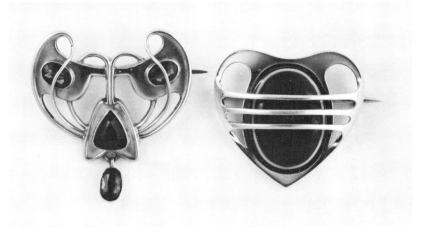

Fig. 20.13. Right: Murrle, Bennett & Co. gold and black onyx brooch, about 1910. Left: Unmarked but equally stylish gold and amethyst brooch. (Sotheby's Belgravia)

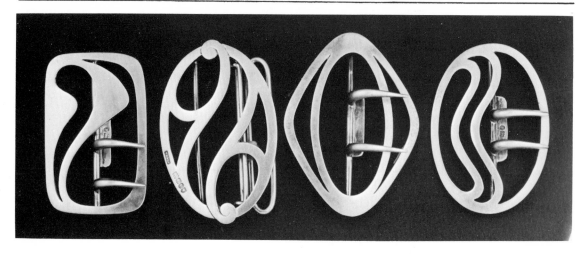

Fig. 20.14. Four silver buckles marked Murrle, Bennett & Co., 1900 to 1902. (Sotheby's Belgravia)

Liberty or their chief designer. For a long time, there has been uncertainty and conjecture on this point, but it now appears that Murrle, Bennett produced many of Liberty's jewels, including Knox designs. The name 'Cymric' appears on stocktaking lists naming some of the Murrle, Bennett ranges; and from this source it would seem that they also made up some Jessie King designs and 'Cymric' plate. Murrle, Bennett did a lot of business with Liberty, but the firm and its reputation was so large that there was obviously no need to 'steal' from or copy Liberty. The silver pendants with floating enamels and Celtic ornament bearing the Murrle, Bennett mark were, no doubt, sold exclusively by Liberty & Company.

However, their most characteristic pieces were made in quite a different style and these were taken from contemporary German designs, with their geometric, plain and strong interpretations of Art Nouveau. Murrle, Bennett called this range 'Modern Art". German Art Nouveau was known as 'Jugendstil', after a magazine called *Jugend* which was published in Munich. Some of these Murrle, Bennett pieces also bear the mark T.F. for Theodor Fahrner, a jewellery manufacturer in Pforzheim, while other Murrle, Bennet pieces are identical to Fahrner's jewellery.

New Light on Murrle, Bennett & Co

A new piece of information about the firm of Murrle, Bennett has just come to light, providing the German link. Ernst Mürrle (the umlaut was used in his name, but not in that of the firm) was German himself, having been born in Pforzheim. He came to London around 1880, and went to work with a cousin, also from Pforzheim, called Mrs Siegele, who was also in the jewellery trade. The firm of Murrle, Bennett & Co was founded on 1 June 1884. Nothing is known of Bennett, the English partner, but it is possible that he died early on in the firm's history, leaving Ernst Mürrle to carry on the business.

In 1915, during the First World War, Mürrle, being a German, was interned. It is interesting that Mürrle was interned on the Isle of Man, where Archibald Knox spent the war years working in the Alien's Detention

Plate 44. (Overleaf from previous page) *Arts and Crafts jewellery. Top right: enamelled gold pendant by Sarah Madeleine Martineau, about 1910. Top left: enamelled plaque of a religious scene by Phoebe Traquair. Below: unmarked gold and enamel necklet by a very skilled Arts and Crafts jeweller.* (John Jesse and Irina Laski)

Plate 45. (Opposite page) *Gold necklet with opal 'mosaic' and pearls. Note the details of the whiplash 'tails', finished with a tiny pearl. Probably made in a Liberty workshop to an A. Knox design, as several of his designs carried notes for such opal work.* (Bellamy)

Plate 46. Turn-of-the-century pendants with Art Nouveau lines and Edwardian elegance. (Left to right) *platinum set with diamonds, rubies, emeralds and pearls; enamelled gold set with diamonds and pearls; simple knot design, reminiscent of negligée pendants, in enamel dotted with gold and set with pearls and turquoise; whiplash Art Nouveau design in enamel, set with peridots and houndstooth pearls.* (S. Rogers and M. Ventura; Brian and Lynn Holmes)

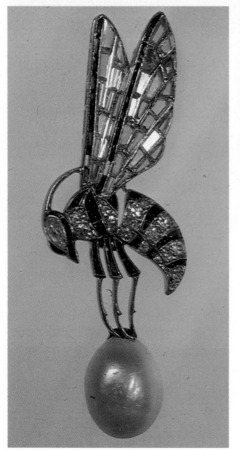

Plate 47. (Top left) *The quintessence of French Art Nouveau: a gold and* plique à jour *enamel brooch by Gautrait, set with blue stones on the peacock's plumes.* (John Jesse and Irina Laski)

Plate 48. (Top right) *Gold and enamel pendant by Lucien Gaillard.* (Hancocks & Co)

Plate 49. (Left) *A French Art Deco wasp brooch, about 1925. The body is of banded diamonds, black onyx and pearls.* (Hancocks & Co)

Plate 50. (Above) *Very fine brooch of abstract design which hovers between Edwardian and Art Deco. The platinum frame uses fine millegrain settings to hold diamonds, rubies, sapphires, emeralds and onyx.* (Johnson, Walker and Tolhurst)

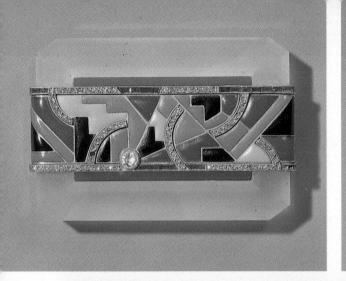

Plate 51. (Previous page) *Gold and enamel necklace with pearl and chrysoprase, by A. J. Cromer-Watt. (John Jesse and Irina Laski)*

Plate 52. (Top left) *Art Deco brooch has enamel around a carved crystal rectangle, with diamonds and rubies possibly by Sandoz. (Bellamy)*

Plate 53. (Top right) *Good Art Deco design on a belt-buckle, enamel on metal. (The Button Queen)*

Plate 54. (Left) *Art Deco 'movie-scene' brooch. Diamonds, rubies, sapphires and carved emerald set in platinum. English, about 1936.*

Plate 55. (Above) *Cocktail ring by Mauboussin, set with diamonds, sapphires and emeralds. (54, 55 Hancocks & Co)*

Camp. In 1916, he was repatriated and returned to Pforzheim, but the firm was confiscated by the British Government, and renamed White, Redgrove and Whyte. Whyte soon left the business, but White and Redgrove continued and is still in existence today.

Murrle, Bennett & Co was definitely only a wholesaler, and it seems that their large premises at 13 Charterhouse Street, with three storeys, did not contain a workshop, just offices and showrooms. Mürrle used a workshop in Pforzheim, where he went at least six times a year, and where he worked with his old schoolfriends Theodor Fahrner and Wilhelm Fühner and others. He had a permanent representative in Pforzheim, a man called Emanuel Saacke, who kept a look-out for designs and jewels which would be suitable for Murrle, Bennett's English outlets.

(My thanks are due to Mr Edward Mürrle and Mr Derek Redgrove for providing this information).

Fig. 20.15. Group of silver Murrle, Bennett & Co. jewels. Top: Very much in the Liberty style with blue and green enamelled leaves. Centre: The typical Murrle, Bennett style of hammered silver, set with amethysts. Right: Pendant with hammered silver, very large misshapen pearl, and the unmistakable 'rivet' pinheads. Left: A Knox design with floating enamel. Below: An unusual silver and mother-of-pearl ring. (Bellamy; John Jesse and Irina Laski)

The Darmstadt Colony

Apparently at this time there was a similar situation in Germany to that created by Liberty in England. A huge industry had developed around Pforzheim, where jewellery was mass-produced in great quantity. Fahrner himself manufactured this inexpensive jewellery, made from silver or low-carat gold and set with semi-precious stones, in the popular Jugendstil designs. Like Liberty, Fahrner employed excellent designers for his project, most of whom lived and worked in an artists' colony in Darmstadt.

This community had been set up under the patronage of the Grand Duke Ernst-Ludwig of Hesse, who took a great interest in the modern Arts and Crafts Movement, and who was anxious to stimulate the growth of artistic talent. Josef Maria Olbrich (1867-1908), Viennese architect, was asked to create this colony for gifted artists and he designed its buildings and interiors. Olbrich was a leading figure in the art movement called the Vienna Sezession, and had studied under its creator, the architect Otto Wagner (1841-1918). The movement was greatly influenced by Mackintosh and the Glasgow School, and developed a style based on similar precise, architectural lines, which was reflected in the jewellery of the period. Olbrich was amongst the designers used by Theodor Fahrner in his jewellery business, but there is no proof or indication of which pieces can be attributed to Olbrich. This is unfortunate, for Olbrich was such an important and talented artist, that any work by him would be classed as a major piece of jewellery.

In the publication *Modern Design in Jewellery and Fans*, a supplement to *Studio International*, the section on modern German jewellery is well illustrated by pieces designed by Olbrich and executed by Fahrner. Olbrich

Fig. 20.16. Silver brooch and buckle, set with amethyst, both marked by Fahrner of Pforzheim. The buckle also bears the initials of the designer Patriz Huber and the mark of Murrle, Bennett & Co. as importers. The brooch bears the initials M. I. G., for Moritz Gradl; a designer whose work was often executed by Fahrner, 1900-02. (John Jesse and Irina Laski)

also designed for another firm called D. and M. Loewenthal. The author says that Olbrich's jewellery is 'the best we have now in Germany because it is superior to fashions and periods. His jewels are pure, thoughtful works of art.' The jewels were made of silver or gold, sometimes hammered, set with lapis, pearls, bloodstones and amethysts, to obtain a very rich and sumptuous effect that at the same time retains simplicity of form and beauty.

Patriz Huber (1878-1902) was another German architect who joined the Darmstadt colony around 1900, and produced many jewel designs for Fahrner. Huber's mark, 'PH', has been found with Fahrner's and, to confuse

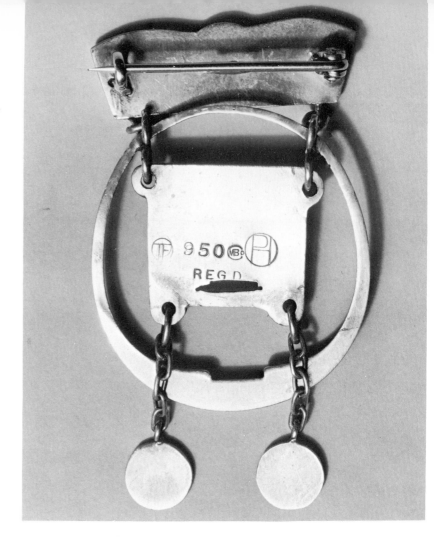

Fig 20.18. Back of the
Fahrner brooch designed by
Patriz Huber showing marks.
Right to left: P.H.; Murrle,
Bennett & Co.; 950 quality
mark; and T F for Fahrner.
(John Jesse and Irina Laski)

matters further, also with a '*déposé*' stamp, meaning that the piece was intended for the French market.

Henry Van de Velde (1863-1957), a Belgian architect and designer, was another who contributed to Fahrner's jewel designs around 1900. Van de Velde was a particularly important artist, a supporter of Art Nouveau, and influential in the development of modern movements. He spent some time in Germany between 1899 and 1917, where he achieved some of his best work.

It is possible then that, due to the connections between Fahrner and Murrle, Bennett, some of the jewellery made by Murrle, Bennett derived from these important designers. One last point, which raised doubts, centres on the marks found on these pieces: some bear the 850 German quality mark; some do not and others have the French *déposé* mark. There were no hard and fast rules as far as the marks were concerned. About eighty per cent of Murrle, Bennett's jewellery must have come from Pforzheim, where Mr Mürrle bought ready-made pieces or ordered new lines from sketches. If he bought ready-made, from Fahrner for example, the item would bear the TF mark already, and possibly the designer's mark. M B & Co would be added as an import mark. Those made up specially for Murrle, Bennett would just bear the firm's mark. A new range would be shown at Pforzheim at least twice a year, so there was an enormous amount of jewellery produced at that time. On an international level, the interchange, or sharing, of designs between Fahrner and Murrle, Bennett is probably unique.

At the London premises, in Charterhouse Street, the windows announced that Murrle, Bennett were 'Importers of Jewellery'; that their specialities were 'Gold, silver, gems' and 'Diamond-set paste'. Contemporary advertisements state the jewels were obtainable through high-class jewellers. The firm was very large, influential and forward-thinking in its production. It offered a very large range of jewels, of which fine paste was an important part. The paste was of very high quality, and stylish design; those made around 1915 had good Art Deco designs. The paste was expensive: the wholesale price of one pendant was £33. Stylish handbag frames were also made in paste. Other lines in the Murrle, Bennett repertoire included 'Scotch goods', a range called 'Mayfair', 'plain wire' jewels, 'treble clefs' (gold wire pins and clips in this shape), Etruscan style, a large chain section looked after by Miss Rose, muff chains, veil fasteners, boa fasteners, dental goods, small gold accessories like pencils and all the traditional items of jewellery of that period. The comprehensive scope of this firm is often not fully appreciated and 'modern art' was only one of its ranges. The business was made up from several different companies: Murrle, Bennett & Co. Ltd., The Artistic Rolled Gold Co., Artistic Novelties Ltd, the L.F. Brenner Co., and the overseas firm, Murrle, Bennett Export Ltd.

When White and Redgrove took over, they kept up the high fashion image, and switched the paste speciality to marcasite. They made excellent marcasite jewellery, between the wars, still in Pforzheim, and also made stylish Art Deco blue chalcedony jewellery.

Apart from this history of the firm, it is important for collectors to distinbuish the firm's stronger, modern style jewels. Murrle, Bennet & Company made a great many gold jewels, usually with a very rich matt sheen, and set with turquoises — usually very large stones speckled with black or brown — or with large misshapen pearls, opal matrix and sometimes carved opal, in the shape of a Red Indian's head, for example. The outlines of these gold pieces were simple but fluid, and the substantial areas of gold narrowed into fine gold wires, which were twisted into Celtic-style knots or interlacing, trailed over the pearl or turquoise to form a kind of cage, or sewed two parts of a pendant or brooch with wire stitches, in imitation of hand-made craftsmanship. The gold was very often cut out into curved shapes, similar to Knox designs, and the whiplash motif was extensively used. A particular characteristic of Murrle, Bennett is the use of straight lines, usually vertical, either as fine gold wires, or as shapes cut out from the main gold-work. Some brooches made of gold only with no stones, consisted of very plain horizontal lines, slightly curved into the familiar pointed shield shape. These forms very closely follow advanced German designs of the time, and are obviously influenced by the first Sezession Exhibition in Vienna in 1898, the year the Darmstadt colony was founded.

Silver jewels were similar to the gold in some ways, but there was also a range of more delicate necklets, decorated with enamels, and brooches with stylised leaves, in the English taste, and in the style usually associated

Fig. 20.19. German silver and amazonite brooch marked C.B. for Carl Braun, and 800 for the silver mark. The design is very modernistic, typical of German and Austrian designers of around 1910. (John Jesse and Irina Laski)

with Liberty. Silver was often set with amethysts, or with mother-of-pearl, and the surface was hammered or scattered very precisely with tiny pin-head bumps which gave the impression of rivets. These rivet-heads are another typical hallmark of Murrle, Bennett jewels, and perhaps they echoed the Crafts revival practice, because they gave the impression of a hand-made piece. Alternatively, the rivet-heads may derive from a French fashion of about the 1860s for jewels with a mechanical look. Apart from delicate festoon necklets, shapes were well-defined and strong, with geometrically curved or straight cut-outs, twisted wires and again the silver stitches linking parts of a pendant. At the start of their production some jewels may have been hand-made, and later machine-produced pieces were hand-finished.

Pendants and brooches, in both silver and gold, are the most common; rings are much harder to find. The mark of the firm was 'M B Co', the B joined to the M inside the C (formed as a circle) for Company. When pieces are unmarked, it is sometimes easy to recognise the Murrle, Bennett German style, but in other cases they look more English, like Liberty jewels. Mr Mürrle was obviously very clever at finding German designs that would appeal to the English. One clue may lie in the materials he used. While designs travel from country to country, it seems that favourite national

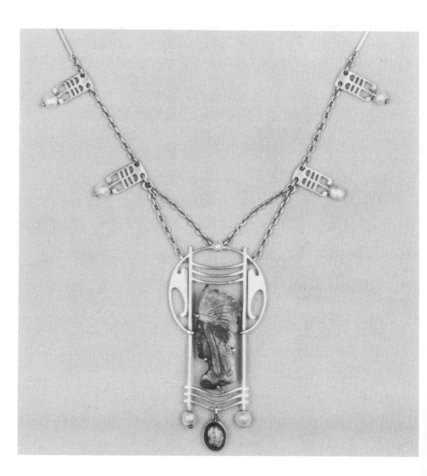

Fig. 20.20. Gold necklace by Murrle, Bennett & Co., set with an opal carved as a Red Indian's head. (Ewing)

materials remain: and although the Murrle, Bennett designs look very German in line, the materials they used — particularly the combinations of gold and turquoise and silver and mother-of-pearl — are very English.

From advertisements of the period, it appears that a firm called Connell tried to compete with Liberty. Around 1909, when the vogue for the 'Tudric' style of pewter wares was declining, Liberty sold several designs to Connell. It is possible that they may also have sold them some jewellery designs. Connell, calling themselves 'modern artists in jewellery and silverware' of 83 Cheapside, London, advertised a range of silver jewels, in styles similar to those described above, and featuring a bracelet which was identical to one shown in a Murrle, Bennett advertisement of the same time. Connell sold through the Goldsmiths and Silversmiths Company, and so were probably wholesalers too. Apart from that, very little else is known about Connell, and presumably there were many other jewellers working in the same way.

C.H. Horner

Moving one step further away from the kind of direct artistic involvement of Liberty & Company, the Halifax firm of Charles Horner was a pioneer of highly commercial mass-production. Charles Horner jewels were mostly silver and enamel, bearing the maker's mark 'C. H.', and made in the early years of the twentieth century. They suddenly became very popular with the growing interest in Art Nouveau jewels, and especially because a name could be attached to them.

Fig. 20.21. Enamelled silver winged scarab brooch by Charles Horner, a speciality of the firm. (Brian and Lynn Holmes)

Charles Henry Horner's father was the inventor of the 'Dorcas' thimble, which proved an enormous success and led to a new factory and a large family company. Two sons carried on the business after their father's death, and it was Charles Henry Horner who was the talent behind the flourishing jewellery concern. He himself was a very good artist and designed most of the pieces which are now considered to be typical of the firm.

Charles Horner was remarkable in his field of mass-production because every stage of the jewellery manufacture was carried out in his factory; i.e. each piece was made from design stage to the finished product on the premises — no other firm at the time was doing this. They even melted the silver grain themselves into ingots and then made sheets and strips. Horner imported special machines from Germany to produce lengths of silver chain from fine silver wire. His factories were large and employed many women.

One of the specialities of the firm was making silver pendants with their own fitted chains. With this new venture, Horner started a trade which had not previously existed north of Birmingham, that still monopolised the industry.

Horner very cleverly adapted the Art Nouveau style to his plans for mass-marketing. He carefully selected the basic, strongest elements of modern design. He simplified forms in many cases and, although many pieces seem very similar, there was a large repertoire of jewels. In all, he came up with the right combination of price, quality and a 'modern' look which was easy to appreciate and to wear. The quality of the jewels is not generally considered equal to that of Liberty or Murrle, Bennett; but considering the huge quantities produced, the jewellery appears consistently well-made, and distinctively enamelled.

There are many standard or ordinary designs, but occasionally you may come across a rather better and more unusual piece of Charles Horner; these can be highly individual and artistic. Silver pendants, brooches and hat-pins were the most plentiful, and some gold jewellery was made as well; rings are very hard to find and were not a speciality of the firm. Mostly the jewellery is characterised by mingled peacock-blue and green or yellow and green enamels; open-work borders and designs which echo rather stiffly the whiplash motifs; Celtic interlacing and stylised rounded leaves. The firm made small simple knot-brooches, sometimes a twist set with a carved amethyst thistle. Another frequent Horner motif, and one of the most pleasing, is the winged scarab, enamelled in blues or greens, and forming a pendant, a tiny brooch or sitting on top of their famous hat-pins.

These hat-pins were particularly popular between 1900 and 1914. Some are executed in gold, but more often they are in silver with enamel decoration, plain Art Nouveau swirls, or knots set with pearls or semi-precious stones (this last type was often sold as a pair). The scarab or winged insect hat-pin motif is often found with the body set with mother-of-pearl and the wings brightly enamelled. The jewels, with the maker's mark 'C. H.', bear a Chester hallmark from the nearby assay offices.

Fig. 20.22. Silver belt buckle in fluid Art Nouveau design made by William Comyns, London 1903. The back is stamped with the Design Registry number. This means that a drawing would have been sent to the Design Registry for the design to be patented. (Bellamy)

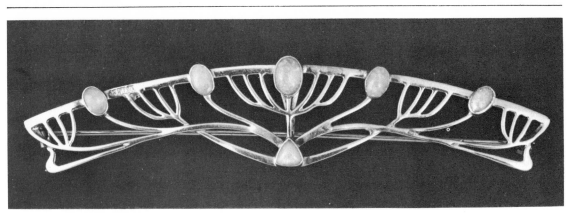

Fig. 20.23. Gold and opal open-work brooch with cabochon opals, made by an unidentified firm, B H J. About 1905. (Sotheby's Belgravia)

Liberty Style Designers

Swirls of silver, with blue, green, lime and yellow enamels, can be found in numerous variations. There were many free-lance designers, including several women, at work at the turn of the century. They were employed by well-established jewellers and silversmiths who needed to keep up with current trends. The quality of designs varied tremendously; some fell more into the Arts and Crafts categories. Some of the best of these designers were Kate Allen, Annie McLeish and Kate Fisher who designed clasps and belt-buckles for the silversmith William Hutton. A traditional silversmith like William Comyns would manufacture silver buckles in stylish floral Art Nouveau designs.

Child and Child was a London firm of silversmiths and jewellers working at the turn of the century, interpreting the new fashion in their own way. The firm was founded in 1880, and later moved to premises in Kensington. After this move, in 1891, they began to manufacture the particular kind of silver and enamel jewellery with which they are now usually associated. 'High fashion' pieces supplemented their usual stock of traditional jewellery and silver, made in the grand Edwardian style and incorporating revived eighteenth century designs of the day. Soon they became jewellers to the Princess of Wales, and always maintained a very high standard of workmanship. Their speciality was enamel-work, particularly a very strong turquoise enamel on engine-turned silver backgrounds (so giving a wavy texture to the colour), which were usually shaped as wings or leaves. They were well-made, appear substantial and even slightly solid; as if the conventional nature of the firm did not quite allow the indulgence in free Art Nouveau forms, materials and mingled enamels.

Buckles made by Child and Child are excellent. One example consisted of butterflies, in turquoise enamel, joined by overlapping wings. Their enamelling skill and experience enabled them to produce good translucent *plique à jour* effects. They made up some jewels designed by the famous artist Edward Burne-Jones, and some of their work shows his influence, particularly in strong lines and deep, rich colours. Their mark was a sunflower with the initials, 'C C', on either side of the stem; but sometimes the signature was hidden on the silver under the enamel.

The area which we have been discussing is a specialised branch of Art

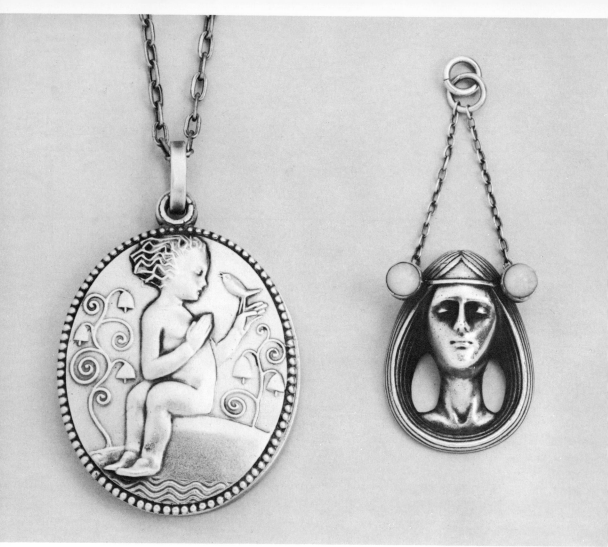

Fig. 20.24. Left: Silver locket made by B. Loethoeur for the Wiener Werkstätte. This is a rare piece and epitomises the Austrian style. (John Jesse and Irina Laski). Right: Fine silver and opal pendant by Austrian designer Gustav Gurschner. He was a sculptor, working in bronze, and his work fully expressed the Viennese style. He did some designs for jewellery. About 1901. (Bellamy)

Nouveau jewellery, far removed from the works of art created by craftsmen like Lalique, but nonetheless part of the same sweeping style. One advantage of the mass-production methods, so often deplored, is that they have left us with a wealth of examples to collect and wear. Marked Liberty jewels have that extra attraction, partly because the designs were very good, and partly because of the close association of the name with Art Nouveau. Murrle, Bennett & Company holds the fascination of the strong, German modernistic style, which may be an acquired taste; and Charles Horner pieces, interesting because he was the original totally-commercial manufacturer, are easier to appreciate, and make a very good starting point in many cases.

Other collectors may prefer to become directly acquainted with the purer styles, and they should try to distinguish between standard pieces and those which feel special, as if they come from a particularly good design. Always buy the best and most distinctive of each firm. A collection based on any one or several of these jewellers will certainly show the results of the commercial interpretations of individual designs, and the success of bringing the academic art movements to the people through jewellery.

21. Edwardian and Art Deco Jewellery

The first three decades of the present century enjoyed some of the most extravagant, elegantly beautiful and outrageous jewellery in the history of personal adornment. It took some time before collectors in general were able to step back far enough to admire early twentieth century jewels, but now these are attracting well-deserved attention.

The opening years of the century were still under the spell of Art Nouveau, and the field of *avant-garde* jewellery was led by French artists like Lalique (see Chapter 17, Signed Art Nouveau Jewellery) Vever, Fouquet, Gaillard. Meanwhile the grand houses, like Cartier and Boucheron, were concentrating on traditional diamond jewellery in the eighteenth century fashion. In England, conventional gem-set pieces were still being worn alongside the more daring Art Nouveau. The Arts and Crafts Movement and the Liberty styles had taken their share of the market, and for smaller budgets the Birmingham factories churned out cheap silver brooches and trinkets. (See Chapters 17, 19 and 20.) These diverse fashions set the scene for the new century, which was so hopefully welcomed, with a new monarch on the throne of England — Edward VII and his elegant queen, Alexandra.

The 'Edwardian' Style

The 'Edwardian' style of the first decade has a very special flavour, but is often neglected for being sandwiched between two such powerful artistic forces as Art Nouveau and Art Deco. Art Nouveau has become such a popular collecting area, so well appreciated and understood in retrospect, that we tend to forget that, at the time, it was treated with distrust or even disgust in some circles. While adventurous individual artists concentrated on design, new materials, and forms, large firms were making headway in improving and revitalising the appearance, setting and cutting of diamond jewellery.

The sobriety of Victoria's reign was thankfully followed by the extravagance and sophistication of the court of Edward VII. High society at last had a pleasure-loving figure to follow and abandoned itself wholeheartedly to the pursuit of luxury and enjoyment and the life of the Belle Époque.

The Edwardian style of jewellery had its roots in the closing years of the

Fig. 21.1. Pearl and diamond négligée pendant, with two different coloured pearls hanging from a hexagonal, flat-cut diamond. Early 20th century, but forecasting the geometry of the 1920s and the adventurous cutting of diamonds. (Sotheby's)

Victorian era, when the Princess of Wales had already become a leader of fashion. She wore pearl dog-collars, diamond star and crescent brooches, and later delicately-coloured gem-set pendants which had just a respectable hint of Art Nouveau (see Chapter 18, Pendants at the Turn of the Century). By the time that Art Nouveau began to wane, the true Edwardian style was in full swing in Britain, and Art Deco was under way on the Continent. Nowhere is the Edwardian style better represented than in the jewels of the period. Diamonds were essential (see Chapter 1, Diamond Brooches) but they had taken on a new and sophisticated look: Edwardian diamond pieces are amongst the finest jewels ever made. In reaction to the heavy, solid sprays of the nineteenth century, diamonds were now made to look as fine and delicate as possible, to match the profusion of lace, silk, feathers and the total femininity of the Edwardian lady.

The new effect was largely achieved by the qualities of platinum, which had been used for setting diamonds since the end of the nineteenth century. Invisible settings of platinum extended and flattered the brilliance and whiteness of the stones and the millegrain method was the most popular. This type of setting required that the thin band of metal gripping the stone should be ridged, or textured with tiny grains or beads, thus creating an extremely fine, almost imperceptible rim for the diamond. Another quality, the strength of platinum, was skilfully exploited so that jewels were remarkably slim and lightweight—masterpieces of engineering. Very precise open-work designs or scalloped patterned edges were possible in platinum and added to the illusion of diamond jewels so that they looked as fine and white as hand-made lace. A major characteristic was the use of 'knife wires', again usually of platinum. These were thin blades of metal, set with the sharp edges facing upwards, so that only a fine, taut thread or 'knife edge' of metal was visible. Efforts to match the flimsy fabrics and hand embroidery always worn by the rich resulted in brooches formed as bows of platinum gauze in a honeycomb pattern, or a kind of fine mesh which resembled *petit point* embroidery.

Brooches, pendants and rings were made to these designs, dominated by diamonds in the same way that fashion was dominated by white. Other popular combinations were sapphires and diamonds, amethysts and diamonds, and opals were still in favour. The French eighteenth century decorative influence could still be detected in the ribbon bows, garlands and baskets of flowers. One recurring motif is the stream, ribbon or line of diamonds, gently flowing but restrained and symmetrical. Many pendants do incorporate traces of Art Nouveau lines, while other brooches herald Art Deco with subtle geometric patterns, and glimpses of sunburst or radial designs.

Several specific forms of jewels emerged at this time, and one of these was the 'négligée' pendant. This had two drops of unequal length hanging from another single stone, all on a slim chain. The 'sautoir', or long necklace, usually of pearls or chain and ending in a tassel, was another favourite piece of Edwardian jewellery.

Technical Advances

The twentieth century coincided with several advances which contributed to the revolution in jewel design and manufacture; the principal one being that

huge progress had been made in gem stone-cutting. The pear shape fitted in well with elegant Edwardian themes, but again there was occasionally a hint of even more adventurous stone-cutting to come, with baguette diamonds or calibré-cut sapphires or emeralds. The inventive use of stones and settings can often be obscured by the subtlety and refinement of the Edwardian style.

Jewellery designs between 1901 and 1911 were not as self-conscious as Art Nouveau or Art Deco, but rather understated — as relaxed and tasteful as the people they adorned — and marked above all by a restrained and noble elegance. There are many pieces of jewellery that bridge the transitional

Fig. 21.3. Quiet Edwardian elegance in delicate pearl and diamond jewels, with an 18th century influence on design evident in the use of ribbon bows and garlands. Tassels were especially popular, and pearl chokers, like the example in the centre, by Cartier; the small rectangular brooch is also by Cartier. (S. Rogers; M. Ventura)

period between Edwardian and Art Deco, and naturally for a while they shared similar elements of design. Apart from this grand and expensive jewellery, many other everyday jewels were still popular: gold bar-brooches; half-hoop bangles set with pearls, diamonds or coloured stones; gypsy rings with stones set into the band, so that the top of the stone is level with the surface of the gold; cross-over rings set with diamonds and sapphires, half-hoop rings; snake rings; and gold chain bracelets set with turquoises or pearls. The bands of gypsy rings were normally wider at the centre, usually set with one or three stones. Occasionally the gem would be dropped into a star-shaped recess, which was known as star-setting. Gypsy rings were worn by both men and women. All these designs were being sold in the 1890s or even earlier, and so are labelled Victorian. However they continued to be worn well into the twentieth century, and most examples found today are in fact Edwardian.

Bar-brooches, first worn in the late nineteenth century, basically consisted of a slim horizontal bar of gold, in the centre of which was placed a decorative motif. Every kind of motif imaginable was used for bar-brooches, and they can be very amusing to collect and attractive to wear. Sporting motifs were popular from the 1890s, with a general vogue for sporting jewellery which was encouraged by women's more active participation in sports. Tiny charms set on to bar-brooches included hunting horns, foxes' heads, riding crops, tennis rackets, jockeys, animals, birds, flowers, lucky charms such as the horseshoe or wishbone, or just pretty designs of gold, pearls or stones. Sometimes there was also a stone or motif set at each end of the bar. Bar-brooches could be made completely of gold, then the twist, knot or bow were among favoured motifs. These little brooches continued as popular accessories during the Edwardian years. However the leisured complacency and prosperity of Edwardian life was brought to an abrupt end by the harsh realities of war in 1914.

After World War I, society emerged in quite a different light. It was transformed by greatly changed ideas and attitudes; it was slightly disillusioned or cynical, but with an eager appetite for life. This appetite was to have a startling effect on the decorative arts, an effect that received extra impetus from a redistribution of wealth among the classes. The Edwardian era could never be recaptured.

Art Deco

It was in this new atmosphere of feverish restlessness and recklessness that Art Deco bloomed. The seeds of the style had been sown before the war, its elements gathered from various sources; these once fused together, completely enveloped the 1920s.

Art Deco is a loose, all-embracing term which is now used to describe the style of decorative arts prevalent during this period between the two World Wars, in Europe and America. The term was derived from the great Paris exhibition of 1925, called the Exposition des Arts Décoratifs et Industriels Modernes. The highly distinctive style has become rather simplified in the public eye; but after looking at some typical examples of the period, it should be quite easy for the collector to recognise a piece of Art Deco jewellery. The 1920s and 1930s, the age of the cocktail party, was itself a sparkling cocktail of social, political and artistic changes, all of which affected jewel design, to some extent. In spite of the seemingly easily-attached label, there were many complex influences at work, and several different stages and styles within the Art Deco framework.

As with so many collecting areas mentioned in this book, a closer look into the social background leads to a fuller enjoyment and appreciation of the jewels. This applies particularly to Art Deco, when 'style' became the essence of life, with the same design themes mirrored in clothes, buildings, furniture, sculptures, advertising posters, everyday objects such as crockery and cutlery, and of course in jewellery.

Two main styles dominated the 1920s and 1930s; Art Deco and Modernism. Art Deco followed the organic fluidity of Art Nouveau. It emerged around 1910 and continued until 1925, the date of the exhibition which gave the style its name, and which signalled both its climax and the start of its decline. To some extent, it was a reaction against Art Nouveau; yet at the same time, it borrowed from and developed out of the earlier style. Very generally, and in contrast to the pale colours and natural lines of Art Nouveau, Art Deco was characterised by vivid colours, formalised floral decoration, spiral motifs and a stronger, more precise use of sinuous curves, spreading into ovals, circles and octagonal panels. A major change of taste was brought about when the Ballet Russe, masterminded by Diaghilev and designed by Léon Bakst, enthralled Paris in 1910. Costumes were very bold,

Fig. 21.4. Group of silver jewels made by Georg Jensen, early 20th century. (Private collection)

Fig. 21.5. Two bronze medallions, by P. Turin and M. Delannoy. (Private collection)

exotic and Eastern, notably those for *Scheherezade*; above all, they were vibrant with strong, bright, clear, primary colours. The formalised flower motifs, found on so many jewels, derived from Charles Rennie Mackintosh's rose design, angular and austere, that reached the Paris world of fashion via Austrian and German artists. Other important elements of early Art Deco design lingered from the Edwardian concentration on graceful eighteenth century design, retaining such motifs as garlands and baskets of flowers.

In the 1920s, the style began to absorb new influences, principally from Negro art and Cubism, which gradually guided designs further towards geometry and simplicity. This period marked the transition from Art Deco to Modernism, which finally took over after 1925.

By the 1930s, the main idea was to banish all unnecessary ornament. Curves were more austere or converted into angles, shapes were streamlined and exact; Cubism and the machine were evidently inspirations. The Depression encouraged this move towards austerity and a new style was created that was very much a product of its own time, moulded from contemporary influences, looking forward instead of back and expressing a consciousness of its own place in history. This then, very basically, sums up the changes which took place in decorative design during this period, which is covered by the collective term Art Deco.

The Art Deco of the 1920s aimed at ornament for its own sake, so that every item in everyday use was decorated to look attractive and fashionable. Perhaps it was intended to distract people from unpleasant memories of wartime. The look was one of total design on every object and every detail, and the effect, far removed from the naturalism of Art Nouveau, was contrived and unreal.

Modernism sprang from a more aesthetic approach, aiming at purity of line in art and architecture. These two distinct styles did to some extent show themselves in jewellery design, but the change is not clearly defined; for collectors of period jewellery, it is still most useful to talk about and look for Art Deco jewels generally, meaning those of the 1920s and 1930s, but keeping an eye open for evidence of the various stages of changing motifs, materials and forms.

Jewellery of this period also divides into separate compartments; either very expensive, i.e. precious jewels; or purely decorative, i.e. costume jewels, including deliberate and effective fakes.

After the War a new class had made its presence felt: this was the new rich or 'Nouveau Riche' who had mostly come from humble origins, made enormous fortunes during the war and then found themselves with a great deal of money — which took them away from the pasts they usually hoped to conceal — but with no real standing in society. The new rich used their wealth to

Fig. 21.6. 1930s costume jewellery: a clip of black plastic, amazonite and marcasite. It is quite convincingly realistic, and effective in wear. (Private collection)

create appearances and to buy their way into society with glamour and fashion. The most lavish and extravagant entertainments were planned to tempt the upper classes and the influential personalities to accept and so include the members of this new class in their magic circle. To win this kind of favour, what was also needed was 'chic' and all this new-found wealth could buy a great deal of that. In this way, a huge new market for luxury goods was created, and Paris was the centre for this artistic activity.

In spite of ravaged countrysides, a nation maimed and devastated by war, Paris continued to lead the world in fashion and taste, and plunged itself into frivolity, self-indulgence, and a world of beauty. Paul Poiret was the foremost fashion designer with unquestionable influence, working towards the total design look. His clothes matched the interiors and, of course, accessories and jewels matched the mood of the clothes and customers. During this period the dressmaker or couturier exerted considerable influence on jewel design.

Another aspect that changed the appearance of jewels was the new role of the woman. During the War, many women had taken on men's jobs and had become used to a taste of emancipation; they were very reluctant to return to their former submissive image. On the contrary, they were determined to display their new-found freedom, often adopting outrageous fashions to prove it and, particularly in the 1930s, choosing fashions that demanded more masculine (i.e. strong and basic) designs and colour combinations in jewels. Women cut their hair short and even wore masculine clothes sometimes. They now joined in more sports and pastimes previously reserved for gentlemen, and again their jewels expressed their ambitions in this area too.

Materials Used in the Jewels

The extravagance and frivolity of the post-war atmosphere permeated jewel design, and coincided with some vital new technical innovations. Valuable stones continued to be set in conventional jewels, but firms such as Cartier,

Fig. 21.7. Carved ivory ring with its own box made by Clement Mère, a furniture designer; and heavy silver ring by Delon, a silversmith working in the manner of the expressionist painters. (Lewis M. Kaplan)

Lacloche, Boucheron and Mauboussin caught the spirit of adventure and experimented with high-fashion designs in costly materials. Never before had such untempered luxury, exquisite craftsmanship and extreme design been expressed in jewels, and in conjunction with a break with the tradition governing the use of precious stones. Platinum was used freely, with great effect in setting diamonds and achieving light and lively mounts, precise shapes and outlines. This valuable metal was widely used until the economical crises of the 1930s meant that white gold was considered a more practical alternative.

Diamonds, always a status symbol, truly became 'a girl's best friend', and were combined with platinum to create an all-white effect of stunning luxury. The value of the diamond no longer paralysed the jeweller into timidity and so new cuts were developed for all precious stones, to fit the new designs with corresponding geometrical and fanciful shapes: triangles or trapeze-cuts, baguettes, oblong or emerald cuts. Any stone cut to a special shape was described as calibré-cut.

Fig. 21.8. An example of a less expensive Art Deco item: a belt buckle with a very stylised scene in black silhouette of a peacock against a pale pink and peach background, in early plastic. (Ingeborg)

The combination of different types of precious stones in one piece of jewellery was unprecedented: rubies, sapphires, emeralds, diamonds echoed the new vogue for bright colours. Colour is a very important factor in Art Deco jewels, linked to the use of materials, and it was originally the Ballet Russe that had stirred this passion for bold and colourful jewels. The tendency towards colour was even stronger after the War.

Apart from precious stones, there were imaginative experiments made with semi-precious stones to stretch the range of colours and to create equally decorative but less expensive jewels. Favourite combinations were onyx, crystal, jade, coral and turquoise: these were mixed with even less valuable but effective materials, like lacquer, enamel and pastes. The Chinese and Oriental influence encouraged the use of certain materials, particularly carved jade, red lacquer and enamels. Semi-precious stones were very often mixed with diamonds, especially to obtain the stark and stunning effect of black onyx and white diamonds, or crystal and diamonds used in the all-white vogue. Pearls are to be found through Art Deco jewellery, either as a contrast to coloured stones, or with diamonds, adding a textural interest to colourless jewels.

Fig. 21.9. Another belt buckle, enamelled in black and white in a cube pattern. (Ingeborg)

Fashion decreed that jewels were to be either the luxurious creations by such names as Boucheron, Van Cleef and Arpels, Chaumet and Cartier, or very obviously and unashamedly fake. Costume jewellery may be more accessible to the collector, and it is a particularly interesting area because designs applied to cheap jewels were excellent and very characteristic. Often they were even more *avant-garde* and zany, because of the low value of the materials. Up-to-the-minute jewellery could quickly go out of fashion, and if it cost relatively little it could then be easily discarded. Their low intrinsic value has also saved many pieces from being broken up, the fate suffered by many more expensive jewels.

Purely decorative or 'costume' jewellery was made of semi-precious stones alone, or of bright enamels on metal, marcasites, plastics, pastes (see Chapter 6, Collecting in Unusual Materials). Sometimes they are such successful imitations of the 'real thing' that it is hard to know if a piece is of, say, plastic and pastes or onyx and diamonds. Lucky collectors might just possibly find that piece of apparently costume jewellery, that looks too good to be real, but is in fact an item of extravagance in precious stones.

It was the legendary couturier, Coco Chanel, who made costume jewellery acceptable, and thereafter fakes, plastics and simulants were not considered to be mere imitations but chic fashion accessories. Fake pearls were particularly associated with Chanel, and these were worn as chokers, or strands of varying lengths, as pins or as part of a brooch or pendant. Sometimes the pretence was flaunted by wearing fake pearls of impossibly large size or outrageous colours.

Plastics added a new dimension to costume jewellery and have been dealt with separately in Chapter 6. They do offer the collector opportunities to capture that all-important style at low prices. During the 1920s and 1930s, the versatility and decorative possibilities of the new material were fully exploited, often by top designers. Such ornaments could be mass-produced in fashionable patterns and at reasonable prices, providing cheap chic.

So materials went from one extreme to another; the whim of the rich for frankly artificial jewels stood them in good stead during the 1930s, when bad financial situations meant fake jewels were often a necessity. As the public began to regard them as direct imitations, they begin to lose their appeal; this accounts for a lull in interest in costume jewellery for some time after this period.

Fig. 21.10. Silver parrot brooch in the style of Georg Jensen, marked with maker's initials, A. K. (Private collection)

Motifs of the 1920s and 1930s

The French were undoubtedly unrivalled in the design and manufacture of jewellery during this period, and it is in French jewellery that the most stunning Art Deco motifs can be found. The fashion designers, led by the versatile Paul Poiret, dominated Art Deco and dictated the kind of accessories that were essential to their creations. In England, women were less affected by this mania, and tended to be more conservative in their choice of jewels.

All the recognised vocabulary of Art Deco ornament can be found on jewellery; the French were particularly skilful at moulding materials to the designs. Oriental influences were powerful in all areas of design. In jewels, they were expressed as carved jade pendants, ear-rings and bracelets; black onyx or black enamel served as a background for Chinese motifs, or for the

Japanese garden scenes that decorated lacquer cigarette-cases. Coral, carved and mounted with a black background also worked towards the Chinese look. Chinese or exotic motifs often appear to control the arrangement of stones in the diamond and platinum set jewels. The shape of an Oriental plant, for example, might be formed by the precise outlines of the diamonds; while a chrysanthemum, the Japanese imperial emblem, would be carved from precious or semi-precious stones, such as lapis-lazuli, with jade leaves.

The discovery of Tutankhamun's tomb in 1923 astonished the world, and the beauty and the colour of the ancient jewels stimulated copies of Egyptian-inspired designs and forms (see Chapter 14, Egyptian Revival Jewellery). These were mainly decorative jewels, stressing the 'stagey' and dramatic character of Art Deco, an aspect of the age that was captured perfectly by the bronze figurative sculptures. It is a good idea to look at some of these, especially those depicting girls in Egyptian or exotic costumes. The outward appearance was all that mattered: the effect of ancient Egyptian ornament was achieved by the use of humble materials such as coloured enamels and by evocative symbols like the sphinx, pyramids, Pharaoh and the serpent. The vogue encouraged the use of turquoise, a favourite stone of the ancient Egyptians, as well as lapis-lazuli, brighly coloured enamels and the use of geometric patterns.

Exoticism became a firm feature of Art Deco design. From a different direction, American Indian Art infiltrated jewellery, and designers made use of the outlines of stepped Aztec temples, which suited the move towards geometry.

Traditional Art Deco motifs — formalised flowers in garlands or baskets, leaves, and octagonal or oblong 'tongue' plaques — are all seen on French jewellery, made before 1925, building up to the height of ornamentation. Art Deco revelled in unreal, man-made flowers and leaves and subjected Nature

Fig. 21.11. Silver belt by Guevel, a French jeweller, showing the influences of Fauvism in its stylised designs of wild animals. About 1925-8. Two brooches by Jean Desprès, with malachite and blue agate set in silver and gold. (Cobra)

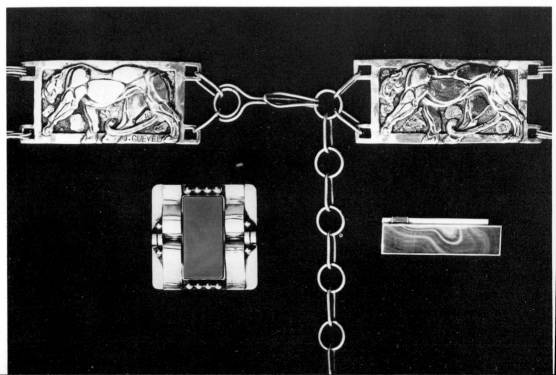

Fig. 21.12. Motor-car brooch in gold with diamonds and rubies, with moving wheels. An example of the combination of 1930s frivolity with style, reflecting the obsession with travel and speed. (Brian and Lynn Holmes)

to the ruling concept of total design. Flowers in jewellery become stylised, petals are shown as having stiff regular curves, leaves are naively angular; all contributing to a flat, contrived but stylish look. The Mackintosh rose — a squared, rolled flower — had a substantial effect on all flower motifs. The simplest of flower and leaf outlines were traced in diamond jewels; precious and semi-precious stones were carved as flowers and leaves, and arranged all together to produce a jewelled bouquet. There was rarely a specific species to identify, except occasionally in the case of oriental blossoms, with their climbing jagged stems.

Movement was a theme which was successfully applied to jewels; not the flowing organic movement of Art Nouveau, but the controlled, frozen, geometrical impressions of the ziggurat, the flash of lightning, a leaping gazelle, a fountain, and the most fashionable of pets, the sleek greyhound. All these ideas occur in jewels, either depicted in enamels, or as carved stones on gold or silver brooches. After the leisurely Edwardian life, the 1920s and 1930s became totally obsessed with speed, with new modes of travel. This preoccupation was boldly stated in jewellery too. The gazelle or greyhound represented streamline, fleet-footed animals, while aeroplanes, motor cars, trains and ocean liners all contributed to the feverish pace of life. Publicity posters then transformed them into major decorative elements. Small brooches were shaped as diamond aeroplanes, motor-car brooches of gold were set with rubies and moveable black enamel wheels. The speed and colour of the racing track was a favourite spectacle, and brooches and tie-pins were created as winning-posts — perfectly plain circles set with diamonds and calibré-cut sapphires, emeralds or rubies — as diamond racehorses ridden by colourful jockeys, or as an enamelled jockey cap.

It was the golden age of ocean liners and luxury cruises: in 1935, the French liner *Normandie* was sent on its maiden voyage as a kind of floating advertisement for French decorative arts. Its lavish interiors had been designed by the most famous artists of the time. Amusing brooches, often in plastic or chrome and enamels, were miniature versions of the great liner.

The speed theme prompted the use of the arrow motif in Art Deco jewellery too: a streamlined strip of diamonds or onyx tipped with diamonds or coloured stones.

While France was the centre of fashion and taste, from America came the wave of Hollywood style. The huge movie industry, the glamour of the stars, the money, the parties, and the movie-moguls added new ideas to the design repertoire. The Hollywood style can usually be found in jewels of the whimsical, amusing type made of artificial materials, but occasionally the theme was adapted to precious stones with exquisite workmanship. One of the best jewel motifs to emerge from the Hollywood style is the palm tree. A brooch could create a scene with the palm tree, perhaps shading a luxurious motor car. The leaves of the palm could be carved in hard stones, jade for example, while the tree trunk would be in gold or platinum, and the car in shiny black enamel. While the vogue was for suppressing colour, white gold set with diamonds might express these symbols of Californian glamour. Similar designs were just as well thought out and detailed in plastics or semi-precious stones.

Through all these motifs and the highly decorative jewels of the 1920s, crept the growing trend towards geometry and abstraction. Ziggurats, sunbursts, fountains were all angular but still representational and used as part of the totally ornamental approach that dominated the 1920s. After 1925, designs began to move towards simplicity, as if the Paris Exposition had provided a surfeit of indigestible decoration. Gradually ornament was discarded and abstract shapes were preferred, while non-representational designs altered the appearance of jewels. Guiding influences were Cubism, Negro art and an interest in machinery. The move towards Modernism can be traced in jewels of the 1930s. Diamond-set pieces were created in more abstract designs, while shapes and outlines became very simple; a ring of diamonds or linked circles of diamonds and onyx; plaque pendants of onyx, coral or crystal; diamonds combined with bright enamels, concentrating on pure shapes and not pictures. Cheaper jewellery became more of a necessity during the financially troubled years of the early 1930s, and looked very attractive with its enamels in jazzy designs, strongly influenced by Cubism.

For a while there was a vogue for heavy, barbaric jewels of ivory, horn or simulants, heavy slave bangles, or jewels that reflected the preoccupation with machinery by using motifs such as screw-heads, ball bearings or girders. Chrome jewellery became distinctive at this stage, and deserves attention from collectors. In spite of the humble material, spectacular modernistic wide bracelets and necklets were made of long flattened, moveable links, very reminiscent of Bauhaus ideas. Some aspects continued from the 1920s into the 1930s of course; the Chinese flavour for instance, the use of black in the form of onyx or enamel, and carved coral and jade.

In fact, the general trend was towards softness, after the harsh boyish look of the mid 1920s. Although jewel motifs became more geometrical and abstract, they were also more relaxed, streamlined, understated and freed from unnecessary clutter, focusing more on a purity of line.

Favoured Forms

Every age has its favourite items of jewellery, usually blending with clothes and fashions, and the Art Deco period had strong preferences. Certain relics of the Victorian years were abhorred, partly because of their associations with the image of the repressed female, partly because they were impractical.

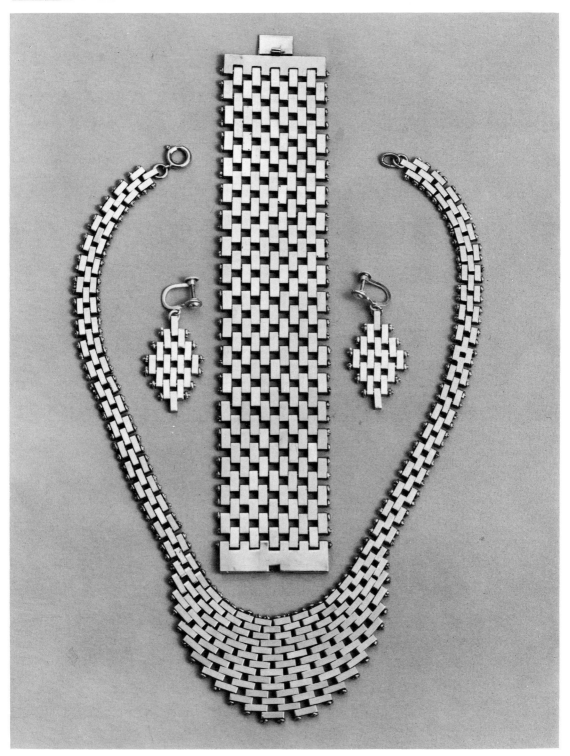

Fig. 21.13. Necklace, ear-rings and bracelet in chrome, very well made in a geometric, modernistic style with articulated links. (Private collection)

*Fig. 21.14. Imaginative use
of colour, materials and
shapes in this group of Art
Deco jewellery. A
chalcedony, lapis-lazuli and
carved cornelian brooch;
diamond, enamel and coral
elegant pendant ear-rings;
Cartier brooch with linked
rings of carved jade; dress
clip of carved smoky quartz
in an 'Odéon' style, set in
gold and platinum with
diamonds and a cabochon
emerald, by Mauboussin.
(Lewis M. Kaplan)*

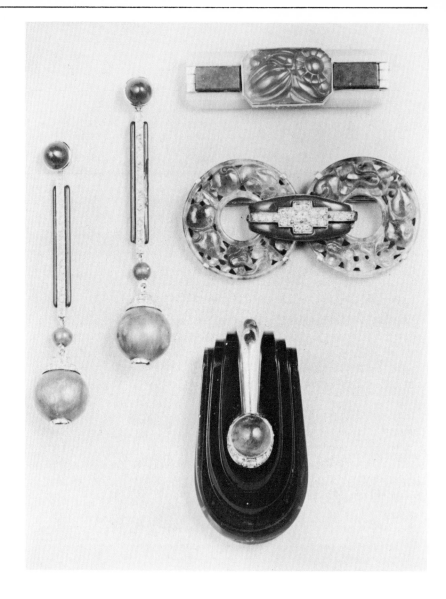

Cameos were never worn for instance, but their place was taken by the French bronze medallions. Many of these commemorated the 1925 Exposition, and were beautifully designed and signed by artists like Delannoy and Pierre Turin.

Brooches were less popular than formerly, although they were still being made and worn, in very different fashions. Arrow brooches — long, slim jabot pins with a decorative motif at either end — were pinned so that only the ends showed, and many brooches were made to show the dress material through the centre of the design. Women were far more active; they worked, they enjoyed sports and their clothes and accessories were adapted accordingly.

Watches changed dramatically, and became major items of decoration, principally due to the efforts and talent of Louis Cartier. The jewelled wristwatch was worn at the cocktail parties which had replaced formal dinner parties as the most popular form of entertaining. Jewelled or enamelled watches were also pinned as brooches to lapels.

Pendants were worn on very long chains to compliment the long line of the body with dropped waistlines, and the flat-chested look asked for long strings of beads in amber, ivory, cornelian, coral or pearl. The sautoir mentioned earlier, which was a long necklace of jewels or pearls ending with a tassel, was also popular. The links of such necklaces or chains were very beautifully engineered to move with the line of the body. Bangles became very popular, but were worn 'slave' style, high on the upper arm, sometimes with a handkerchief tucked through it. Short necklaces of novelty designs were made of moulded glass or from flat, stylish beads of plastic or chrome. The négligée pendant was worn through the 1920s.

Short-cropped or bobbed hairstyles demanded long ear-rings. Following the feminine outline these were usually sleek and slim, echoing the movement of the body, with perhaps a design of linked circles, oblongs or triangles. Other accessories became jewels by virtue of their decoration, and enamelled powder compacts with mirror and powder puff inside, might be hung on silk ropes with a dangling tassel.

The introduction of the minaudière transformed the evening bag into a jewel. This was a stiff metal or plastic bag or box fitted with compartments for lipstick, cigarettes, money, mirror and other items, which solved the problem of having to find an evening bag to match each evening gown. The minaudière was first sold in England by Asprey, but other jewellers soon copied the idea. The bag could be of silver or gold, often engine-turned, with a tiny cabochon ruby or sapphire clasp; or it could be made of plastic, with marcasite or chromium decoration.

The cocktail party inspired other jewels like the dress or 'cocktail' ring, traditionally in a geometrical, oblong or so-called tablet design, perhaps of onyx and diamonds, diamonds and sapphires, or any stark contrast in colours that was considered smart. The oblong background can be found covered with diamonds and then set with cabochon sapphires, or a circled self-patterned motif. An onyx slab might have diamonds set into the dark shiny background.

The flexible diamond (or paste) bracelet could also be worn for a similar occasion, and these were made in vast numbers and an amazing choice of designs within the limitations of the lines of the bracelet. They varied in width, either a slim slither of stones, or a band about two inches (5cm) wide. However the platinum settings always enabled them to be very slim and beautifully flexible; either of open-work diamond design, or with a geometrical or floral pattern running along the bracelet in specially-cut coloured stones. As with all jewels of the period, there was a corresponding fashion in cheap or artificial materials. Usually, in this case, they were bracelets made of pastes, marcasites or semi-precious stones.

Perhaps the most typical item of jewellery from the 1920s and 1930s is the buckle or clip. These could form the basis for an interesting collection of Art Deco or Modernist designs. The utilitarian aspect of the clip appealed to the fashion-conscious generations and it became an essential part of the wardrobe in the 1930s. Clips were made in pairs, so that they could be joined together

Fig. 21.15. Enamelled watch, the gold background is decorated with blue, black and white design. (Anne Bloom)

to form a brooch, or separate to clip individually on to a cloche hat or into the neckline of a dress. In spite of the depression, innumerable versions were made in precious stones, but they were also produced in paste by very good firms, including Cartier, and in plastics. Quite an extraordinary range of varied designs was produced, and these clips, usually very well made, were obviously by far the most popular item of jewellery.

Belt buckles received similar treatment, and those made of metal or copper were decorated, most frequently, with enamels in bright colours in jazzy or Cubist designs, or in the earlier floral patterns, with ziggurats, gazelles and sunburst motifs. Occasionally, *plique à jour* translucent enamel was used, although it was most popular with Art Nouveau jewellers. It is always interesting to find *plique à jour* enamel on an item of purely decorative or costume jewellery, because it demanded a great deal of skill and time. In the early years of its revival, it was saved for exquisite and costly jewels.

Important Designers

The finest jewellery of this period was the work of the large, well-established firms of jewellers, particularly in Paris. The names of jewellers were important then, as now, adding to the value of a status symbol. Buying jewellery involved a ritual for the rich, who lingered in luxurious salons, pondering over the array of sumptuous gems spread out before them. Parisian jewellers, such as Cartier, Boucheron, Mauboussin, Chaumet, Lacloche, and Van Cleef and Arpels created jewels of the highest standard of workmanship and design and all boasted very wealthy and eminent customers amongst their clientèle (see Chapter 16, The Famous Jewel Houses). There was a small group of distinguished designers whose work has stood the test of time and whose jewels are amongst the most highly-prized of the period.

Georges Fouquet (1862-1957) had made superb Art Nouveau jewels. He adapted well to the new style and created spectacular Art Deco jewellery. About 1922 he fully adopted a modern style, rejecting his earlier ideas of

Fig. 21.16. Platinum, jet and diamond brooch designed by Jean Fouquet. (Sotheby's)

figurative and floral decoration, to produce brooches, bracelets, belt clasps and pendants with very stylised abstract motifs. He replaced traditional precious stones with new materials chosen for their strong, dense colours: onyx, coral, jade, which he combined with the misty translucency of amethysts, topazes, aquamarines and crystal. Stones were beautifully carved and shaped; and textures and colours were varied by the use of enamel and lacquer. He drew on other contemporary artists for fresh ideas and, in 1925, he presented at the International Exposition, work by his leading craftsman, Louis Fertey, along with his own designs and those of his son, Jean, plus jewels from designs by architect Eric Bagge, painter André Léveillé, and poster artist Adolphe Mouron, known as Cassandre. He presided over the jewellery section in 1925. In 1936 he commissioned designs from the sculptor Lambert-Rucki.

Jean Fouquet, his son, started on a literary career, after completing classical studies, but went into his father's business in about 1919. He exhibited at the 1925 and 1937 exhibitions, and was awarded a prize. Jean Fouquet preferred a far more geometric approach than his father and belonged to the school of designers who directly translated contemporary art into jewels, building up designs from geometric shapes. He used a great deal of lacquer and skilful enamels.

Jean Desprès was born into a famous glass-making family at Souvigny-Allier in 1889. His parents also had a jewellery business in Paris and, as a young boy, he went to learn the jeweller's craft in Paris, while studying design in the evenings. Early on in his career he showed a tendency towards painting, and while living in Montmartre, he became friendly with Georges Braque, Joan Miró, and other modern artists. In 1914 he joined the war effort, and while working on the production of aeroplanes, he became fascinated by metals, machinery and techniques. After the War, he worked only in metal, silver, gold and pewter, but his earlier involvement with contemporary painting showed itself in his jewels.

His work was resolutely modernistic in appearance and abstract in design. It also shows evidence of his interest in machines. Characteristics of his work include black lacquer; strong, austere and geometrical patterns and motifs; hammered silver surfaces; and machine-like details such as balls which resemble ball-bearings. He too exhibited at the 1925 Exposition.

Jean Dunand (1877-1942) was an important Swiss craftsman of the period, and is best known for his lacquer work. He was an admirer of Ruskin and of the Arts and Crafts Movement and began his career as a sculptor between 1896 and 1902. From Art Nouveau he progressed towards a more geometric style around 1913. In 1912 he had started his important studies of lacquering techniques, working with a Japanese master. With growing interest in metal wares, he saw the possibilities of lacquer as a decoration for metal. He resumed work after the war in 1919, concentrating on his lacquer techniques; the jewels he created were geometric, usually with black or red lacquer decoration.

Gérard Sandoz, born in Paris in 1902, was another designer who aimed to translate modern art into jewellery. He came from a family of jewellers and worked with his father, but became involved in modern decorative art through his uncle, Paul Follot, a sculptor and decorator. Sandoz painted and

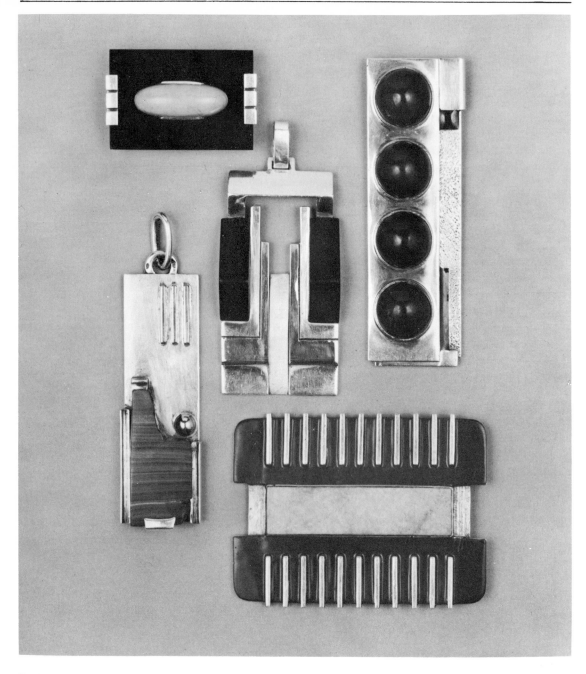

Fig. 21.17. The strong, architectural style of Desprès. Black onyx, jade, silver and gold brooch; pendant showing African influence in its resemblance to an African Zairese mask, using ebony, ivory, gold and silver; oblong brooch with four balls of lapis-lazuli, black enamel, silver and gold; oblong pendant in silver and gold set with malachite left with a jagged edge; and brooch that copies a primitive African comb, in subdued blue enamel, central panel of jade and silver and gold. All signed by Jean Desprès, made around 1925-30. (Lewis M. Kaplan)

designed posters. At the same time, he designed jewels for his father's shop. He worked on purely geometric patterns; the simplicity of his designs grew from a group of basic, abstract shapes, rather than from a planned, forced design.

Raymond Templier (1891-1968) was a member of a Paris family of jewellers. He studied at the École des Beaux Arts from 1909 to 1912, and in that year he entered his father's business. He exhibited at the 1925 and 1937 Expositions, and became a partner in his father's firm, with his own premises in the Rue Auber. From 1929 he employed the designer Marcel Percheron, who continued to be a close and valuable colleague for 36 years. It was Percheron who acted as a technical translator for Templier's *avant-garde* ideas. Like his contemporaries, Fouquet and Sandoz, he banished ornament completely, emphasising geometry, the influence of the machine, and discipline of form and design.

The severity of his jewels was compensated by the use of varied and unusual materials, in particular black lacquer, or eggshell lacquer. He also made many modernistic jewels in diamonds and platinum. A favourite stone of many of these designers was the aquamarine, which seemed to blend well with the bluish tones of white metals and with black lacquer. Small objects for the modern woman were made by Templier, in particular excellent cigarette-cases. In London, Templier jewellery could be bought at the *avant-garde* gallery in Fitzroy Square owned by Curtis Moffat, an American photographer.

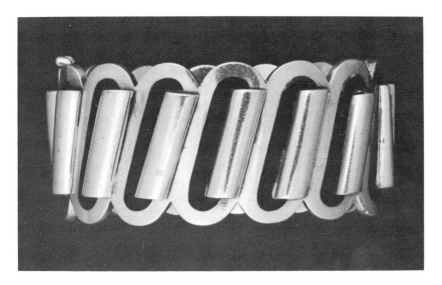

Fig. 21.18. Modernist part-lacquered bracelet by Raymond Templier, late 1920s. (Sotheby's Belgravia)

Paul Brandt was another jeweller with an artistic background; he was also a geometricist working in enamels.

Georg Jensen (1866-1935) is a name well known for distinctive jewellery and silverware which is still made today. Jensen was a Danish silversmith, goldsmith and sculptor, who trained in Copenhagen. There, some time in the late 1890s, he became friendly with the artist Mogens Ballin. Ballin was also working with silver and pewter about 1899, and Jensen started to work with him in 1901, making jewellery in silver and semi-precious stones. In 1904, Jensen started to design and manufacture jewellery which he sold in his own shop. He developed a very distinctive style of silver jewels with highly stylised motifs. They were not as aggressively modern or abstract as those of the other designers mentioned here, but more in the style of early Art Deco, using stylised flowers, leaves, birds and animals.

Lacloche was one Parisian firm which was best known for its Art Deco jewels. It was actually founded in Madrid in 1875 by four brothers; they opened branches in San Sebastian, Biarritz and finally in Paris about 1898. In about 1920, they opened a shop in London, taking over Fabergé's former retail premises, and also taking charge of the remaining stock. The business closed down in 1931; then Jacques Lacloche reopened in Cannes in 1934-5, and in Paris in 1937. The shops were later converted to art galleries. They created very stylish, high-class jewels, using skilful combinations of coloured precious stones and diamonds.

Among the other great Paris jewellers, Boucheron took a large part in the 1925 Exposition with many innovative jewels in semi-precious stones and diamonds set in black enamel. Cartiers were world famous for the watches which they had transformed into fashionable jewels, and for the jewelled clips so popular in the late 1930s.

In general, English jewellers were slow to pick up the fanciful and adventurous lead taken by Paris, and the English tastes were more conservative. In the 1920s and 1930s, many jewellers were still working in the Arts and Crafts tradition, notably Sybil Dunlop (see Chapter 20, Arts and Crafts Jewellery). The relatively quiet jewels set with semi-precious stones suited the tastes of the majority; Liberty, that barometer of popular taste, was certainly still selling Arts and Crafts style jewels in the 1920s. When the English did adapt to

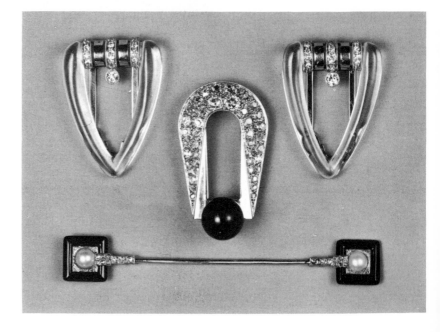

Fig. 21.19. The 1930s fashion for black and white was interpreted in fine jewels. Pair of crystal and diamond dress clips; modernistic dress clip in platinum, diamond and black onyx by Raymond Templier about 1925; 'jabot' pin with diamonds, pearls and onyx, by Lacloche. (Lewis M. Kaplan)

Art Deco, it was with restraint and reservation; because of this, this chapter has concentrated on the stylish French jewellery which epitomised the period.

After the 1925 Exposition, Americans took wholeheartedly to Art Deco: they embraced its way of life, and helped create it in some ways. The new American millionaire travelled to Europe or lived in Paris, and tried to find a way into society through clothes, objects, jewels and the patronage of fashionable designers. In New York, the leading jewellers were Tiffany and Company, but there was also Cartier New York, Van Cleef and Arpels, and other, less well-known but excellent jewellers working in the Art Deco style.

Collecting Art Deco

Collecting Art Deco jewellery means collecting the style and designs of the period expressed in an ideal medium of pure decoration. It is quite easy to recognise the style broadly, and to appreciate those jewels made in the finest quality and most sumptuous materials. However, for most of us, the jewels of the 1920s and 1930s are too expensive and impractical. It can be just as much, if not more, fun to search for Art Deco or Modernist styles applied to cheap or fake jewellery, and it is more of a challenge to the collector in a way.

Mostly, signatures were limited to costly jewels. Without the help of a name or some certainty of intrinsic value, the collector must trust his judgment and taste and pay solely for design. It is, in fact, very much like buying a painting, but with the added advantage that you should gain a piece of decorative and period jewellery that you will enjoy wearing.

Bibliography

Aldred, Cyril: *Jewels of the Pharoahs;* Thames and Hudson.
Arwas, Victor: *Art Deco;* Academy Editions.
Battersby, Martin: *The Decorative Thirties;* Studio Vista;
——*The Decorative Twenties;* Studio Vista.
Billing, A.: *The Science of Gems, Jewels, Coins and Medals.*
Clifford, Anne: *Cut Steel and Berlin Iron Jewellery;* Adams & Deane.
Crisp, F.A.: *Memorial Rings (1694-1837).*
Cooper, Diana and Battershill, N.: *Victorian Sentimental Jewellery;* David & Charles.
Dent, Hubert C.: *Piqué — a beautiful minor art;* Connoisseur Books.
Evans, Joan: *A History of Jewellery, 1100-1870;* Faber & Faber.
Flower, Margaret: *Victorian Jewellery;* Cassell.
Gere, Charlotte: *European and American Jewellery 1830-1914;* Heinemann.
--*Victorian Jewellery Design;* Kimber & Co.
——, and Anscombe, Isabelle: *Arts and Crafts in Britain and America;* Academy Editions.
Hinks, Peter: *Nineteenth Century Jewellery;* Faber & Faber.
Janson, Dora Jane: *From Slave to Siren;* Duke Museum of Art, North Carolina.
Kendall, Hugh P.: *The Story of Whitby Jet;* Whitby Museum.
Lewis, M.D.S.: *Antique Paste Jewellery;* Faber & Faber.
Mason, Anita and Packer, Diane: *An Illustrated Dictionary of Jewellery;* Osprey.
Purtell, Joseph: *The Tiffany Touch.*
Roche, J.C.: *The History, Development and Organisation of the Birmingham Jewellery and Allied Trades;* Supplement to *The Dial* 1927.
Snowman, K.: *The Art of Karl Fabergé;* Faber & Faber.
Tilbrook, Adrian: *The Designs of Archibald Knox for Liberty & Co.;* Ornament Press.
Vever, Henri: *La Bijouterie Française au XIXeme Siècle;* 63 volumes) Paris 1904-8.
Von Hase, Ulrike: *Schmuck in Deutschland und Osterreich 1895-1914;* Prestel.
Art Nouveau Jewellery and Fans; Dover Publications (Reprint).
The Jeweller's Art: an introduction to the Hull-Grundy Gift to the British Museum; British Museum Publications.

Index

NOTE All references in italic, which come at the end of an entry, refer to specific pictures in the text. The first number refers to the chapter, the second to its position within the chapter. So for example: *6.18* means that the eighteenth picture in Chapter 6 provides additional information. All picture captions start with a unique reference number.

Adam, Robert, influence of 41
Aesthetic Movement 46, 49, 52, 246
agates 68, 105, 115, 117, 137, 141, *12.1, 12.2, 12.3*
Aguatti, Antonio 161-2, *13.3*
Ah-Hopte, Queen 167
aigrettes 63, 77
Alexandra, Princess of Wales and Queen 17, 18, 52, 212, 265, 268
Allen, Kate 265
Amastini 145
amethysts 18, 27, 95, 105, 115, 121, 136, 172, 228, 261, 268
ammonites 69
amulets 170
animals 17, 127-33, 136, 137, 161, 212, *13.3, 21.10*
annular brooches, *see* ring brooches
aquamarine 27, 287
archaeological influence on designs 28, 31, 168, 178, 187, *3.6, 3.9, 3.11, 14.2, 14.3 See also* Egyptian style
Argy-Rousseau *6.8*
Arnauld *18.2*
arrow motif 279, 282
Art Deco 20, 63, 80, 138, 271-89, *1.11, 1.12, 11.5, 14.6, 16.2, 16.4*
    American 289
Art Nouveau 18, 72, 126, 131, 198, 199-213, 216, 237, 244-5, 267, *1.10*
    English 237, 265
    hair-combs *6.22*
    pendants 214-22
    stick-pins *11.1*

Art Workers' Guild 225
Artificers' Guild 226, 240
Arts and Crafts Movement 18, 68, 210, 215, 223-43, 245, 247-8, 288
    American 208, 210, 243
    jewellery 223-43
    principles 226-9
Ashbee, C.R. 216, 225-6, 230, 238, 240, 251, *19.9, 19.12*
Asprey 283
asymmetry 51
Aucoc, Louis 199, *17.1*
Aztec influences 278

Baekeland, Leo Hendrick 80
Bagge, Eric 285
Bakelite 80
Baker, Oliver 238, 253, *19.2, 20.4*
Ballin, Mogens 287-8
bar-brooches 32, 117, 131, 163, 180, 271
Barberi, Michelangelo 162
basket-weave design 41
Bassi 149
beads 283
    coral 21-4, 67
    jet 102-3
    piqué 43
bee motif 17, 131
Belleek 68
Berini, Antonio 145
Berlin iron jewellery 75, *6.15*
Bernhardt, Sarah 173, 198, 200

Berquem, Louis de 12
Bing, Samuel 49, 208
Birmingham Guild of Handicraft 226, *19.16*
Birmingham trade 52, 55, 58, 117, 124, 215
Black, Starr & Frost 209-10, 211
'bloom' 32, 45
'Blue John' 69
bog-oak 74, 105
Bohemian garnets 69
Bonavita, Giovanni Bianchi 156
bone 71
Bonelli, Angelo 143-4
botanical jewellery, *see* flowers in jewellery
Bott, Thomas 68
Boucheron 192-4, 200, 277, 288
Boulle, C.A. 38
Boulton, Matthew 76, 151
bouquet motif 119, 121, 126
bow-brooches 13, 63, 117, 268, *7.24*
boxes 162, 203, *4.5*
bracelets 28, 43, 67, 71, 77, 108, 115, 130,
174, 271, 283, *5.5, 5.10*
    bangles 32, 46, 51, 122, 163, 271, 280,
    283, *3.9, 4.4, 17.3*
    jet 102
    pinchbeck 67
    piqué 43, *4.2*
Bragg, T. & J. 168
Brandebourgs 12
Brandt, Paul 287
Braun, Carl *20.19*
Breguet 196
bright-cutting 91
Briot, Count Epinay da *17.7*
Brogden, John 31, 150, 187
Bromsgrove Guild of Applied Art 226
brooches 28, 32, 43, 71, 83, 112, 115, 182,
203, 251, 261, 268, 271, 282
    bar- 32, 117, 131, 163, 180, 271
    bow- 13, 63, 117, 268, *7.24*
    crescent 14, 69, 268, *1.1*
    diamond 11-20
    Egyptian Revival 168, 174
    flower 118-26, *17.2*
    jet 103
    Jubilee 58
    love 55-7, *5.6, 5.8*
    'Mizpah' 57
    mourning 95, 98, 106, 107, 110, *7.21*

    name 57
    ring 112
    spray 13, 15, *1.2*
Brown, Charles and William 145, *12.1*
buckles 67, 43, 83, 229, 238, 253-4, 264,
265, 284, *17.13, 19.5, 19.12, 20.4, 20.13,
21.8, 21.9*
    shoe 63, 76, *9.1*
'buhl' 38
bulla 31, 182, *3.8*
Burch, Edward 145
Burne-Jones, Edward, 265
butterfly motif 17, 43, 51, 73, 77, 128, 131,
165, 265, *1.9, 2.1, 6.17, 6.18, 15.10, 19.12*
buttons 43, 77

cabochon 63, 69, 228
Caetani, Michelangelo 179
cairngorms 115
Caldwell, J. E., & Co. 208
cameos 68, 127, 135, 139-54, 182, *15.1*
    coral 23, *2.4*
    habillés 148
    imitations 141, 151-3
    jet 102, 103
    Neo-classical 140, 142-5
    Renaissance 140
    shell 143, 146-9
    Thorwaldsen, in the manner of *12.6*
    Victorian 145-50
cameo-cutting 141-2
Canino, Princess of 178-9
cannetille 25, 161 *See also* gold-work
Canning jewel 128
Cartier 63, 191-2, 200, 277, 282, 284, 288,
21.3, 21.14
casein 80
Cassandre, *see* Mowron, Adolphe
Castellani, Alessandro 179, 182
Castellani, Alfredo 180
Castellani, Augusto 179, 185
Castellani, F. P. 28-31, 150, 162, 177-82,
214
Celluloid 80
Celtic ornament 237, 249-50, 256, 261, 264
Celtic Revival 249
Century Guild 225

chains 28, 75, 107, 130, 219, *3.10, 6.6*
  ivory 71
  pinchbeck 67
Chaise, Jules 192, 198
Chanel, Coco 277
Charlton 210
chatelaine 77
Chaumet 194-6, 277
Child & Child 265
chrome 280, 283, *21.13*
cigarette-cases 278, 287
citrines 113, 115, 121, 136
clip, dress 283-4, 288, *21.6*
cloisonné enamel 49, 172, 196-7, *16.8*
closed-back settings 13
collars 172, 268, *16.2, 17.8*
colour symbolism in Egyptian
jewellery 171
coloured stones, use of 219, 276
commemorative jewels 84, 85, 94, *7.2 See
also* mourning jewels
compact, powder *16.3, 16.7*
Comstock Lode 45
Comyns, William 219, 265, *20.8*
Connell 262-3
Connemara marble 68, 126
Cooper, John Paul 228, 234
coral 20, 21-4, 67, 95, 122, 136, 276, 278
  branch 22-3
  cameos 150
  imitation 80
cornelian 171, 228
cornucopia motif 120
corsage ornament 13
costume jewellery 274, 277, 283, 284
Cosway, Richard 96
cravat-pins, *see* tie-pins
crescent shape 14, 69, 268, *1.1*
Crisp collection 86, 92, 94
cross 43, 44, 71, 74, 105, 113, 162, *4.7, 6.9,
7.15*
crystal 87, 88, 94, 95, 112, 115, 130-1, 136,
275, *11.2*
Cubism 273, 290
cuff-links *16.6*
culet facet 17
cut-steel 76-7
cuts, baguette 20, 269, 275
  brilliant 12, 14, 16, 17, 121

calibré 269, 275
  diamond 23
  emerald 20, 275
  Mazarin 11
  rose 11, 14, 16, 17, 60, 69, 92, 212, 219
  table 11
  trapeze 275
  triangle 275
cutting, stone 11, 115, 269, 275, *21.1*
Cuzner, Bernard 233, 238, 253
Cymric range 219, 237, 243, 248-51

Darmstadt, Artists' colony at 256-8, 261
Dawson, Edith 236, *19.10*
Dawson, Nelson 226, 236, 240, *19.10*
Debût, Jules 194
Deleanoy, M. *21.5*
Delon *21.7*
Dent, Herbert C. 35
Derby marble 165, *13.9*
Desprès, Jean 285, *21.11, 21.17*
Desrosiers 198
diamonds 11-20, 120, 189, 219, 268, 275,
280, 283
  and colourless stones 45
  in mourning rings 92
dog-collar 268
Doria, Carlo, *see* Robert Phillips
Dreicer, Theodore 210-11
Duchesse d'Aumale 22
Dunand, Jean 285
Dunlop, Sybil 240, 288, *19.13*

ear-rings 24, 32, 34, 43, 71, 103, 115, 122,
148, 197, 277, 283, *2.2, 3.11, 4.6, 6.1, 7.24,
13.6*
  pinchbeck 67
ebonite, *see* Vulcanite
Edward VII 191, 212, 267
Edwardian style 18, 220, 254, 265, 267-71,
1.7, 1.9, 20.12
Egyptian style 59, 67, 127, 163-4, 167-76,
184, 211, 278, *13.7*
emancipation of women, effect of 275, 282
emeralds 20

Emmanuel, Harry 182
'en esclavage' 161
enamel 12, 18, 28, 32, 49, 85, 87, 91-2, 94, 118, 184, 196-7, 212, 220, 236, 238, 250, 256, 264, 265, *19.10*
   black, use of 98, 277, 280, 288
   cloisonné 49, 172, 196-7, *16.8*
   floating 250, 256
   guilloché 91, 212
   opaline 92, *18.2*
   peacock 239
   plique à jour 133, 176, 201, 204, 210, 265, 284, *10.6, 16.9, 17.4, 17.11, 18.1*
   revival 238-40
   turquoise 230, 240
   white, significance of 88, 99
Etruscan influence and style 28, 31, 177-82, 214, *3.8 See also* archaeological influences
Eugénie, Empress 189, 191, 196
exhibitions 16, 79, 80, 102, 105, 108, 109, 121, 149, 168, 182, 194, 200, 203, 204, 205, 212, 223, 271, 285, 288, 289
eye motif 96, *7.12*
   of Horus (wedjet) 170-1

Fabergé, Peter Carl 188, 211-13
Fahrner, Theodor 256-61, *20.12, 20.19*
Falize, Alexis 196
Falize, André 197
Falize, Lucien 49, 196
'Falsework' 63
fan motif 51
Ferty, Louis 285
Fisher, Alexander 236, 240
Fisher, Kate 265
flowers in jewellery 12, 15, 16, 22, 27, 39, 41, 43, 46, 51, 52, 55-6, 64, 68, 72-4, 76, 96, 103, 118-26, 201, *2.2, 3.4, 3.5*
   Art Deco 278-9
   formalised 273, 278-9
   grapes and vine leaves 39, 123, 165, *9.7*
   Japanese style 49, 278
   language of 55-6, 96, 122
   leaf motif, Arts & Crafts 236, 240
   lotus 28, 171, *3.6, 3.8*
   mosaic 165, *13.8*
   on mourning jewellery 96

flower-basket motif 120, 278
Foggini, Geovanni Battista 156
foiling paste and stones 12, 14, 27, 63, 120
Fontenay, Eugène *15.5*
fossils 69
Fossin, Jean-Baptiste 195
Fossin, Jules 195
Fouquet, Alphonse 197-8
Fouquet, Georges 198, 284-5, *18.6*
Fouquet, Jean 285, *21.16*
French jet 64, 105
fringing, gold 32-4, *3.12*
frog motif 130, *10.7*
frogs, fastenings 12
Froment-Meurice, F. D. 111

Gaillard, Ernest 203
Gaillard, Lucien 72-3, 203-4, *6.14, 6.15*
galleon motif 240
garnet 28, 32, 45, 88, 91, 228, *3.7*
   almandine 95
   Bohemian (pyrope) 69
   demantoid (green) 131
Gaskin, Arthur 228, 233, 236, 238, 253, *19.6, 19.7, 19.17*
Gaskin, Georgina 233
Gautrait 202, *18.1*
geometric designs 32, 51, 115, 261, 273, 280, 285, 287
German Art Nouveau design 256, *20.19*
Girometti, Guiseppe 145
Giuliano, Carlo 31, 180, 182-6, 214, *14.1*
Giuliano, Carlo & Arthur (sons of C.G.) 185, 186
Giuliano, Federico 184-5
Giuliano, Ferdinando 185
Glasgow School 240, 243, 258
glass 60, 63, 105, 207, 283, *6.5*
gold 23, 24, 171, 179, 261
   backing 17, 25
   blooming 24, 32, 34, 45
   coloured 27, 51, 121
gold-work 25-34
   cannetille 25, 161, *3.3*
   chasing 97, 192, 211
   Murrle Bennett 261
   repoussé 27, *3.1, 3.2, 3.7*

Gorham Corporation 209
Gothic revival 111, 115, 214, 224-5
Gradl, Moritz *20.12, 20.19*
granulation 31, 32, 34, 179-80, 184, 186, 187
Grasset, Eugene 202
Gregory, Lady 99
Guevel *21.11*
Guild of Handicraft 225-6, 230, 238, *19.1, 19.2*
    Birmingham 226, *19.16*
    other Guilds 225-6 *See also* Arts and Crafts Movement
guilloché enamel 91, 212
Gulbenkian, Calouste 201
gunmetal 75
Gurschner, Gustav *20.24*

hair, in jewellery 87, 88, 89, 91, 94, 95, 97
    hair-work 105-10, *7.24*
hair ornaments 18, 43, 67, 77, 105, 204, 230, *4.1, 6.7, 6.18, 6.21, 9.6, 17.6*
hand motif 22, 71, 74, 103, 105, *2.3, 5.10, 6.11*
Hardman & Co. 111
Haseler, W. H. & Son 251-3
hat-pins 72-3, 117, 264
heart motif 28, 56, 88, 95, 97, 112, *3.5, 8.2*
Hoffman, Joseph 244
Hollywood style 83, 280
horn 49, 72-3, 133, 201, 204, 233, *6.13, 6.14, 10.4, 17.5, 17.6*
Horner, Charles 219, 263-4, 266, *20.10, 20.21*
Hornick, Erasmus 128
horsehair 107
Huber, Patriz 258, *20.12, 20.19*
Hunt & Roskell 16, 121, 182
Hunt, George 240
Hurst, Godfrey *7.15*
Hutton, William 265
Hyatt, John Wesley 80

Imperial Crest, Japanese 49, 278
inscriptions on mourning jewellery 92

insect 17, 39, 73, 129, 131, 133, 136, *10.4*
    fly, in Egyptian jewellery 171
intaglio 135, 141 *See also* cameos
    reverse crystal 130-1, 136
iron and steel jewellery 74-9
Isler, Luigi 149
ivory 35, 41, 68, 71, 91, 122, 126, *6.11, 6.9, 6.10, 9.5*

jabot pins 282
jade 20, 276, 277, *21.14*
Japanese influence 46-52, 72, 196, 203-4, 208, 246, 278
'Jasper' cameos 68, 151, *12.11*
Jeffroy 142
Jensen, Georg 287-8, *21.4*
jet 71, 85, 98, 99-105, 150, 166
    French 63, 105
    imitations 105
Jones, A. E. 68
Jones, Owen, *Grammar of Ornament* 224
Jubilee, 1887 52, 58, 110, 124
Jugendstil 256

Kauffman, Angelica 91
Kerr & Co. 211
kilt pins 113, *8.3*
King, Jessie M. 243, 253
knot motif 32, 56, 103, 108, 250, 261, 264, *3.2, 11.1*
knot and tassel 28
'knife wires' 268
Knox, Archibald 237, 248-50, 254, 255-6, *19.13, 20.6*
Koehler, Florence 243
Kollin, Eric 188, *15.14*

lace pin 17, 69, 131
lace-work in diamonds 18, 268, *1.8*
Lacloche, Maison 205, 288, *21.19*
lacquer 276, 285, 287
Lalique, René 64, 72-3, 83, 174, 199-201, 245, *14.5*

Lambert-Rucki 285
language of flowers 55-6, 96, 122
lapis-lazuli 161, 171
lava cameos 150, *12.10*
La Belle Assembleé 109
Le Japon Artistique 49
leaf motif 236, 240, 250
Leblanc of Paris 67
Légaré, Gilles 12, 14, 119
Lévéillé, André 285
Liberty, Arthur Lazenby 49
Liberty & Co. 219, 237-40, 244-66, 288, *18.5, 19.6*
Limmonier of Paris 109
Littledale 179
Lizard motif 131
lockets 32, 45, 75, 110, 119, 122, 130, *3.12, 5.4*
Loethoeur, Bernhardt, *20.22*
Lowenthal, D. & M. 258
lorgnettes 35, 39, *17.5*
lotus flower motif 28, 171, *3.6, 3.8*
love brooches 55-7
Luckenbooth brooches 88, 112, *8.2*

Macdonald, Margaret & Frances 240
machine-made silver items 55, 211, 215
machinery motifs 280
Mackintosh, Charles Rennie 240, 244, 258, 273, 279
Mackintosh, Rose 279
Mackmurdo, A. H. 225
MacNair, J. Herbert 240, 243
Maison Lacloche 205, 288
Maison Mauboisson 205
Maison Mellerio 196
Maison Moderne *17.5*
Maison Vever 205
Makers' marks 182, 185, 186, 187, 188, 197, 198, 205, 208, 253, 256, 258, 261, 263, 264
marcasites 77, 283
Marchant 144-5
Marcus & Co 210, 243
Mariette, Auguste 167
Martineau, Sarah Madeleine 236, *19.11*
Masriera, Luis 205
Massim, Oscar 15, 16, 121

match-cases 55, 76
Mauboussin 205, *21.14*
Maurice, F. D. 224
Mazarin cut 11
McLeish, Annie 265
medallions, bronze 282
Medusa 148, 186, *12.9*
Meier-Graefe, M. *17.5*
Melillo, Giacinto 186
Mellerio, Maison 196
Memento Mori pieces 85, *7.1*
Mère, Clement *21.7*
message brooches 57-8
millegrain setting 268
minaudière 83, 283
miniatures 89-91, 110, *7.3, 7.7, 7.12*
   eye 96, *7.12*
'Mizpah' motif 57-8, *5.6, 5.7*
Moderne, Maison *17.5*
Modernism 273-274, 280, 285, *21.18*
moonstones 69, 229
Moore, Edward C. 50, 208
Morel, J. V., & Co. 16, 121
Morel, Prosper 195
Morelli 145
Morris, May 64
Morris, Talwyn 243
Morris, William 49, 64, 223-4
mosaics 31, 105, 123, 129, 155-66, 169, *9.7*
   micromosaics 159
'Moses basket' motif 176
mother-of-pearl 35, 36, 41, 43, 72, 228, 250, 261
mourning jewellery 44, 74, 84-110, 124, 135
Mouron, Adolphe 285
movement, motifs of 279
Mucha, Alphonse 198, *18.6*
'mummy' motif 176
Murrle, Bennett & Co 219, 220, 255-63, 266, *19.16*
Mürrle, Ernst 256-7

name brooches 57, *5.6*
Napoleon 140, 142, 167, 195
Natter, Jean Laurent 144
necklaces 18, 31, 64, 77, 83, 174, 182, 184, 185, 197, 216, 229, 254, 261, 283, *14.5, 15.7, 17.11, 19.11*

Neo-classical designs 86, 88-91, 139
   on cameos 140, 142-5
   on mosaics 158
   on mourning jewellery 88-92
Neri 149
niello 79, 105, 203, *6.20*
Nitot, Etienne 194-5
Normandie, S.S. 279
Novissimo, Pasquale 185-6

Olbrich, Josef Maria 244, 258
onyx 20, 96, 98, 105, 276, 277, 283
opal 18, 133, 229, 250, 261, 268, *20.20*
   paste 63
open-work 250, *5.5*
Opificio delle Pietre Dure 155-6
organic jewellery 69-73
   motifs 72 *See also* flowers in jewellery
oriental influence 245, 277-8 *See also*
Japanese influence
      Chinoiserie 41
      Japonaiserie 46, 246

paillons, in enamelling 236
pale stones, fashion for 18
pampilles 16, 121
Parian 68, 122
Parkes, Alexander 80
'Parkesine' 80
Partridge, Fred T. 230-3
paste 13, 59-63, 65, 91, 120, 128, 135, 276,
283, 284, *10.2*
pâte de verre 6.8
patriotic motifs, 56, 135, *11.6*
Patti, Adeline *9.9*
pavé setting 13, 17, 23, 32, 77, *1.1, 3.11*
peacock motif 39, 133
pearls 20, 22, 32, 91, 95, 128, 136, 217, 228-
9, 250, 261, 268, 276, *9.8, 18.4, 21.3*
   fake pearls 277
   See also seed-pearls
pectorals, Egyptian 172, 174
Pellatt, Apsley 153
pendants, Art Nouveau 244
   Arts and Crafts 229

Egyptian Revival 174
   mourning 87-8
   négligée 268, 283, *21.1*
   turn-of-the-century 201, 214-222, 254,
   256, 261, 268, 283, *16.9, 17.14*
Percheron, Marcel 287
peridots 18, 184, 229
Peruzzi, Vincenzo 12
Pforzheim 256, 260
Phillips, Alfred 187
Phillips, Robert, of Cockspur Street, 22, 31,
68, 150, 168, 182, 187
photograph lockets 46, 110
Pichler, Giovanni 143
Pichler, Luigi 145, 153
pierced metal-work 51
pietra-dura, *see* mosaics
pinchbeck 45, 65-7, *6.7, 6.6*
Pinchbeck, Christopher 65
piqué 35-44, 71, 105, 123
Pistrucci, Benedetto 143-4
Pistrucci, Elena & Eliza Maria 149
plaid pins 113, *8.1*
plaques 174
plastics 79-83, 277, 283, *21.6*
platinum 17, 20, 211, 268, 275, 283
plique à jour enamelling 133, 176, 201, 204,
210, 265, 284, *10.6, 16.9, 17.4, 17.11, 18.1*
Poiret, Paul 274
political motif 137-8
pottery and porcelain 67-8
Prince of Wales 'twist' pattern 219
Pugin, A.W.N. 111, 224

Queen Mary brooches 112
quizzing glass *3.10*

Raffaelli, Giacomo 159, 161, 162
Ramsden, Omar *19.14*
rattle, with coral 21
Ravenscroft, George 60
Rega, Philippo 145
Regent diamond 195
registration mark 117
Renty of Lille 67

repoussé work, fashion for 27
Rico, F. 261
rings 271, *17.1, 19.13*
  cocktail 283
  cross-over 271
  Egyptian Revival 176
  gypsy 271
  half-hoop 271
  'Mizpah' 58
  mourning 84, 86-7, 89, 90, 92, 94, 96, 97
  piqué *4.3*
  snake 130
ring brooches 112
rivet-head effect 261, *20.14*
rock crystals 115
Romanticism 96, 97, 105, 139, 141 *See also* sentiment in jewels
rubies 20
Rudder, Isidore de 205
Ruskin, John 68, 223, 224, 225, 228
  pottery 68, *19.12*

St George's Art Society 225
Sandoz, Gérard 285-7
sapphires 20, 268
sardonyx 141, 150
Saulini, Luigi 149-50, 182
Saulini, Tommasso 149
sautoir 268, 283, *16.6, 21.2*
scarab 127, 170, 174, 176, 182, 264, *14.4, 14.5, 15.2 See also* Egyptian style
  heart 170
Scarf Pin Society 138
Scottish jewellery 68, 88, 111-17, 136
seals 27, 67, 128, *6.22*
seed-pearls 72, 89, 92, 123, *6.12*
semi-precious stones, fashion for 25-7, 219, 228, 251, 276
sentiment in jewels 55-8, 67, 71, 87-8, 96, 106, 122, 135, 161, *3.4*
serpent motif 27, 88, 95, 102, 108, 127, 128, 129, 130, 136, 174, 271, *7.18, 10.2*
  snake chains 28, 34
settings 14, 229, 268
  of cameos 150
  claw 13

closed 13
collet 17
millegrain 268
open 17, 121, *1.1, 1.3*
pavé 13, 17, 23, 32
silver 17
Sévignés 13
shakudo 46, *5.2, 5.3*
shell cameos 146, 149, *12.5, 12.6 See also* cameos
shibuichi 46
shoe buckles *9.1*
silver 34, 45-58, 69, 79, 176, 203, 228, 251, 261, 263
  marking of 50, 52
  silver gilt 174
Silver, Arthur 247
Silver, Rex 247, 253
'Silver Studio' 247
'silvering' paste stones 63
Simpson, Edgar 233
skean-dhus 113
slides, mourning 84, 87
smalti filati 159
speed motifs 279
Spencer, Edward 240, *19.15*
sporting motifs 17, 131, 136-7, 271, *5.9, 11.2, 13.2*
sprays 13, 27, 120, 121, *1.4*
star shape 17, 69, 268
  star-setting 32, 271
steel, iron and, jewellery 74-9
stick-pins 108, 131, 134-138
Stile Liberty 245
strap and buckle motif 102, 113
Strass, G. F. 60
Streeter, Edwin 168-9
Studio International 247, 248, 255, 261
style cathédrale 111
suites, Victorian gold 45, 117, *3.3, 3.7*
'Sylvia' pendant 202

Tard 49
'targe' brooches 115
Tassie, James 63, 151-3
Taylor, W. Howson 68
'tear' jewellery 96, *7.12*

Templier, Raymond 287, *21.8, 21.19*
tesserae 155
tiaras 63, 67, 174, *6.7, 6.19, 12.5, 16.6*
tie-pins, *see* stick-pins
Tiffany, Charles Lewis 205-8
Tiffany, Louis C. 49, 51, 52, 208, 289, *11.5*
topaz 27
Torricelli, G.A.B. 156
tortoise-shell 35-44, 105, *4.1, 6.22, 12.9*
Tourette 202
Toutin, Jean 119
Traquair, Phoebe 240
tremblant 16, 121, *9.3, 9.6*
Tremlett, Captain 102
'Tudric' 248, 262
Turin, P. *21.5*
turquoises 27, 32, 76, 123, 130, 136, 173-4,
228, 250, 261, 276, 278, *3.11*
Tutankhamun, discovery of tomb of 174

Unger Brothers 211
unusual materials 59-83

Van Cleef & Arpels 284, *16.7*
Van de Velde, Henry 260
Varley, Charles F. 238-9, 240
Vauxhall glass 63, *6.4*
vestas, *see* match-cases
Vever, Maison 202, 245, *1.5*

Victoria, Queen, influence on jewellery 92,
96, 97, 98, 110, 111, 129, 141, 146
Vienna Sezession 244, 258, 261
visiting card motif 56
Vovert, Jean 119
Vulcanite 74, 105

watches 85, 119, 192, 282, 288, *21.15*
Wedgwood 67, 76, 77, 151
'wedjet' eye of Horus 170-1
whiplash motif 237, 250, 261
Whitby, Yorks 100, 102-5
white enamel, significance of, in mourning
jewellery 88
Wickes & Netherton 63
Wiener Werkstätte *20.24*
Wièse, Jules *15.4*
Wilson, Henry 233-4, *19.9*
Win, R. 261
Witch's heart brooches 88, *8.2*
Wolfers, Philippe 205
Wyon, Benjamin 145

Xylonite 70

Yard, Raymond C. 211
Young, John B. 207